MEN IN BATTLE

by ALVAH BESSIE

Novels:

The Symbol
The un-Americans
Bread & a Stone
Dwell in the Wilderness
One for My Baby (in process)
The Serpent was More Subtil (in process)

Autobiography:

Spain Again
Inquisition in Eden
Men in Battle

Anthology:

The Heart of Spain (editor)

MEN IN BATTLE

A Story of Americans in Spain

By

Alvah Bessie

CHANDLER & SHARP PUBLISHERS, INC.

SAN FRANCISCO

Grateful acknowledgment is made to Mary Rolfe for use of the map "Where the Lincoln Battalion Fought in Spain," from *The Lincoln Battalion*, by Edwin Rolfe (Random House, 1939), and to Professor Gabriel Jackson for the use of the two maps of the Ebro offensive (Jackson, *A Concise History of the Spanish Civil War*, John Day, 1974) and for his permission to condense and somewhat rewrite his excellent chronology of that war (Jackson, *The Spanish Republic and the Civil War, 1931–1939*, Princeton University Press, 1965).

.A.B.

Publishing History, *Men in Battle*:

Scribners, 1939
Veterans of the Abraham Lincoln Brigade, 1954
Seven Seas Books, 1959 (paperback)
Ediciones ERA (Mexico), 1969 (*Hombres en Guerra*, paperback)

Library of Congress Cataloging in Publication Data

Bessie, Alvah Cecil, 1904-
    Men in battle.

    Reprint, with some new material, of the ed. published by Scribner, New York.
      1. Spain—History—Civil War, 1936-1939—Personal narra-
tives.   2. Bessie, Alvah Cecil, 1904-   3. Spain—History
—Civil War, 1926-1939—Foreign participation—American.
I. Title.
DP269.9.B39   1975   946.081'092'2   78-28743
ISBN 0-88316-513-9

This edition of *Men in Battle* is dedicated to the people of Spain for whom the men of the International Brigades had the honor to fight.

Much has changed in Spain, but not its valiant people. They are as committed as ever to the overthrow of the Franco regime and to the restoration of—and the improvement of—their Republic.

For some time now their struggle has been moving closer to the surface; masses of people are in action; unity is being cemented between workers, students, women, even priests—a unity that cannot be broken by any oppressive measures and that will eventually bring to flaming life their great slogan of 1936:

Madrid será la tumba del fascismo.

A. B.

CONTENTS

PREFACE: 1936–1975

Thirty-eight years ago last July Francisco Franco, aided by his Nazi German and Italian fascist allies, started a rebellion against the legally elected Spanish Republic he had sworn to defend. That rebellion ended three years later with the defeat of the Republic by the fascist powers, but the people of Spain have not yet spoken the last word and their voices are heard more loudly every day.

The Franco regime would not have lasted this long were it not for the support given Franco during his treasonous uprising by the Axis, as well as the passive complicity and later the active assistance provided by the great capitalist democracies—especially the United States of America.

Had we sold arms to the Republic—its right under international law—the rebellion would have ended in its first month. Had we armed the thousands of Spanish refugees in France the last days of World War II—and they were ready and anxious to move, and many did—Franco would have gone down the drain with Hitler and Mussolini. Had we not taken the place of Germany and Italy as procurer of arms, money and political support, beginning almost immediately after World War II ended, the new regime would have foundered in bankruptcy and could have been removed by the Spanish people with no loss of blood.*

---

* As a matter of fact more gasoline, oil and trucks came to Franco from the United States than he got from the Axis powers.

The guilt our government bears for this triple betrayal of the Spanish people has yet to be purged. To the contrary, it is compounded every time we renew the leases on our air, naval, military and atomic arsenals and missile bases in Spain. We also have a *de facto* if not *de jure* agreement to come to the aid of the regime should anyone attempt to overthrow it, and our troops have even held joint maneuvers with Franco's, suppressing hypothetical rebellions.

More than 3,000 young Americans left our country during the Spanish war in violation of our "neutrality" act, to give what aid they could to the Republican cause. It was these volunteers' contention that if Spain lost its battle against subversion and the Axis invasion, World War II would be inevitable.

They joined a force of foreign volunteers from over 20 countries that was called The International Brigades, which never numbered more than 30,000 men in all. Of the 3,200 Americans who went to Spain, 1,300 returned.

This narrative, written by one of those Americans, represents an additional effort on his part to mitigate the guilt of his own country in its criminal support of Franco in terms of arms and money. Whatever effect it has had in the over 35 years since it was written and the several editions through which it has gone can be measured in the only terms that count: the degree to which it has moved readers to support the Spanish people and to oppose their oppressors. That it has moved Howard Chandler and Jonathan Sharp to reissue it—with a companion volume called *Spain Again*—is enormously gratifying to its author.

It is of course only one man's story of that crucial conflict—the opening battle of World War II. It tells truly and scrupulously, insofar as a single individual may see clearly and write honestly, precisely what he saw, felt, learned and experienced during one year (1938) as a soldier in the American battalion of the Brigades.

The battalion's name—Abraham Lincoln—was not chosen idly, for Lincoln represented to us all that aspect of the American democratic tradition that will live forever and forever honor the name of the United States: the struggle against human slavery, against exploitation of the poor by the rich, the fight for decency and human progress against those forces that would hold all peoples back from the achievement of their great potential.

It is therefore a matter of considerable shame and horror to this particular American that as these words are written, the forces of retrogression in the world today still parade under the Stars and Stripes and have found their most beastly expression under our last four administrations: in Korea and the Bay of Pigs, in Santo Domingo and Chile and Vietnam, and in too many other places on the surface of our earth.

We Americans who fought in Spain have been called "premature antifascists" and Spain has been called a lost cause. Premature antifascists have been honored in every nation that fought the Axis—except our own—but we do not seek honors and we have never believed in lost causes.

We know that the opposition of our people can and has forced changes in the policies of our leaders, even though it did not do so during the Spanish war itself. It did force Lyndon Johnson out of office; it did force Richard Nixon to campaign on a promise to end the Vietnam obscenity (just as Johnson had promised before him) and it neutralized and forced Nixon out of office as the depths of his own corruption, arrogance and cynicism became known.

Our people and the entire world have changed greatly since February 1939 when Franco, following his Moorish troops at a safe distance, entered a betrayed Madrid that had never been captured in three years of cruel and bloody fighting. It has taken a long time but Franco's regime is on its last legs today—literally and figuratively.

The forces for world peace and decency are far stronger today than they were 36 years ago. The United States stands alone in its support of Franco's fascism, as it stood alone during Vietnam while the valiant people of a tiny Asian country single-handedly fought to a standstill and forced the withdrawal of one of the most powerful military machines on earth today.

The Vietnamese people did battle as did the Spanish almost four decades ago, and for identical reasons: the right to live their own lives as they saw fit; the right to determine their own destiny, free of foreign interference. They won; the Spanish people lost.

Ultimately, of course, neither decency nor progress can lose to indecency and retrogression. The martyred dead from Auschwitz to Hanoi to the "model" prison in Madrid proclaim this simple fact, this simple truth. We do not mourn them the less but we struggle to spare our contemporaries and our children the agony of such martyrdom.

To do so will require more than books; more than courageous statements by prominent individuals; more than protest demonstrations by millions throughout the civilized world.

It will require the mobilization of those millions—as they are mobilizing in Spain again today—and these millions will force upon the killers a final realization: that their further pursuit of profits, of exploitation, hatred, indecency and death will accomplish nothing less than their total destruction. They will also bring to the earth a regime of decency, security, life, love and peace for which men, women and children have struggled for centuries.

A. B.

San Rafael, California
18 January 1975

A NOTE

The question most frequently asked of the American volunteers who returned from fighting for the Spanish Loyalist Government in the second war of Spain's independence, is: "Why did you go?" Even people whose experience has made them aware of the world-wide peril to democracy cannot somehow take the logical step in thinking that would answer the question for them. They want to know (and they have a right to know) why American citizens, young men—and some older men—who had families, friends, work and obligations in their native land, could abandon those families and friends and jobs, and apparently forget their obligations to the extent of going 3500 miles to fight in a foreign country, in a war that was "not their own." Yet it is precisely because these volunteers were able—some 3800 of them—to bridge that gap in the average man's thinking, and to see that the war in Spain *was* their fight, that they went. For although there were some who went for adventure, and some who went on impulse, the vast majority left their own country (which they loved) as the result of irresistible determination to take their place in a struggle whose front-lines are not confined to Spain.

This book, whose chronology covers only my own experience in Spain, and whose sentiments are purely my own, is intended to elaborate and explain (by indirection) the role that these Americans played in what is still called the "Spanish Civil War." I say "by indirection" because I am neither a political economist nor a historian; I am a fiction writer. (Yet there is no fiction in this narrative.) But the method I have chosen in writing it is, for my own purposes, the only one that I am able to use with any degree of effectiveness. It may leave certain questions unanswered, but I think that it will answer the majority. And it is intended to answer them through its exposition of our life in a foreign country; through its dialogue, its scenes of men in war. By revealing the nature of the life we lived, the things we thought and felt and spoke of, by revealing the sort of men we were and the nature and effect on human beings of modern warfare, it should explain what we were doing there, and why we had to go.

A. B.

A NOTE FOR 1954

The question most frequently asked of the American volunteers who returned from fighting for the Spanish Republic in the second war of Spain's independence, was: "Why did you go?" Even people whose experience had made them aware of the world-wide peril to democracy could not somehow take the logical step in thinking that would have answered the question for them.

They wanted to know why Americans who had families, friends, work and obligations in their native land could leave those families and friends and jobs and apparently forget their obligations to the extent of going 3,500 miles to fight in a foreign country, in a war that was "not their own."

This book, whose chronology covers only my own experience and whose sentiments are entirely my own, was intended to elaborate and explain the role that these Americans played in what *is* still called the "Spanish Civil War."

That it has now been reprinted, fifteen years after it was written, must be flattering to any writer and I am deeply appreciative that my comrades of the Lincoln Brigade feel my book retains enough validity to warrant its reappearance at this time. Whether they are correct the reader will determine for himself.

But it is certain that the emotions and convictions that inspired this narrative are still very much alive in millions of human beings who were involved in the Spanish war, either directly or indirectly.

During that struggle we partisans of the Republic said that if Spain was lost there would be a second World War. Since World War II ended we have been saying that if

Spain remains fascist, the danger of a third is always imminent.

The alliance our spokesmen have made with the Spanish
butcher, we regard today as the second American betrayal
of the Spanish people, as well as treason to our own. It
cannot be justified on any grounds except the obvious fact
that a third world war *is* in preparation.

For the maintenance—by force and violence—of Franco's
grip on Spain explodes the pretensions of our government
to the leadership of the "free world." It also constitutes a
cynical repudiation of every American (and United Nations)
soldier who died to accomplish the final destruction of
fascism.

Those Americans who went to Spain to fight Franco and
to stave off World War II have never minded being called
"premature anti-fascists." They were proud of the label.

And it is therefore inevitable that an Administration that
considers Franco an ally must consider us veterans of the
anti-Franco war "subversives" and "traitors" to its cause:
the cause of maintaining fascism on the Iberian Peninsula.

But it is much easier for the Administration to rewrite
history than to reverse its motion. And that is why most of
us confidently expect to live to see Madrid become the tomb
of fascism, as the Spanish people in 1936 said that it would
be.

We will live to see Franco meet the end of Hitler and
Mussolini—and the Spanish land returned to a people
whose kindliness, whose dignity and whose spirit we have
not forgotten for a single day during the fifteen years that
have passed since the war in Spain "ended."

The same understanding of history that inspires this
confidence convinces us, too, that we will live to see the

McCarrans, the McCarthys and the proliferating breed of witch-hunters that plague our own beloved land return to the dust from which they were created, and the American earth returned to the rank and file Americans in whom the Founders placed their ultimate confidence.

We have long memories. We have developed a relative immunity to the endless barrage of propaganda, slander and outright lies that has been laid upon us. And especially, we are immune to the Big Lie that destroyed Spain and which Hitler developed to such a point of perfection that it was necessary for millions of human beings to die to achieve the defeat of the Axis.

Yet the Big Lie survives and flourishes mightily in our own country today. As it is promulgated daily, hourly and every minute of the day through every medium of communication, so it must be answered—until our own people see it for what it is and explode it in their own good time.

Whenever we hear it said that Communism threatens us from within and without; whenever we are told that the Soviet Union menaces our "way of life" and wants to conquer the world; whenever we are summoned to a Holy Crusade that—if it is allowed to begin—will ravish the entire earth, we recall the following simple facts of history.

- Mussolini killed whatever democracy existed in Italy by claiming that Italy was threatened by Communism;
- Hitler destroyed the German Republic with the same weapon;
- Tojo broke the resistance of the people of Japan by using the identical thesis;
- Franco murdered the Spanish Republic in the name of the "Red menace";
- The Axis launched World War II under the slogan of saving the world from Communism.

These simple facts will not vanish no matter what the real enemies of the people do to conceal them or to give them a new or "one hundred per cent American" coloration.

We are faced, within the boundaries of our country, with a "dynamic crusade" to destroy the liberties of the American people in the name of "national security." We are faced with a major and desperate attempt to return the American worker to the days of the open shop; to deny the American Negro people their rightful place in society.

In the field of foreign affairs, actions are taken daily in the name of the American people which have—in the space of nine short years—made us hated throughout the world, and feared more than we are hated.

It is a safe bet that the "dynamic crusade" will fail, but thousands of Americans will suffer deeply before it peters out in the face of the resistance of a people which has never accepted any tyranny, foreign or domestic.

If the republication of this book serves in any way to inform a generation that has grown up since Spain about the issues of that war and the Americans who helped to fight it, and to illuminate the shocking parallels between the actions of the Franco regime and the intentions of our native reactionaries, the paper and ink used in this edition will not have been consumed in vain.

This writer, at least, is prouder of his membership in the Veterans of the Abraham Lincoln Brigade than he is of any other action he has taken in the fifty years of his life.

A. B.

San Francisco, 19 September 1954

"Mothers! Women! When the years pass by and the wounds of the war are being stanched; when the cloudy memory of the sorrowful, bloody days returns in a present of freedom, peace and well-being; when the feelings of rancour are dying away and when pride in a free country is felt equally by all Spaniards, then speak to your children. Tell them of these men of the International Brigades.

"Tell them how, coming over seas and mountains, crossing frontiers bristling with bayonets . . . these men reached our country as crusaders for freedom, to fight and die for Spain's liberty and independence which were threatened by German and Italian Fascism. They gave up everything: their loves, their countries, home and fortune; fathers, mothers, wives, brothers, sisters and children, and they came and told us: 'We are here. Your cause, Spain's cause, is ours—it is the cause of all advanced and progressive mankind.'"

DOLORES IBARRURI
('LA PASIONARIA')

1

THE RETREAT

I

THE SHIP was several hours late at Le Havre, and so we did not arrive in Paris until one o'clock in the morning. Paris late at night is a dead city, but it could not diminish our excitement, and we were all sorry that we were so tired and that no places were open at that hour. So we took a cab to a hotel near the Gare St. Lazare, and rang the doorbell. A sleepy young man finally answered.

"We're expected?" we said.

"No," he said.

"Weren't you informed that six Americans would arrive today?"

"No."

We looked at each other, then asked for rooms; three rooms for six men. We wondered what had become of the three other men who had been on the ship, and were going to the same place—Hoover and Garfield and Earl, all from California.

"This way," the concierge said, and we followed him to the top floor, where he opened the three rooms. There was a double bed in each room, and immediately Proios, the Greek, announced that he would sleep on the floor. Looking at Merkel, the enormous German-American seaman, we couldn't blame him, but that was his affair. We couldn't understand a word that Proios said, but he made himself

3

understood nevertheless. Without a word of English at his
command, he had even managed to clean out the third-class
passengers at poker. He could laugh; he laughed every time
he raked in a pot and spread his hands in an apologetic
manner. He had beautiful teeth, framed in gold.

The two Cubans, Prieto and Diaz, were content to sleep
together, and 'Lopez' and I drew the other room. Looking at 'Lopez' I laughed. A New York Jew, he had managed to get a Spanish passport that, he confidently believed,
would carry him into Spain aboard a train. 'After all, I'm
a Spanish citizen,' he said. 'But you can't speak a word of
Spanish,' we had said. 'That's all right; I was brought to
America when I was a kid.'

"What're you laughing at?" he said.

"The furnishings." There was the inevitable Roman-
striped wallpaper, the red carpet, the nineteenth-century gilt
clock under a glass bell, the deep closet, the push-button
that turned on the light if you kept pushing it long enough.
I left a note outside, "Please wake me at seven o'clock," and
we turned in. We knew there was a committee that assisted
men anxious to get to Spain, but I had a feeling that no one
would be there at that time of night.

Early the next morning I reported, by cab, to the Committee and received a few hundred francs, six tickets to a
coöperative restaurant near by and instructions to bring the
others to the Committee's headquarters at two that afternoon. I asked about Hoover and Garfield and Earl, but
they had not yet turned up. I taxied back to the hotel near
St. Lazare, where the other boys were waking up, and we
went out to see the town. I had wanted to show them the
Sainte Chapelle, Notre Dame and the chastity-belts in the

Musée de Cluny, but there was little time to spend and nothing much to see; only thousands of people going to work, who looked just the same as other people going to work all over the world; dejected, tired, defeated but content. Our job was to keep our mouths shut and not attract attention, and we were even hesitant about walking together on the street.

The free meal was bad, and 'Lopez' wasted a lot of time sending a cablegram signed 'Hy' to some one in America. But we got to the Committee at two, and sat on low benches in a lecture hall. There were other men there; one I recall who was wearing a blue beret and a leather glove on an obviously artificial hand. "You guys just get back?" he said, and we said, "No, we're just going." "Oh," he mumbled, "more suckers." We looked at him but he retired into himself, sitting in the back of the room for a time, and then suddenly leaving.

The committee-man said, "I can't impress on you too seriously the need for caution. The French Government is nominally sympathetic to Spain, but the border is officially closed. Non-intervention, you understand. We can't do anything that might give our enemies, and Spain's enemies, an opportunity to make our difficulties greater . . ." We glanced over at Hoover and Garfield and Earl, who had been drunk from one shore to the other, and had made no bones about where they all were going. ". . . I advise you guys to watch your step. Don't drink too much, and avoid whores; there are plenty of Fascist spies in Paris, who're very interested in what we're doing. You guys came here to go to Spain, not to paint the town red; keep that in mind at all times and I'm sure we won't have any trouble."

They said to us, "I think you'd better take the train to-night. Be in your rooms at four this afternoon, and stay there till we come. Pack as little as possible in a paper parcel; we'll pick up your suitcases and pay the hotel bill after you've gone." "What'll happen with our suitcases?" Prieto said. "You'll get them back," they said, "when . . . when you come back." Prieto grinned.

We spent the next hour and a quarter buying a few essentials we felt that we would need—tobacco, cigarettes, pipes, chocolate, a couple flasks of *Martell*. We wrote letters, packed a shirt, a change of underwear, an extra pair of socks, shaving equipment, toothbrush and soap, handkerchiefs, making a neat paper parcel and looking longingly at the stuff that would have to be left behind. Hoover and Garfield and Earl showed up, considerably sobered. (The Committee had apparently given them our address.) Garfield, who had been a small-time actor in Hollywood, needed a shave badly and seemed to have lost the bounce he spent so much time exhibiting on shipboard. We laughed again at his last-night performance, when he'd been particularly plastered, and getting hold of a pack of baggage-stickers, had escaped from third class. He pasted one on every door in first class, on the shoes waiting to be shined in the corridor, on a remonstrating steward's nose. We laughed, and then we sat twiddling our thumbs till five o'clock, when three men from the Paris committee came in the door.

They gave us money and tickets for the train that was to leave at 9:10 from the Gare de Lyons. The speaker said, "This comrade will be your guide; look for him at the station, but do not speak to him. Follow him aboard the train, but do not speak to him aboard the train. There will be a lot of other men aboard; do not speak to them either. You're supposed to be tourists; so act the part . . ." (We wondered how we could look like tourists; eight men with identical paper parcels getting off at the same station. Eight men? Perhaps eighty men. We didn't ask.) ". . . At ten-thirty tomorrow you'll reach your first stop, and go to this hotel by cab. They'll be expecting you and will show you to your rooms. Stay in those rooms, no matter how long it is, until this other comrade"—he indicated the other, who looked French—"comes to you. Don't leave your rooms; good luck." The three of them turned to go, and then the speaker said, "Go to the station in three separate taxis."

We were certain the cab was being followed, we saw dozens of plainclothes men in the Gare de Lyons and we were terrified when the guide, a short stocky fellow wearing no hat and carrying a briefcase, nodded quite perceptibly to us; but we followed him at a distance, positive that our group was attracting attention but fearful of losing each other in the crowd. In the third-class coach the compartments were filled with men studiously looking out the windows onto the platforms, paper parcels in their laps or on the racks. They were foreign in appearance; they looked more like workingmen than we. Hoover, Garfield and Earl were nowhere in sight, but the five of us found an empty compartment, and sat saying nothing to each other, aching for the train to pull out.

The guide wandered down the corridor, looked in at us and nodded slightly and passed on. The leather seats were hard; the coach was poorly heated. Merkel lit his pipe and winked at me; 'Lopez' blew his nose; Garcia and Diaz sat staring through each other; Proios had been left, temporarily, in Paris to get treatment for an infected eye. The whistles blew and I thought again of my two little kids back in Brooklyn, and of the post-card I had sent them from the ship.

There was no sleep that night. There had been little sleep the night before and practically none the last night aboard ship. We put our feet up on the leather-covered benches opposite, begging our fellow-travelers' pardon. But there was no sleep.

Merkel winked again, and said, "Sprechen Sie Deutsch?"

"Nein," I said. "Ich hab es nur ein Yahr studiert."

He laughed, 'Lopez' threw in a few words in Yiddish and we began to speak in low tones. I remembered having had a "premonition" the night I met these men. Seeing this enormously fat man for the first time, I had thought, 'He'll be the first to go.' Now we began to feel each other out; find out who we were and where we'd come from. 'Lopez' was a New York student; Merkel a sea-cook from the West Coast; Prieto had lived for some time in the States and spoke a curious sort of English, very formal. Diaz spoke not a word, but he sang a lot. Dark of skin, he was a magnificently built animal wearing high boots under his city overcoat; he was bowlegged, had been a cavalryman in the Cuban Army for a time. He smiled, showing magnificent white teeth; but he was just as likely to be surly, and he switched these two personalities on and off like an electric-light bulb.

"I was four years in the war," Merkel said. "German army."

"What was it like?"

"It ain't bad," he said. "It ain't bad at all; you get used to it. You never see the enemy; you shoot and shoot and you never see 'em. It ain't bad at all."

We talked of the World War and of the Spanish War. Merkel told us that he had done underground work in Germany, and of the discontent among the German workers. "Every ship what comes to Hamburg," he said, "brings literature for 'em; they eat it up. I fight against Hitler, that bastard," he said. We talked of conditions back home; of Roosevelt's popularity and liberalism, and of the reactionary opposition they were trying to whip up again; of its chances of success. "In the end," said Merkel, "you can't fool the workers. Takes 'em maybe a long time to wake up with the newspapers saying lies all the time, but you can't fool 'em."

We switched out the light and tried to sleep again; the windows were clouded with steam as the train shrieked along the tracks, and we thought of the thousands from all countries who had traveled this way before, and of those who had not come back. We thought of the volunteer organizations throughout the world that were helping to get these men to Spain; we thought of the men from Fascist countries, who had known the enemy at first hand, had escaped from their own countries and traveled thousands of miles to get to Spain to fight that enemy on another front, and who would have no homes if they survived the war. We were optimistic of the outcome. The Loyalists had retaken Teruel; their Army was now an integer; they had resolved the internal struggle between the various political parties who each had had its own idea of how to fight the war; they were fighting it together now. A friend of mine had said, "I envy you; you'll be in at the kill." Every one back home thought that Teruel meant the turning of the tide.

We dozed and woke (Merkel did not sleep a wink; I could see his pipe glowing all night long); we looked out of the windows when the windows were clear of steam. At one twenty-five we were in Dijon; at four in Lyons, and dawn came slowly over southern France. It was cold in the compartment, cold and damp and stuffy. Earlier in the night the guide had come into the compartment and talked to us. He spoke only a few words of English, but he talked a fluent Spanish to Diaz and Prieto (who translated for us), he spoke German to Merkel, French to me and Yiddish to 'Lopez.' He told us that he spoke four other languages, and we asked how many men were on the train.

"Over a hundred," he said. "Mostly Poles, Rumanians and Czechs."

"How often do you make this trip?" we said.

"Three times a week."

We were cold and hungry; the apples, the chocolate, the oranges and small cakes we had purchased in the station all were gone. The dawn brought a sharper cold that seeped through the steamed windowpanes, rose from the carriage floor. We passed Valence, Avignon, Tarascon, Vimes, Montpellier. Below Avignon ('Lopez' and I inevitably sang, 'Sur le pont, d'Avignon, l'on y danse, l'on y danse') there were the first gray olive trees; rock rose through the soil, gray and rugged; there were masonry houses with tile roofs, and there were walls around the houses. It was a peaceful countryside, and the inexperienced mind immediately imagined a contrast that would be noticed once the Spanish border had been crossed. The mind expected the country-side to show immediate signs of war, if not actual troops in motion, big guns, airplanes. With the approach to the Spanish land our excitement must have been mounting; we knew that we were finally going somewhere; it was revealed in our animation, the light that shone in our eyes, our rapid gestures, our exuberance. As the train slowed to a stop at Béziers, the guide passed through the corridor, indicated that this was our station, and we stretched our heavy legs.

Emerging from the train, every man glanced at the man near by; there were dozens, scores, getting down from the train, crossing the platform, carrying almost identical paper parcels, wearing city overcoats, felt hats or caps, sedulously paying no attention to their fellows. We got into a cab, gave the name of our particular hotel to the driver and watched the town through the windows. It was built on a hill, and we climbed that hill; the road twisting and turning over the rough cobbles, the houses painted in pastel colors, pale pink, light blue, shades of brown. There were palm trees, narrow streets and a broad main boulevard; many people on the streets seemed to notice us riding in the cab. At the entrance to the hotel we climbed out, and went in a door that was held open for us by a buxom French-woman of early middle age. She smiled, greeted us as "Cama-rades," and told us to go right upstairs, our rooms were waiting. "Dinner will be ready in ten minutes," she said.

It was cold in the room; there was no way of heating it. We washed in cold water, tested the enormous feather beds, looked out of the small window that looked down into the town. The guide and the other man from the Paris committee came in the door. The guide seemed angry.

"I thought I told you to go to *this* hotel," he said, showing us a card.

We were bewildered.

"This hotel," he said, "is across the street; you are in the wrong hotel."

"We gave this name," we said, wondering how and why it could matter. The two of them withdrew for consultation, then returned. "It doesn't matter," they said. "Send two of your men across to this other hotel. There is a certain rivalry. . . . " We all laughed. "You will be here all day, tonight, and part of tomorrow. Tomorrow after lunch a taxicab will call for you and take you to the next point; be on hand to watch for it. You're free to visit the town, but talk to no one. If you want to spend what money you have, we advise you to buy tobacco and chocolate, but mostly tobacco. You will find very little tobacco in Spain."

We went down to the combined dining and sitting room, where there was a score of other men. The meal was plain; this was a working-class hotel. Plenty of bread with the soup, cold cuts of various types of sausages, good beer or wine, a hot green vegetable. Conversation did not lag at the long table. Men seemed to feel at home immediately, though few could speak a common tongue. Here there were two Frenchmen, three Poles, some Rumanians—all young. We tried our hand at various languages. Most of these Europeans could speak French and German and we carried on long, halting conversations by piecing together the few words we knew of at least five languages. We laughed a good deal at each other's efforts; there was a definite desire to communicate; it made you feel good. Here were students, engineers, dock-workers, clerks and labor-organizers, farm-

ers. Most were unacquainted with each other, but they
came together now with the warmth and familiarity of old
friends; they told each other of their work in their respective countries; of their friends and families. They spoke of
the European political scene, of the imperative necessity for
the Loyalist Government to drive the foreign invader from
Spain; you felt that with each of them, no matter how
diverse his previous training, the Spanish struggle was a
personal issue; something deep and close. This in itself,
considering the disparity of their origin, was a major political phenomenon. They spoke no word of the actual
business of war; they did not speculate on the nature of
artillery or air attacks, of machine-gun fire. You felt: many
of these men will never see their friends or families again;
they don't know what they're getting into; their idealism
has blinded them to the reality of what they will have to
face. And you knew immediately that you were wrong;
that they were so far from being blind that it might be
said of them that they were among the first soldiers in the
history of the world who really knew what they were about,
what they were going to fight for—and that they were ready
and eager to fight. Their very presence on the French frontier was an earnest of their understanding and their clarity;
no one had made them come, no force but an inner force
had brought them.

They contrasted strangely with the three other Americans
who had been on our ship—Hoover and Garfield and Earl.
Hoover and Earl had worked for a living too, as sheet-
metal workers in a California aircraft factory; they had
participated in a bitter strike, but they were not, inevitably,
a part of that majority of human beings the world over

who have nothing to look forward to from day to day except work. They were floaters. Earl had been a small-time pugilist; Hoover a Jack-of-all-trades and Garfield a hanger-on of the artistic world. He was strangely feminine although he talked a great deal of his wife, whom he had left, and of his various love affairs. 'I'm going to work in a hospital,' he had told me. 'I'm not going to be a front-line soldier. I'm willing to work in hospitals even if they do drop a few bombs on our heads once in awhile.' I had asked him why he was going to Spain. 'To make a man of myself,' he said, and I think he half believed it, in a romantic fashion. He was twenty-five years old and more of a woman than a man. On shipboard he and Earl had rapidly taken a dislike to Hoover; Hoover was loud, attracted attention to himself and to his past experiences. He said he was a pilot; he showed a picture of himself standing beside an airplane; he showed a photograph of a pretty girl who had been killed in an automobile accident. 'Since that happened,' he said with a conscious, bitter smile, 'I haven't cared whether I lived or died. I hope I get killed.' 'We hope he does too,' Earl and Garfield said. 'It's no great loss.'

Whenever the mind has led the body to an important decision, events have a way of assuming, momentarily, a half-symbolic nature. The mind plays that trick on you, and everything you see seems to partake of the quality of the decision you have made. The town of Béziers was the incarnation of peace itself as we walked its narrow, quiet streets. The small purchases we made—American cigarettes and tobacco, pipe-cleaners, a cigarette lighter, postcards to send home (*Dear Dan and Dave, I'm here far away across the ocean, in France. Mom will show you a picture of France on the map . . .*)—all these assumed a finality that could be terrifying if you allowed yourself to dwell on it. Merkel wanted to walk, but something drew me to a moving-picture theater that was playing a matinée. I wanted to see an American moving-picture; it would re-establish contact for me.

But even the picture, "Black Legion" (in French), seemed to confirm the decision that had brought me thus far, and it re-established contact, not only with my own country but with progressive forces that were at work around the world. Watching the typical American workingman, in the film, succumb to and accept ideals diametrically opposed to the very attributes that made him an American, you could feel again the power of the evil that was at work. An evil power that would split man from man, brother from brother the world over—and you knew again the necessity to fight that power. For here was Fascism in its American manifestation, at work in terms of human beings, not in terms of words set down on paper. Here was the objectification of a conscious force that had as its aim the maintenance of human subjection—by force and violence. Here was something that could make you mad again, and the decent human being finds it difficult to harbor hatred in his heart for any considerable length of time.

We slept well in the French feather beds despite the cold and the Mediterranean fog that came in the open window. We awoke early, and promptly after the noon meal a taxi drove up to the door, the concièrge nodded to us, gave us all a *fine* on the house and we piled in. The cab drove into the countryside, going north, for about twenty minutes;

and turned into the dooryard of a well-kept farm. Around behind the farmhouse there was a large stone barn with a sliding door, and we were told to go into the barn and wait. The door was closed behind us; it was cold. The barn was empty except for a few barrels, a work-bench with rusting farm tools, a long table made by placing three doors across carpenters' horses. There was a hayloft and an entrance to the farmhouse that was kept closed. There were three small children; exceptionally beautiful children with dark eyes and hair, who might have been either French or Spanish.

This was the home of a sympathetic peasant family, who spoke both French and Spanish with equal fluency. They paid little attention to us, except to warn us not to show ourselves outside the barnyard. Other taxis arrived with other men; Germans, Danes, more Poles, a Japanese, some Englishmen. The barn was crowded and the men were becoming bored. They horsed around, laughed at inconsequentialities, tried various acrobatic stunts on the rafters, competed in the sort of mild gymnastics that can be performed in a parlor—hand-wrestling, contortionistic stunts. Garfield had been trying for some time to open a wine barrel, with little success. It was bunged up, but the bung had a small hole in it. A group stood, laughing, between him and the entrance to the farmhouse, hoping that he could find some way to the wine, giggling like twelve-year-olds, offering impossible advice. He was popular with the men; he sang Mexican, French, German or Italian songs between bouts with the wine barrel; he and Hoover and Earl repeated a favorite of theirs that had amused the third-class passengers: "There was an old man and he had an

old sow, umph, humph (grunting like pigs) hy-diddle-
dow . . ." This they claimed was an old English folksong,
and it may well have been, but only the English-speaking
could understand it, and the other men laughed at the
noises the trio made. "Now this old sow had nine little
pigs . . ."

Some men were trying to sleep on the long table, their
coats draped over them, their heads in each other's lap.
Some played cards, but their fingers grew cold. Some walked
up and down, soberly. It was said that we were only a short
distance from the border. It was said we'd only have an
hour's walk to cross the frontier. Mention was made of
men who had been shot at, some killed, by the French
border-guards, but this seemed to worry no one; in fact it
added spice to the adventure. "We'll be shot at soon enough
anyhow," a Pole said, in French.

Garfield had found a hollow metal tube that was long
and thin enough to tap the cask. He sucked on it as though
it were a straw; he laughed; the red wine trickled from the
corners of his wet red mouth, like blood. *"La cucarácha,
la cucarácha!"* he shouted, *"ya no puedo caminar!"* Others
took their turn at the barrel. The barn reverberated with the
noise of shouting, singing men.

"Arise! Ye prisoners of starvation," sang 'Lopez' in a
timid, nasal voice, "Arise! Ye wretched of the earth!" The
song was taken up in a half-dozen languages. *"Das Recht,
wie Glut im Kraterherde,"* Merkel thundered, and Diaz,
plucking an imaginary guitar, cried, *"Guerra hast' el fin
de la opresión!"*

The door into the farmhouse opened and one of the
peasant men stood there, holding the smallest girl-child in

his arms. She was wearing only a short dirty white dress; her little brown bottom pressed against his arm. Behind him stood his wife, his brother, the two other children. He spoke in French.

"Comrades," he said. "I must ask you not to sing that song so loud." He smiled.

After dark two buses came for the men in the stone barn, and stood waiting in a lane off the main road, their lights turned off. Silently we boarded them and sat still and nervous as the cars bored their way through the darkness, dark inside, their headlights tunneling the night ahead. There was a light rain and the black road ahead was slippery; the bus moved through the mist as though it rode on wings, seemingly unattached to the earth. We were moving fast and after a time we passed through Narbonne. In the darkness we put on the rope-soled slippers we later came to know as *alpargatas,* and tied the tapes about our ankles.

Beyond Narbonne it was no surprise to see French soldiers in the beam of the headlights, and we sat tense and quiet as the bus came to a stop in response to their command. Soldiers moved about the bus, shining their flashlights into the interior, and the motionless and silent men sat looking stonily ahead. We felt this inspection to be an unnecessary piece of sadism, for they must have known who we were and where we were going, and after a consultation with the driver they told us to move on. This happened again a half an hour later, only this time they were *hirondelles,* bicycle-police examining the scene of an accident. Then we continued, moving faster in the darkness, listening to the hiss of the tires on the wet pavement, straining our eyes in vain to see the countryside.

The road wound up through the foothills of the Pyrenees and on a black road, with no other light showing, the bus stopped, switched off its lights and waited. We got down and stood on a path that led into the road, in the drizzle. It was dark and cold. In ten minutes the other bus came, switched off its lights, and when the men got down they joined us. We moved off, slightly down grade toward the mountains in the distance, that could be felt rather than seen. We kept close together and, as if by common consent, we did not speak. We moved cross-country for a time, our feet immediately wet through the rope-soled *alpargatas,* our faces wet by the drifting haze and drizzle. There were lights of houses in the distance, but we seemed to be avoiding them. A dog barked near by, furious at the sound of moving men, but as it seemed to be chained and came no closer, we continued moving through an orchard toward the distant hills.

At their base we crossed a broad and shallow stream, moving delicately across long thin poles laid across the water. (I slipped, fell in, the bundle, that was already damp, burst and packages of cigarettes fell out, floated away.) We trudged through marshy soil on the far side of the stream, cursing silently, stumbling and falling, running when we could feel the men ahead were moving faster. By now it was raining and snowing alternately; the wind stung our cheeks, drove the snowflakes into our eyes like tiny points of ice. And the ground rose under our feet, slowly at first, and then more sharply. For a time we moved on a narrow, hard-surfaced road in single file, but then there was a light ahead of us, like a white dawn rising in the mist, and within a fraction of a second there was not a man on the road. We had run to the side, leaped the ditches and the low stone walls and flattened ourselves in the mud as the car roared by.

The ground rose under our feet and the going became hard. There were tough bushes and slippery rocks, shrubs that caught at our city overcoats. The felt hat was sodden on my head, drooping around my ears. The package had completely disintegrated, and had to be held together in both arms. We did not slow down, we did not halt for rest, but we left the path and climbed the hillsides, scrambling and stumbling through the bushes and the light second growth of trees, slipping on the moss, grunting with the effort. The path made itself felt again through the thin-soled sandals, and we were grateful for it. It was pitch-black but below us we could see the agglomeration of lights that meant a town— light and warmth and comfort, and people tucked in feather beds. Here there were only the huddled men in the darkness, cold and wet, steaming in their own sweat, anxious to keep close together, as though mere proximity meant safety, anxious not to be seen. In the dark the path wound swiftly back and forth, lacing the mountain side, skirting tall pines and great overhanging rocks, dipping and rising. Word came back in half a dozen languages during a brief pause, that from this point on we were not to smoke, not to talk. We thought we were near the border; it cheered us. Men knelt in the path in the mud, and we passed the flasks of _Martell_ around; they didn't go very far but the cognac heated our bellies and our limbs. The men stole a swift drag of smoke under cover of their overcoats.

The guide went ahead, feeling for the path in the darkness. Earlier we had seen him; a short fat man, a former Portugese smuggler they had told us, who was wearing a raincoat and carrying an umbrella. He let out a low whistle and we followed. It was so dark you could not see the man ahead unless you could touch him, so we stayed close enough together to be able to put out our hands and touch the dark and reassuring back ahead. The meaning of the word 'comrade,' so often heard in Spain, began to become clear. We were tired; our ankles were sore; our feet were tender. The path rose ever steeper and we were bent to the path, as though carrying heavy loads. Our chests ached with the effort to breathe deeply, normally; our thighs with the long hours of walking. Yet there seemed to be no end to it; we crossed a low summit, slid down the other side and saw the next ridge of hills looming steep and dark before us, like a head sea. An hour from the border! We had already been walking four; that meant that it was after two o'clock. Two o'clock in France; nine o'clock in Brooklyn.

In the darkness I walked straight off the path, felt myself falling and bent double, rolled down the embankment till a tree stopped me with a thud. The bundle, now wrapped in a suede-leather jacket, was still in my arms, but my hat was gone. I hunted for it a moment in the dark, heard the men passing above me and scrambled back toward the path. A hand reached out and helped me onto it, and I thought of the hat lying abandoned in one of the passes of the Pyrenees; a dark blue felt hat (made in Paris for Lord & Taylor Co.), stamped with the initials of the actor Morris Carnovsky, worn in the production of "Wings Over Europe." It made me laugh to think of it lying there.

There was some commotion in the dark, voices spoke

quietly in several languages; some men straggling behind
had been lost from the Indian file and were calling quietly.
We halted and a guide went back for them. It was a blessed
rest and we lay in the path on the wet stony soil, feeling the
rain in our hair, feeling the cold drops trickle down our
faces. Far below, behind, in the thickening mist, the jeweled
town still shone in the darkness; but there were fewer lights;
most folks had gone to bed. Then we were up and on again,
moving with one hand outstretched before us, like elephants
in a circus-procession, holding onto each other's tails. The
exertion stimulated our intestinal muscles; all night long
the men were breaking wind from the unaccustomed exercise. *"Merde alors!"* the man behind me said, and whistled
quietly. *"Pas exactement,"* I replied. . . .

. . . The pace accelerated; dawn was near and it would
have to find us over the frontier. The men, largely untrained and in no physical condition for a trek like this,
were catching a second wind, but we knew there was a section far behind. Courage, determination you could feel all
around you in the first faint glow of dawn. Shapes began
to emerge gradually from the darkness; it was possible to
recognize a man you had seen before on the train, in the
barn. Garfield was just in front of me, his dark curly hair
matted in the high cold wind that swept down from the
peaks. In the dark I passed a small man, moving doggedly
ahead, sobbing quietly to himself; the sound it made was
barely perceptible in the whining of the wind. Above we
could see the towering summit of the range, seeming over-
balanced in the half-light of dawn. It was a long way off,
and every step we took seemed to carry us backward, like

the indefatigable frog in the well. It floated before our eyes like a mirage and it had about it that exasperating impersonality that one sees in every natural phenomenon—a storm at sea, a forest fire, an elecric storm. It was a challenge we were trying to accept.

The men struggled up the slope in the growing light; the timber-line was far below us and we moved among giant boulders, over close-cropped grass; grass close-cropped by the high winds of the peaks. There was snow in the folds of the rock; snow underfoot, in patches. Two men were carrying another; one man was limping, supported by a comrade. One man's face was streaked with streaming blood. The wind stiffened and we leaned against it, our overcoats flapping around us, hampering our movements; our legs kept moving though our minds had already stopped far down the farthest slopes. We leaned sideways against the wind, presenting less surface, moving like crabs across the wide open expanse. There were huge rounded stones rising from the soil, like molars, fangs, and the sky was swept clean of clouds, a pale washed blue that was as cold to look at as the wind on our faces. The brilliant light hurt our eyes and we narrowed them; you could feel the grit in the corners of your eyes; you could feel your beard growing. The men's clothes were the color of the earth.

They broke into a run ahead, slanting across the crest of the peak, leaning parallel to each other like fence-posts. There were a few trees, stunted and twisted by the wind and cold, their trunks covered with thick, ironlike bark. The men were running as though they were being pursued, and we all followed, heaving like spavined horses, gasping and groaning aloud as we ran. On the far side of the peak they had run a few hundred yards more, then dropped onto the ground. It was hard to know what to look at first, the men lying spread-eagled on the ground in the biting wind, or the sight of Spain lying below us for fifty miles stretched out beyond the mountains. Dirty, exhausted, their faces scratched, their city clothes ragged, they lay there laughing, weeping. One man was frankly sobbing into his hands, his shoulders working. Two were wrestling with each other; others stood in what seemed to be heroic postures, a hand to their foreheads, gazing at the land that lay ahead.

Far below and flat to the eye lay Spain, beyond the rugged mountains to the west. There were rivers winding far away, gleaming silver in the sun like fragile woven threads. It was a peaceful countryside; there was not a cloud in the sky, not a bird flying. You could not see a house from where we stood. The wind was strong and moaned across the summit; you had to lean against it. You felt that you were in the presence of Time and Death, the top of the world and the end of it. You felt that you would like to lift your arms, soar into the face of the wind like a sail-plane, circle and bank and gently float to earth.

2

[*February*]

You CANNOT really believe in the existence of a foreign country until you see it. Sliding, trotting down the Spanish slope of the Pyrenees recalled a trip to France nine years before when, after thirteen days at sea, bored by the immensity of it and its great power, I awoke late at night to see, half-waking, half-sleeping, great white lights moving, one by one, past the cabin port-holes; and later, coming out on deck in the early morning, saw a sign on the pier, in French! Here the immediate sense-data were different, but the emotion remained. Here was magnificent rugged scenery, mountains thrown together in theatrical and monstrous forms, cork-trees whose trunks were stripped of their bark as a whale is stripped of its blubber; the dull gray-green of olive-trees, the olives ripening; lemon-trees with their bright lanternlike fruit hanging from their branches, in February!

Below us were houses perched on the mountain side; houses of masonry and composite stone; brick, field-stone and blocks, with tile roofs. Three women dressed in black were climbing the hillside toward us, looking up at us as we approached. When we passed we saw that they were poor peasants; one young, one middle-aged, one old. They smiled and said, *"Salud! Salud compañeros!"* The oldest said nothing. We were cold, hungry and exhausted and continued to stumble down the mountain side, occasionally looking back at the women, the first three Spanish people we had seen. We wondered what they thought of us, foreign men dressed in foreign clothes, climbing over the Pyrenees in dead of night, coming to fight beside their men. They could not speak our language, nor we theirs.

Below there was a hard-surfaced road, shining white in the distance, and as we approached it our hearts beat faster. Two soldiers had appeared from nowhere; blankets were thrown over their shoulders instead of capes or overcoats, and they carried rifles. On their caps they wore a red five-pointed star, the star of the Republic. They smiled at us and headed the column of perhaps fifty men, trying to

establish communication with us. Three or four of the men
had been home on leave and were now returning; they
could speak a few words of Spanish. But most of us bunched
up near the soldiers, trying vainly to understand what
they were saying, offering cigarettes and chocolates. We sat
on the side of the hard road in the sun, which was not very
warm, and shivered, waiting for the trucks we had been
told would come. We sat there almost two hours, tried to
sleep or smoked, until two trucks came rolling down the
road from the west, with soldiers standing on the running-
board waving their rifles in greeting to us. The men awoke;
their strength returned; they vaulted into the open trucks
as though they had unlimited reserves of energy, and the
trucks moved on again, still going west.

Jammed into the open metal bodies, falling all over each
other at every jolt, we laughed and shouted, greeting every
one we saw with loud cries of *"Salud!"* and *"Viva la República!"* Peasants in donkey-carts smiled at us, lifting their
arms in the clenched-fist Popular Front salute, shook that
arm with determination. Peasants in the fields beside the
road lifted their arms at a distance, held them aloft until
we rounded the bend in the road, passed out of sight. The
driver, like all Spanish drivers (cars were a novelty before
the war) was mad for speed; he blew his horn continuously and roared down the road, frightening the *burros,*
the occasional people walking on the edge; he was out to
see how much the truck could take. At odd points there
were traffic jams—trucks, carts, donkeys being led—and at
one of these points we were stalled beside a truck full of
Spanish soldiers moving the other way. They threw over
several bottles labeled *coñac* and we shouted with delight.

"Viva los extranjeros!" they cried. *"Viva las Brigadas Internacionales!"* and we answered, *"Viva!"* The *coñac* tasted like a mixture of paint-remover and vanilla.

There was a town in sight, and a group of soldiers in the middle of the road waved us to a stop. Those who could understand what they were saying translated for us: "The town is being bombed." But the truck picked up speed immediately, and if anything it rolled faster than before. Peasants standing in the fields outside the town, beside the entrances of *refugios,* looked at us with curiosity as we burned up the road leading into town, then returned their attention to the sky. Their faces were calm, impassive but full of hate; and in the pause when the soldiers had stopped us, we had heard the planes droning in the sky. Their sound was different from the sound of any plane that I had ever heard; their motors pulsed and throbbed in the sky (so blue you could not look at it), beating and beating with ominous overtone. Beauty had become enormity, more horrible for its persisting lovelieness. We saw them, tiny sparks of silver tinsel flashing in the blue immensity, two Italian all-metal monoplanes soaring at eight thousand feet above the peaceful town. Then they were cut off from view as the houses surrounded us; we crouched in the trucks, instinctively, and they turned a corner, coming out onto a broad, curving road that wound uphill to a fortress at the crest. We stood balancing in the trucks, watching the planes, hearing their propeller-roar now over the whining of the truck in second gear, and we rolled into a broad courtyard where men in uniform herded us immediately into the cellars of the fort—high, vaulted masonry caverns dripping with moisture and cold to the skin. Here we stayed until the alarm was over, in the caverns of the ancient fortress of Figueras. . . .

. . . There was bread to eat and a hot black fluid we called coffee; it was bitter. Then we reported in single file to the office, where a Greek who spoke English with a British accent (and a dozen other languages as well) registered us all and said, "You know, of course, that you are here for the duration of the war." We said, "Of course." "What address to notify in case of accident?"

We wandered in the courtyard; we were shown to our bunks in long rooms that all opened on the courtyard. There were long rows of beds made of planks and covered with straw-filled ticks wide enough for two men; that was all the furniture. There was a latrine in one of the empty rooms; the usual European hole in the floor; it stank. We climbed on the battlements of the fortress, looking back at the snow-covered Pyrenees; forward into the plain country that lay beyond. Then a whistle blew and we returned to the long whitewashed room that was a mess hall, where the plank tables were laid with tin dishes, tin spoons. The end men at each table reported to the kitchen in the courtyard and returned carrying washtubs of potatoes and stew. There were crocks of red wine on the tables, tin cups into which to pour the wine. It was bad. There was a short speech of welcome made in good German, good Polish and French, and in bad English. There was absoloute silence as the officer spoke, and after lunch we went to bed, sleeping until late that afternoon. It was cool in the long room; hot in the sun.

In the reading room next to the mess hall the walls were

covered with crude mural paintings: scenes of the war, por-
traits of Negrin, Azaña, Lenin, La Pasionaria, Dimitrov,
Marx and Diaz, and the Loyalist commanders, Rojo, Modesto, Lister and "El Campesino." There were notices posted
in every language you could and could not read, urging discipline, coöperation, cleanliness, comradeliness. There were
drawings of how to take shelter from various types of fire
—artillery, air-bombs, machine-guns; how not to expose
yourself in moving across a field. There was a small, meticu-
lous model of modern fortifications, trenches, communication trenches, machine-gun nests and dug-outs, completely
furnished with toy soldiers, stretcher-bearers, ambulances
and barbed wire. There were publications from every country, *The London Times,* the *Paris-Soir* and *L'Humanité,*
the *Daily Worker, Colliers, Mundo Obrero, International
Press Correspondence, Punch, Rote Fahne, La Vanguardia,
Life* and *Time, Frente Rojo,* working-class publications of
all sorts. There were exhortations painted on the walls:

Proletarios de Todos Paises! Unios!
Proletarier, Alle Länder, Vereinigt Euch!
Proletaires de Tous Pays, Unissez-vous!
Proletari di Tutti i Paesi Unitevi!
Proletar JUSZEWSZYSTICH KRAJOW ta CZeIESIE!
WORKERS OF THE WORLD, UNITE!

Every one was friendly, every one was smiling. Men were
trying to establish contact with each other in their various
languages, laughing over their difficulties. Men were writing letters and postcards home; their faces were serious.
Some were playing checkers or chess, some were reading
the innumerable publications, pamphlets and books. Poles,

Germans, French and English, Welsh, Irish, Scots, Americans and Rumanians wandered in the courtyard and over the battlements (we were not permitted to leave the fortress grounds), bought oranges by the kilo and a bottled chemical drink in the *cantina* where the concessionaire obviously did not care much for his customers. He sat frowning at the light-hearted men, raking in the pesetas we had received for our francs or dollars, with eager, grasping fingers. He was fat; his wife was even fatter. We had learned the word for foreigners; we heard him use the word with contempt but we could not be angry with him. We were in a country where his money-grubbing class was rapidly losing its place, just as it would eventually lose its place throughout the world. We believed there would some day be a world of people who would see in money no more than a medium of exchange, the fruit of honest labor, not the symbol of superiority, of human bondage.

It grew dark rapidly and after a supper of soup, white beans, bread and wine, we wandered in the courtyard or turned in. There was a light in the long room next to the one in which the Americans were quartered, and we opened the huge barnlike doors. Men were sitting on the bunks, on the floor, listening to an American standing at the end of the room, who was speaking to them in a shy, embarrassed voice. He did not know what to do with his hands, and he continued to smile in an embarrassed fashion as he spoke. The Englishmen, Scots and Welsh and Irish, the Canadians who listened, gave him their entire attention.

"My comrade and I," he said, "stowed away aboard a ship, and hid in a compartment of the hold. We had decided that there must be sympathizers of Spain among the crew; we had been told they would find us and feed us. But whether they were there or not, or whether they were afraid to contact us, we never knew. . . ."

It was a simple story he was telling: of ten days of hunger, filth and lack of sleep in the hold of the luxury ship (the little food they had was garbage); of how they had jumped the ship in France, swum ashore and made contact with the Committee there. Even now he looked hollow-cheeked and tired, and when he had finished his story of privation and determination, saying simply and with a childlike smile, "Here we are," the men applauded, shouting, "Bloody good, comrade! Bravo the Yanks!" pounding him on the back and shouting. Then the impromptu chairman, an Englishman, said. "We have all heard Comrade Tabb's story, and I am sure we have a better understanding of why the people of Spain, whatever may happen, cannot lose this war. This comrade's story is typical of many stories that we could all tell, and it is an indication of what the working people of the world feel about Spain. They know that here is a country that is determined to fight for its independence and its freely elected institutions in spite of great odds placed in its way by the Fascist powers and by our own bloody government——"

"No bloody speeches, you bleeding sod!" some one shouted, and the men laughed.

"All right," he laughed, "no speeches. Comrade—I can't pronounce his name—has promised to sing."

A young Hungarian with gold teeth stood smiling before the men and then launched into melodramatic song, waving his arms and holding the high notes until the men yelled, "Cut it, you bloody nightingale!" But he continued to smile and to sing, enjoying himself, bursting with music until they rushed him and tumbled him onto a bed.

Then a little Irishman got up, and standing in the middle of the room said, "I would like to recite."

"Hear! hear!" they shouted. He held up his hand for silence, composed his face into a serious pattern, stretched forth his hand in an appealing gesture. The men were silent.

"I was once as pure as the lily," he said, batting his eyes, "And nobody called me a cow.

"My c... was as sweet as a rosebud;

"Look at the fuckin' thing now!"

They screamed and laughed and fell onto the floor; they wrestled with each other, lifted the little Irishman in the air and tossed him back and forth. The place broke into a bedlam of conversation and was quieted with difficulty.

"No more bloody recitations!" some one shouted.

"Hear! hear!"

"Music!" they shouted. "Music!"

"We have a Polish comrade here," the chairman said, "who brought his violin along." (I remembered having seen him in the coöperative restaurant in Paris; on the Pyrenees, sweating like a pig, his violin case under his arm, no other baggage.)

He sat on a bunk and played fairly well; some Chopin, some Strauss, *The Blue Danube*. He understood English and the men demanded other songs, most of which he knew. They definitely preferred the more sentimental tunes, and he played *The Last Rose of Summer* and *The Roses of Picardy,* and with some assistance from the little Irishman, who plucked out the melody first, he played *Kevin Barry*.

In the light of the dim bulb that hung from the high, vaulted ceiling of the room, the men, grouped around the Polish violinist, sang that folksong of the Irish Republican Revolution of 1916:

> Early on a Sunday morning,
> High upon a gallows tree,
> Kevin Barry gave his young life
> For the cause of liberty . . .

There were heavy shadows on the walls; the men lay on their bunks, smoking, staring at the ceiling. Those who did not sing hummed the chorus:

> Shoot me like an Irish soldier,
> Do not hang me like a dog.
> For I fought for Ireland's freedom
> On that bright September morn——

Watching them there in that whitewashed room of an old Spanish fortress, these men from foreign lands, you knew they were brothers in the only sense in which the word has meaning . . . comrade was the word they used . . . you knew they were together.

For two days we learned the elementary military formations in Figueras. It was all very informal; there was a lot of fun in learning the commands in Spanish from a chinless American drill-sergeant whose Yankee accents made it impossible to guess at the true pronunciation of the words. Men who had previous military experience took turns at drilling the others, dropping all pretence of learning the Spanish commands. Garfield, the actor, who, it developed, had once belonged to a cavalry unit of the National Guard, made a stab at drilling us; one squad would march off to the right, the second to the left, the third stand still, uncertain. We all laughed. He was particularly amusing, attempting to cover his femininity with a mask of military abruptness, but he had picked up the Spanish words and pronounced them like a pedant.

Merkel drilled us in German (his marching revealed a trace of the goose-step); an Englishman who had spent years in the British Army put us through the paces, his normally red face bursting with blood as he barked the commands that were almost as difficult to understand as the Spanish; Diaz tried his hand in Cuban Spanish. Then we sat in the shade listening to a lecture by the chinless sergeant in the baggy pants; a lecture on air-raid precautions. We learned a few marching songs in English, Spanish, French: Connolly's *Rebel Song, Hold the Fort* (with the word 'Madrid' substituted for 'fort' and 'I. B. men' for 'union men'), *Joven Guardia,* the *Marseillaise.* And on that Friday night they paid us for five days, thirty pesetas, six pesetas a day. The rumor went around that we were moving, and the rumor was correct.

At four-thirty the next afternoon we rode in trucks to the station of Figueras where a dilapidated train was waiting for us. The coaches, seating six men on one side and two on the other, were worn ragged; the windows had been broken and some of them were stopped with boards or slatted shutters, others were wide open. We were told to pull up the shutters till we left the station, so we could only guess at the size of the civilian crowd that had come down to see us off. We heard them murmuring and talking on the platforms, and we tried to look through the cracks of the shutters. There was no limit to our excitement; men rushed up and down the aisles, stowing their parcels on the overhead racks, dividing up oranges, cigarettes, talking and yelling at the top of their lungs. We were uneasy about the scant protection offered by the thin wooden roofs; we wondered if we had a machine-gun mounted on the car for protection against air-raids; we were certain that some one would be posted to watch for planes.

The whistle blew, the train moved, but we missed the drama of ordinary departures on American, French or British trains. The train moved out of the station like a snail, and like a snail it continued to move along the track. For hours on end it picked up no speed, and we pulled the shutters down, hung out the windows looking at the scenery, waving at the peasants in the fields, watching the sky for possible airplanes, feeling in our bones that some pilot must even now be watching us from far above, giving the word to a Fascist squadron warming its motors at some distant field. No plane appeared. There were four hundred men on the train, packed in like sardines, standing in the aisles, hanging onto the front and rear platforms. We wondered when we would eat, what it would be. We had bought oranges in Figueras, sent out an illegal detail to scour the town (that had barely caught the train), but there was no chocolate to be had; there were a few hard crackers.

Hour after hour in the bright February sun the train moved slowly along the track and we got bored looking out the windows. We decided that its speed was a precaution; that it moved so slowly, not because it could not move faster, but because in the event of a raid, it would be able to stop suddenly and let us pile out of the windows without injury. We stopped worrying too much about air-raids; sat and talked, sang songs. We sang *The International*, the *Marseillaise, Casey Jones, I've Been Workin' on the Railroad*. The British sang their own songs, whose words we could not catch. The Americans then hit upon a device that was to pass many hours—trying to remember old-time songs. We sang *Rosy O'Grady, Red Wing, Ev'ry Little Movement, A Bicycle Built for Two, The Bowery, Everybody's Doin' It* (doin' what? Turkey Trot), *Black Eyes* (why are you blue?), *Has Anybody Here Seen Kelly? America, The Star-Spangled Banner, Tell Me, Pretty Gipsy, When It's Appleblossom Time in Normandy, When It's Springtime in the Rockies, Home on the Range, The Rose of No-Man's Land, Tipperary* (with the British), *Lorraine, Lorraine* (my bee-utiful Alsace-Lorraine), *Keep the Home Fires Burning, I Didn't Raise My Boy to Be a Soldier, Over There.*

The small towns were relatively close together, and at every one the same performance was repeated. As the train drew into the station the men crowded to the windows, jammed their bodies half-way through the frames. Children and grown-ups rushed down from the town, from the fields, carrying baskets and bags of oranges—large, full, solid oranges. From the train windows came showers of cigarettes, English, American, French, Belgian, Dutch; into the windows came showers of oranges; bushels of them. We ate oranges one after another, dropping the peels on the floor, flinging them from the windows, tossing them at sleeping comrades in the wooden benches. Our fingers were sticky and yellow, our growing beards showed traces of the juice. Those we could not eat we stowed on the baggage-racks, crammed in our pockets. There were orchards beside the tracks for kilometers, heavy with the fruit, glowing in the sunlight. Some men had bread; the children begged for it: *"Pan, pan,"* they said. *"Un poco de pan, camarada?"* *"Tienes pan?"* They had nothing but oranges or an occasional jar of wine to exchange and the men were generous with their bread and cigarettes. *"Tienes tabaco por mi padre?"* the children said. We had been issued a loaf of bread per man, a small piece of petrified sausage, a small can of bully-beef. We gave the tobacco for their fathers, and we showered our bread from the windows. Little girls or sad-eyed women gathered it in their aprons, moving slowly from car to car, looking up at the foreign men in the windows, saying *"Pan? Tienes pan, camarada?"* Little children held their mothers' skirts as they moved along the platform, looking up at the men in the train. Little children, plain and beautiful, played on the platforms, the littlest wearing no more than a short dress that could not cover their naked limbs. They were generally clean and they seemed mostly undernourished; they had large bellies and thin arms and legs, large dark eyes.

Then as the station-master came out, looked at the large clock at the station wall and deliberately yanked on the bell-cord, the men in the train started to sing, spontaneously —"Arise, ye prisoners of starvation!" and the people on the platform lifted their arms, clenched their fists, stood with their arms raised singing with the men until the train had moved out of the platform into the distance. Little babies in their mothers' arms held their tiny fists aloft, their mothers smiling, looking at them. Our hearts were full, watching them, knowing that they knew who we were and what we were doing there; that we were with them; that we felt their fight was our fight too. They were plain people, working people, peasants and small urban workers, and intelligence shone out of their hard, brown faces, their deep, black eyes.

'Lopez,' sitting next to me, said, "It's good to hear the *International* sung some place else but Madison Square Garden; it's good to think there's a place where you can sing it openly." Garfield was close to tears; Merkel smoked a cigar; Diaz and Prieto were shouting at each other in Spanish—since we had entered Spain their services had been at a premium; they had become important, and they enjoyed the feeling. Hoover, the loud-mouth, was somewhat subdued, for Earl, the little pugilist, had taken some of the bounce out of him by picking on him and never letting up. He challenged everything that Hoover said; he made it apparent that anything that Hoover said was likely to be somewhat less than worth hearing. It got on Hoover's nerve, and he was silent. . . .

. . . The Mediterranean was as blue as they say it is; it was so blue that it was unbelievable. Hour after hour we saw it on our left; that way lay Majorca and the Italian air-base, from which the Capronis and the Fiats and the Savoias (whose government was non-intervening in the Spanish conflict) came to drop their demolition-bombs on the women and children of these coastal cities. But the Mediterranean was beautiful as antiquity, and you could think of Venus rising from the foam and the canals of Venice and the long Phœnician ships that used to tack among the Ægean Islands in the days before men could ride the air. It was growing dark, and by instruction of the committee in charge of the convoy we pulled up the slatted shutters and the blue-painted bulbs came on, casting a lugubrious light over the crowded cars.

Come Work-ers sing a reb-el song,
A song of love and hate;
Of love un-to the low-ly and of hat-red to the great . . .

In the darkened car the English-speaking men took up that song again, and it seemed to go well with the clicking of the wheels. ("We got flat wheels on this train," Garfield said.)

Then sing a reb-el song
As we proud-ly march a-long
To end the age-old tyr-an-ny that makes for human tears.
Our march is near-er done
With the set-ting of the sun
And the ty-rant's might is pass-ing with the pass-ing of the
    years . . .

. . . The blue bulbs cast a poor light in the crowded cars. It was cold at night and the wooden shutters could not keep out the Mediterranean fog. When you went onto the platform for a leak you could look at the sea that Mr. Mussolini claimed as his own, flat and dark and brooding on our left, hour after hour. There were a few white breakers, curling like an edge of lace upon the shore. Then you came back into the rattling car, stepping carefully over and around the half-sleeping, exhausted men lying on the floor in grotesque positions, like the dead. They lay in the aisles and under the wooden benches; some had followed Garfield's humorous example and were performing the contortionistic feat of sleeping in the net baggage-racks overhead. (Garfield claimed he slept like a top.) But no one slept; they just pretended to.

All night the train moved slowly south, stopping in the yards at Barcelona at eleven-thirty for an hour or so, then moving on. There was nothing to see there; we were in the industrial suburbs and the tracks were bordered by high warehouses; there was no light in the city. Solitary guards paced the tracks occasionally, looked at the train, moved on. So you sat huddled on the wooden benches, sore all over, hungry and cold, wanting nothing more than a steaming hot cup of coffee and a place to stretch at full length and sleep. Some few men in the far corner of the car kept up the pretence of singing in quiet tones, but the majority dozed and awoke, nodded and stared at their nodding comrades.

You could think of the beauty of the country, the orange trees and the lemons with their bright ripe fruit, the almond trees dressed in fragile pink-white blossoms, the kilometers of grapevines, cut now to within a foot of the ground, waiting for spring to bring them to leaf and growth again. The mountains skirted the coast on our right; fantastic peaks and curves, pinnacles and hollows, and on the slopes there were many small towns that all seemed to have been cast in a mould, built after an endless pattern. Even from the train you were startled by the medievalism of the country, which had persisted down into this twentieth century and had again precipitated this conflict between the poor and those who owned the poor. For each little town consisted of a huddle of wretched, tight-packed houses, thrown together in confusion or revealing the traits of an organic growth over centuries, one house tacked onto the wall of

the next. And towering above each town, generally built
on a height commanding it, stood the church, its finger
pointed to heaven, its masonry rich and heavy, permanent
and menacing, a constant reminder of the domination of
the Church down all the ages. For although this deeply
Catholic people had been burning their churches for centuries, the Church and its allies had always reasserted their
power over the people, and this power was in dispute again
today. And for final contrast or corroboration you looked
again to the endless hills, carved from root to summit with
stone-shored terraces to hold the olives and the vine fields,
quiet evidence of thousands upon thousands of years of
grinding hours of man and woman labor. Sunny Spain,
land of mañana, where nothing was done today that could
be put off till tomorrow!

Or you could think of the children you had seen, standing beside the railroad tracks or on the platforms, thousands of bright-eyed children dressed in rags, their feet
unshod, covered with the red dust of the earth, holding
their fists aloft, crying *"Salud!"* to the international soldiers. These children were very close to us; we came to
know them well. And from thinking of them, undernourished from conception to the grave, uneducated except in
the Catechism, apt as slaves for a slave society, you thought
of the dozing men in the trains and the first Spanish soldiers we had seen that afternoon, loaded into box-cars and
on flat-cars, armed with rifles and machine-guns, moving
the other way; their brothers, their fathers. And the dozing
tired men who had come this long way to a distant foreign
country, fathers of children themselves, or future fathers
of future children, or fathers of children who never would

be born . . . children themselves of working fathers the
world over, who had come prepared to face death, if death
were necessary, to defend their living and their unborn
children on a foreign soil.

And so you came to think of something Abraham Lincoln had said: "The strongest bond of human sympathy,
outside of the family relation, should be one of uniting all
working people, of all nations, and tongues, and kindreds."
And from these foreign fathers and their Spanish children
with their Spanish fathers, you could bear to think of your
own children again, two small children back in the United
States, who would not be able to understand, for years,
why their father had left them and gone away for a long
time. And it made it easier (though it was not easy), to
think of them as they should be thought of—not as *your*
children, unique possession of the mother who had borne
them and the father who had begotten them on their
mother, but as just two children, two kids among millions
of kids the world over, any two kids whom you happened
to know a little better because they were your own. And
you wondered what they would think if their father never
came back, and would they ever understand . . . for it was
important that they should some day understand.

And it all tied up as you sat there in the jolting car early
in the morning among the half-sleeping men: the foreigners, the workers from distant lands; the Spanish people
fighting, dying here; the hills terraced by the million hands
and the bowed backs of Spanish men and women; those
men and women, their dark, lined, strong, hard, kind faces
and their eyes; and their children with their thin legs and
big heads and deep understanding eyes; and the huddled

rubble towns with crumbling walls; and the domination of the Church, buttressed in permanent stone; and the shrewd Italian bombers paid for by the men who lived graciously on the bitter labor of these people whom they deeply hate and fear; and your own children. It was all of a piece . . .

. . . All that next day the train moved slowly south and at five in the afternoon we detrained in Valencia, formed up in the station and marched a few blocks through the streets to a great and luxurious house that might once have belonged to a member of the Spanish royalty. The staircases were of marble and the walls of marble too, and we waited in groups in the smaller salons until the large drawing rooms, that were being used as mess halls, could be emptied of the men who had come before. We began to realize how much of war there was in merely waiting, for we waited two hours for our meager supper and then we waited two more hours when we had finished and marched back to the train again.

The journey was endless and we were endlessly bored; we spent hours just sitting on the ends of our aching spines on the hard wooden benches, our chins in our hands, staring out the windows, and it became more and more difficult to rise to the occasion that each small town and railroad village presented. For it is not easy to sustain the most genuine emotion for any length of time. We sang and we tried to sleep, and the long day passed and we chewed on the petrified sausage and opened the cold cans of watery bully-beef and gnawed on the bread and sucked endless oranges. And the night came on and still the train crawled slowly along the narrow tracks, moving with the deter-

mination of endless patience through the night. And all
the next day we continued to move inland from Valencia.
We looked at each other, dirty, disheveled, unshaved, our
clothes filthy from lying on the carriage floors, from two
days and nights of confinement in an overcrowded train
with no opportunity for change.

But the old excitement rose again as the train pulled into
Albacete late that afternoon, just as slowly as it had pulled
out of Figueras in the north two days before. The platforms
were crowded with soldiers and civilians, Internationals and
Spanish; there was a brass band, its instruments blazing in
the steady sun, and there is something about a brass band
that elevates the human spirit. We sloughed off a good
part of our fatigue; we were rejoiced to feel the enthusiasm
of the Spanish crowds in the streets of the town—they
seemed to be more excited by our presence there than the
few people we had seen in Valencia. Everywhere we were
saluted with the clenched fist, the universal salute of the
Popular Front, that seems somehow to signalize at once
the lifted arm of international labor, the everlasting determination to be free, the strength of universal brotherhood.

Voices called, English voices, "Any Canucks here?" "Any
guys from Chicago?" "Manchester, Leeds?" "Hi comrade,
got a fag?" (But by now we were beginning to be careful
with our cigarettes.) The band played us into town with
a tinkling tune and the untrained men tried to march in
step. The crowds followed us; little kids ran alongside us,
smiling, saying, *"Saloo! saloo! Pan? Tienes pan? Hay
tabaco por mi padre?"*

There was a certain solemnity about the parade; the enthusiasm began, you felt, to be channelled into the paths of a certain purpose; it was no longer diffuse, though just as spontaneous, just as stirring to the heart. We marched through the streets shouting at the girls, and through the vast portals of a great house, into a huge square courtyard that was circled by a continuous balcony at the second story. The flags of Great Britain, France, America, the Soviet Union, Czechoslovakia and Finland, Norway and the Irish Free State, Cuba, Catalonia and Spain, Sweden and China hung from the balcony that was crowded with men in uniform, men wearing dazzling white bandages, men on crutches. There were hundreds in the courtyard, standing on the cobbles, looking up at the balcony. Posters such as we had seen reproduced in our native lands were pasted on the walls; exhortations to unity, to conquest, to death for Fascism. A streamer said: '1938—*Año de la Victoria*—1938.' Another quoted the slogan that had been coined by Spain's great woman leader, *"La Pasionaria"*: "Better to die on your feet than to live on your knees."

The band played from the balcony, the *Marseillaise*, the *International*, the *Star-Spangled Banner*, the *Hymn of Riego*, national anthem of the Spanish Republic. We did not know this song, but as we saw the others come to attention and salute, clenched fist to forehead, we did the same. We felt light on our feet, exhilarated, eager to do something, anything. A bugle called all to attention, and we were welcomed by five speakers in uniform, who spoke, respectively, in French, German, English, Polish and Spanish. The new men were herded into a corner of the court, where a section furnished with tables and benches had been set apart, and we were registered, filling out enormous questionnaires.

We ate in a long mess hall that had once been the stables and coach houses of this mansion—soup, beans, bread and red wine. We shared our cigarettes, which were running low; we talked endlessly and at the top of our lungs, shouting across the tables to each other. . . .

It was beginning to grow dark when we lined up in the courtyard for our baths and army clothes. It was growing cold; we were tired and peevish, but men who tried to cut in front of the others, in order to be done with the business of cleaning and dressing, were loudly cried down and pushed to the rear for this display of selfishness. In the shower room dozens of men stood on the slatted cat-walks, luxuriating in the steaming water. "Hot water!" they cried, "hot water!" as though hot water were a luxury they had not known in months. (Later we came to appreciate it even more; crave it; almost worship the very idea of hot water.) Men of every size and form stood naked there, bathing, thin men and fat, short and tall, powerfully built workers and men showing every sign of malnutrition, even congenital defects. There were men covered with hair, bow-legged men, men with the skin of young girls and their soft curves, men with the scars of wounds suffered in the World War.

Still naked, our civilian clothes thrown into a great heap in the corner of the room, we lined up before a wicket, where a comrade looked at us casually, then handed us a neatly tied-up bundle of clothes. This bundle contained a heavy undershirt and drawers, a pair of socks, a knitted sleeveless sweater, a pair of pants (breeches or long baggy trousers that tied at the ankle), a heavy tunic, a wooly cap that could be pulled down around the ears, an overcoat or a woolen poncho. A German rushed us from the room the minute we got these clothes, and men were dressing everywhere, in the courtyard, in a room that opened on the courtyard, in the latrine. We had been asked, "What size shoes?" and had been handed a pair; they were of poor quality; we were told they were captured Fascist shoes, Italian-make. I drew a pair of breeches and roll puttees, and since I am bowlegged, I could not make the puttees stay put on my crooked legs and was disconsolate. I bumped into Diaz, who was furious at having received a long pair of the baggy trousers that seemed to be peculiar to the Spanish People's Army, and we swapped. (He had high leather boots.) Everywhere you looked you could find material for laughter: enormous men trying to shoe-horn themselves into tiny garments, thin men in colossal trousers that could be wrapped around their waists, tall men with short pants and short men with coats that would fit a giant. The caps, coats, jackets, overcoats and ponchos were gray, green, olive-drab, khaki, of all manner of styles; no two looked alike. They were apparently the hand-me-downs of a dozen different foreign armies (there were even clothes with the United States Army's eagle-stamped buttons); some one or some firm had profited greatly at the expense of the government. Men were wandering in a bewildered fashion through the room and the courtyard, trying to find some one who had clothes that would fit them, offering to swap. Men stormed the wickets when they could get inside, arguing and pleading, blustering and shouting, "Comrade, this is too small for me; comrade, this is too big for me; comrade, look at this, it's ridiculous." If it were too obviously ridiculous the men in charge would consent to change it for something else, but largely they paid no attention; they were swamped. And they flatly turned down all requests for the long baggy pants by men who did not like the breeches, all requests for breeches by men who did not like the baggy pants. I considered myself lucky; I'm something of a standard size, so I could afford to laugh uncharitably at "Lopez," who was grinning in an oversized jacket whose collar would have fit Jack Dempsey, and we both could feel sorry for the close-to-three-hundred-pound Merkel. Nothing could possibly fit him, and he was only interested, at the moment, in trying to draw the jacket and pants together, where they gaped across his swollen belly. (But his belly was really smaller than it had been when we started across the Pyrenees.)

The night was cold, the sky was bright with stars and the waiting trucks were humming in the courtyard. They were large, canvas-covered *General Motors* trucks that resembled covered wagons and each truck was packed with forty men. We sat in them a long time, waiting till all the English-speaking had been rounded up and directed to the trucks, and then we rolled out of Albacete onto a straight hard road. It was cold and the men huddled together for warmth and comradeship. We smoked in the dark or nodded with sleep, and we sang:

> There's a long, long trail a-winding
> Into the land of, my dreams,
> Where the night-in-gale is sing-ing
> And a white moon beams. . . .

3

[*February-March*]

THE TRAINING base of Tarrazona was a small town in the plain country of Albacete Province, and even in early February the days were like summer. The nights, however, were bitter-cold, and we were never warm, lying on our straw ticks on the stone floors of the unheated barracks. At night we wore all our clothes, our caps that could be pulled down over our ears, our gloves (if we had any); and our overcoats and woolen ponchos were draped over the single thin blanket with which it was possible to provide us. Winter nights are long; it was dark by six o'clock and the lights went out at nine. Colds and the grippe were common among the men, and had to be cured solely by the passage of time, for medical supplies in the camp's infirmary were elementary, if not entirely lacking. Yet there was surprisingly little serious illness, and the fact that men who appeared regularly on sick-parade got to be known as 'goldbricks' (whether they were truly ill or not) may have had something to do with it. No one wanted to report sick if he could possibly stand on his feet, and few did.

There must have been fifteen hundred men in the town when we arrived, British, Canadian, American, Cuban, Puerto Rican, Irish. The French, the Germans, Czechs and other nationalities were quartered and trained in other towns that we never visited. All day and every day the units that were in training marched through the narrow packed-dirt streets, between the two-story mud-and-stone houses. Peasants passed through the streets at all hours, driving donkeys loaded with paniers full of dried olives, or pulling little carts full of evergreen boughs which were used as kindling wood. You saw women on line daily to buy oranges or get their bread or milk ration; dumpy, short-legged women dressed in peasant black, with shawls around their heads and felt slippers on their feet. They were friendly. The streets were full of tiny children who wore a single garment, a short linen or cotton smock that rarely came more than an inch or so below their buttocks. They were singularly beautiful children, who played normally in the streets and followed the soldiers around, begging for bread. Few had any shoes to wear, but they seemed to be fairly well-nourished and they were generally clean.

(I had tried to write to my kids, and I *had* written to them, but it grieved me that there was so little I could say; that the contact had to be so feeble. What can you write to a boy of six, what can you write to a babe of three, that will explain your absence or your loss? You could write: *Well, kids, pretty soon now the Spanish mailman ought to be bringing me a letter from you. In fact, by the time this letter goes across all of Spain and all of France and the whole Atlantic Ocean and is brought to you in Brooklyn by your mailman, I should have received that letter of yours. I hope it will tell me that you are both well, that Dan is going to school and Dave is helping Mom every morning; and that both of you are good boys and help her every afternoon.* And then what could you say? Could you explain why it is necessary sometimes for a father or a mother to leave their children for awhile? Could you explain why a father had to go across an ocean to fight in a foreign war? Perhaps to die? Could you say, and hope for understanding, *I have come here to help the Spanish people fight their enemies, the Fascists. The Spanish people are mostly poor people, good people who want their children to be healthy and happy and go to school and have enough to eat, and the Fascists are trying—and there are Fascists all over the world —to keep the poor people poor. So here in Spain the people have taken up guns to fight for their homes and children and their right to live the way they want to?* I said it, God knows, but what could it mean? But you could say, *All of a sudden some day you will wake up and you will both be maybe a year older than you are now, and Mom will say, 'Pop is coming home soon,' and I will come to see you both again, and we will all go to the airport together to ride in Eddie's cabin-plane.* And you could say, *I sent you two soldier caps that the Spanish soldiers wear, and two pairs of slippers just like the little Spanish children wear.* And you could say, *I am thinking of you, and love you both, and send you both a great big kiss. Goodnight Dan, goodnight Dave, Your Pop.* And you could hope that would mean something to them.)

The stores were empty; there was nothing to sell. There were no street lights, and at night all windows were darkened against air raids, and the entire population of the town walked out through the streets, strolling, conversing in low tones. (On such a dark night I bumped into a Cuban comrade, apologized, and discovered that he had lived across the street from me in Brooklyn, and was a member of a workers' flying club we both had helped to organize.) It was a strange sensation, at first, to walk in absolute darkness, feeling your way along by hand and foot, but after a time you got used to it. For the contrast of a town full of people, people sitting in their simple homes behind closed shutters with their lights on, and the darkness of the town streets, was the contrast between peace and war. But after a time you could find your way in the dark from one point in the town to another. You could come from the library in the powerfully built church on the *plaza* and go up one street, across another, around the corners with confidence and ease, back to the recruit barracks where the men were turning in, horsing around, singing, reading or writing on their straw bedticks.

The sky was full of stars when we awoke cold before dawn, formed in the vine-covered patio of the house that served as barracks, and marched in column of fours to the mess hall that once had been a theater. The mess kits we had been issued in Albacete had been turned in to the kitchen, because of its shortage of equipment, and the tin plates and cups awaited us on the long bare tables. A streamer on the wall said: DO NOT WASTE BREAD; IT HELPS OUR ENEMY. Soldiers served one plateful of the steaming brew we dignified by the name of coffee, and depending on your taste, you broke your third-loaf of bread into the coffee, or ate it separately, or saved it for the day's maneuvers. Another streamer said: SPAIN'S CHILDREN NEED BREAD; DO NOT WASTE IT.

At eight we formed, with formality, in the *plaza,* the recruit company, the regular companies, and saluted the red, gold and mauve Republican flag as it was raised. This was a ceremony that was always witnessed by the people who lived near the square, the oldest men and women and children, for the young men were away to war and the younger women and the men who still could work were already at work in the fields beyond the town, doing their plowing for the spring, gathering what little wood grew in that part of the country, tending small garden patches. And after we had raised the flag and thought, while watching it rise on the flagpole, of what it stood for and what our relationship to it meant, we marched out of the town and through the vineyards, empty now of all but short stems that had not yet turned green. In these vineyards and in the pine woods on the hills beyond, we were beginning to learn the trade of the soldier.

It is a hard trade, and one that does things to you as a man; that changes you from one sort of man into another. It is not easy to be a good soldier, and for a middle-class intellectual who had spent most of his conscious life in the sedentary pursuit of finding words for things he believed he felt, it was an almost impossible life. For years I had not waked in the morning before ten, and loved to lie abed; now I was up daily before dawn. I had always avoided walking when I could ride; and now spent hours every day marching all over the landscape. And the intellectual is likely to find his greatest satisfaction (perverted as it is) in long periods of solitude when he can justify his loneliness by looking down upon his fellow man. "You're in the ar-my now," the boys would sing, "you're not be-hind the plow. You'll never get rich, you son of a bitch . . ."

You're in the army now, and when you're in the army you learn to keep a large part of your precious individualism to yourself. An army of individualists cannot function in the field, and this the Spanish people had learned to their sorrow earlier in the war, when individualized units recruited independently by dozens of political parties and trade unions had done a beautiful job of failing to coöperate with each other—while demonstrating determination and heroism that will be remembered so long as there are men to whom the defense of democracy is more than a hackneyed phrase. But now the People's Army was under a unified command and many of the earliest idealisms had been laid aside. It was required now that a soldier salute his superior officer—the first flush of equalitarianism had seen in this a degrading gesture. It was understood that soldiers would obey their officers' commands in action; question them later. And therein lies the distinction that made this army unique in military history. For while certain manifestations of individualism had to be restrained in the interest of unified action, every soldier retained the right to question his command, his officers and commissars, and to bring his grievance to the attention of his fellow soldiers and his superiors. This was done in an organized and democratic fashion through the medium of the political meeting, for this was a political army first to last.

We were not an army of automatons under the absolute authority of an unquestionable command. We were an army of responsible, thinking men. We elected our political delegates—an officer who does not exist in any of the finance-controlled armies of the so-called democracies. This political delegate, known as a commissar, was responsible to us. Meetings were called at his, or our, request, where every problem of discipline, of food, clothing, shelter, military orders, mail, tobacco (or largely the absence thereof), tactics and personal behavior was thrashed out. The majority opinion ruled; it was the commissar's obligation to see that abuses

and complaints were referred to the proper authority, and
to implement the will of the soldiers as well as the desires
of the command. It was his obligation to explain (and ours
to understand) the conduct of the war, the significance of
events in and out of Spain—political, economic, social, military. He was entrusted with the political education of the
soldiers, which was at a high level among the Interationals,
and became progressively higher among the Spanish as the
struggle became sharper. These soldiers not only knew how
to obey, but they understood the reasons for their obedience,
and the rigid discipline that was imposed on them in action was self-imposed within reasonable limits. Through
their understanding of their convictions and the motives
that underlay the war they could be obedient without being
puppets; and at the same time their advice, their complaints
and their suggestions were solicited and desired by the
command. Out of hours they addressed their officers as
'comrade,' or by their first names. They were so addressed
by their officers; and this solidarity within our army accounted for military miracles inexplicable to the traditional
'foreign military observers,' who cannot understand how
men furnished with the most primitive of arms and handi-
capped by the most scanty provisions of food, medical supplies and munitions, could and did withstand for months
and years the enormously overwhelming superiority of the
Fascist enemy's materiel.

Yet our preparation followed the accepted outlines of
infantry-training in practice the world over. We marched
and counter-marched to toughen our muscles; we trotted
and ran; we ran and fell with our rifles, learning how to fall
without hurting ourselves or damaging our arms. We prac-

tised close-order drill (the Americans never learned to march properly) and we practised infiltration over the terrain—advancing by squads and platoons and sections; seeking cover, advancing, charging. We dug various types of fortifications—fox-holes, firing-pits, dugouts and trenches, and we learned how to camouflage them. We received instruction in musketry—dry-firing, triangulation, target practice, fire and movement. We learned how to strip and clean our arms and reassemble them, even in the dark. We were taught how to take cover from various types of fire—artillery, machine-gun, rifle, airplane. We were shown how to handle every type of arm the infantry was using, and we were taught how to care for the wounded; and men who felt they had a flair for the more specialized services—first-aid, transmissions, topography, scouting, sniping, anti-aircraft and transport—were given an opportunity at these specialties when men were needed.

In training most men received the chance to command at one time or another, as corporals or sergeants, and they held the jobs (in training) so long as they demonstrated the ability to command. But it was understood by all the men that stripes, as such, were only won in action, and we had many lieutenants who went to the front as common soldiers and many soldiers who emerged from action, officers. This was considered only just, and was never questioned by the men; and it was no uncommon thing for a man to be a sergeant one day, a corporal the next, a machine-gun loader on the next, and vice-versa. It was expected, too, that soldiers could be interchanged; that a squad-leader could be used as a scout or a stretcher-bearer; that a machine-gunner might work on fortifications or be used as a runner; and men were so used. Elasticity thus made for greater efficiency, and compensated for understaffed *cadres*.

Garfield did manage to be made company *practicante* (first-aid man), and then he got himself transferred to orderly work in the primitive hospital across the street from recruit barracks. It was work that he enjoyed doing; that, by his feminine sensibilities, he was eminently fitted for. But with the exception of Merkel (who was drafted to work in the kitchen), those of us who had come down from Figueras together remained in the ranks. Prieto was made secretary for a company of Cubans and Americans; Diaz was a soldier who kept complaining that he wanted to transfer into the cavalry (he could never learn to march in step); I managed to evade being wangled onto the 'cultural commission,' where I would have had to prepare articles and items of entertainment for the training-base; Tabb got into an anti-gas school that was being organized and 'Lopez' somehow found himself in a school for non-commissioned officers. He was in deadly earnest, determined to become a good sergeant and to hold the job once he got into the lines. He read innumerable manuals of infantry training, picking out the words with the aid of a Spanish dictionary, but his clothes were still too large for him. And we all went to class, one hour a day, in the great fortresslike church on the *plaza* which was like an icebox inside, and there we learned the rudiments of Spanish. It was told that in the first days of General Franco's rebellion, the people's anti-clericalism found expression in an attack on the church, and that the parish priest and the local landlords had fired on the people from the tower, with rifles.

We were shown the casement from which the cleric had fired, and from which he had fallen in his turn. We always looked at it as we marched to class past the women lined up to buy oranges for their children; we admired the narrow slots in the ancient four-foot masonry, excellent rifle and machine-gun emplacements.

Returning from the church (which was also used as a town hall and a moving-picture theater), we sang:

> Hold, Mad-rid, for we are com-ing,
> I. B. men be strong . . .
> Side-by-side, we'll battle on-ward,
> Vic-tory will come!

(I always recalled the streamer the towns-people had hung in the church: *Long Live the Soviet Union, Best Friend of the Spanish People,* and I could not help but laugh.) And after the noon and evening meals (beans or rice with *burro* meat, which has a smell and a taste all its own) we frequented the canteen on a neighboring street. Here it was possible slightly to alleviate the permanent hunger that plagued us, for we were always hungry. Here you could occasionally buy a ham sandwich ($1\frac{1}{2}$ pesetas), a cup of burnt barley called coffee (50 centimos), or you could drink muscatel or rum, málaga, anis or vermouth, all bad. There was no tobacco to be had, and the men were dependent on the weekly issue of twenty *Gaulois* (blue) or letters from home enclosing cigarettes. The hunt for tobacco was pursued by every one with determination and deathless patience. No man could be seen smoking without being asked for the butt, and the butt generally went the rounds of from five to fifteen men. Each man carried a cigarette case in which he collected butts; his own or o.p.'s, and the streets were combed with a fine comb for shreds of tobacco. There was a place in town we called Sloppy Joe's, where bootleg wine could be had out of hours, and although it was strictly against orders to buy bread (and thus diminish the civilian supply), you could see men at certain hours of the day, emerging cautiously from a certain house, looking slightly pregnant. A variety of scallion could be picked in the fields if the peasants were not watching; with a cake of soap or some tobacco it was possible to arrange to eat occasionally in a private home—a bit of chicken, an omelet and wine. Money could not buy anything in the line of food except *avellanoes* (hazel nuts), india nuts or an occasional slab of stiff marmalade; with soap you could buy eggs. With soap you could get your laundry done; without it no amount of money purchased washing. With soap you could buy anything.

But the money—we had been raised to ten pesetas a day—had to be spent, and we spent it in the canteen on military badges (red stars, and the emblems of transmissions, transport, aviation, tanks, machine-guns, first-aid), on belts made of a paper composition, on writing paper and envelopes (both scarce), on socks of a poor quality, handkerchiefs, caps, knives (with tin blades and horn handles), shaving brushes whose bristles came out, razor blades, needle and thread, toothpaste, brushes, postcards, dictionaries. For a peseta you could be shaved in the canteen (if you waited long enough), by a Spanish barber who had once lived on 14th Street in New York, and had imported the American custom of the hot towel; the only barber shop in Spain that offered this inestimable luxury. (All others shaved you with cold water.) In the canteen our social life (such as it was) was centered, for if enough men crowded in, it was warm, and here we could talk with our officers as man to man and get to know them.

I remember Mitchell, a handsome Negro who commanded our recruit company for a time and wore lieutenant's stripes. He walked like a king or like a panther; he had one of the most beautiful speaking voices I have ever heard, and a sense of humor about his job that was beyond cavil. He went to the front later as a soldier; I have never seen him since. I remember Gregory, short, powerful, Scotch longshoreman with the peaches-and-cream complexion of a girl and a girl's gentle voice, who also commanded us for a time and was at once the sternest disciplinarian and the gentlest man I can remember meeting. They say he was killed the last night the XVth International Brigade was in action—the same night Ring Lardner's son Jim was lost. I remember George Watt, New York student, political delegate and later commissar of the Lincoln Battalion, whose extreme youth and diffident air always seemed to me out of place in an army. And best of all the non-coms in the training camp I liked British Allan Logan, ex-stock-exchange man and landscape gardener who had lost most of his hair (except a patch or so), and who was liked by no one else. He was shy, and therefore forward; he was uncertain, and therefore positive. He showed me a picture of a girl he had loved for years, who had married some one else, and he told me privately that he did not much care whether he went home or not. And it was possible to believe him, as it had not been possible to believe Hoover. If he got home I have not heard of it, for he was captured in the Aragon, and General Franco did not like the Internationals. . . .

. . . There were hundreds of homeless, hungry, starving dogs in the town and they ran the streets freely, copulating in the *plaza* and in the gutters, their ribs bursting through their skin, their smell augmenting the normal smell of the town whose sewage flowed through open drains covered only with flagstones. They were of all sizes, shapes and breeds, small dogs with short legs and huge anomalous beasts with long rangy limbs, and they were in everybody's way. Their eyes were red and they had an expression in their eyes, of permanent reproach, that it was not easy to look at.

On the afternoon of the 12th of February they seemed more numerous than ever, criss-crossing the streets and receiving more than their normal share of curses and kicks, for the town was at a high pitch of excitement. An emergency meeting had been called in the church, and the rumor flew through the town that a draft was going to the front. Men ran through the streets for their barracks, shaking hands with each other, laughing, shouting. We knew that the Fascists had been counter-attacking at Teruel ever since the Government had retaken it on December 22, after a brilliant offensive that had lasted but five days. Teruel was a key town and the Fascist command was bent on its recapture; for that purpose enormous reserves of men and materiel had been immediately brought up, and on the 30th of that month they reached the gates of the town, where they were immobilized by the Government forces. It was on this memorable occasion that Mr. William P. Carney of *The New York Times,* writing from a point far and safe behind the lines, described the delight with which the population greeted the 'liberating' army of the invaders, and Mr. Herbert Matthews followed a day later with a despatch from Teruel itself. How we did laugh back home!

All the new recruits stood guard duty on the hillside that led to the main road to Albacete and the railroad terminal. For two hours we stood there, holding the population from the road, our hearts in our throats with excitement, and then they came. Starving dogs and laughing children preceded them, running back and forth across the streets; and they were laughing too—seven hundred men from the training camp, Americans and British, Canadians and Irish and some Cubans, were going to the front. There was no band, but they sang as they marched up the hill in columns of four, making their own music as they came. You saw no thoughtful face, a universal smile lit them all; they joked and shoved each other as they waited in line at the top of the hill for their rations—three loaves of bread for each man, large tins of bully-beef and smaller ones of corned beef, marmalade, a piece of chocolate (*Baker's*) and two packs of *Lucky Strikes*.

"Damn it," said 'Lopez,' "why can't we go?"

"Trade places with ya, he! he!" shouted Merkel.

"Damn it," said 'Lopez,' "it's Lincoln's Birthday."

Then we saw Hoover and Earl, who had wangled their way into the draft by claiming previous military experience; they had none. Hoover had a fine fur hat he had picked up somewhere; Earl was wearing a tin helmet. They waved their packs of *Lucky Strikes* at us and we abandoned our guard duty to wring their hands. Hoover was feeling pretty cocky; Earl, as always, was quiet and reserved. I remembered how, on shipboard, he had sat hours in the smoking room, talking to no one; had leaned against the rail and watched the sea. He was a likable little guy and I think we shook his hand with greater feeling than we exhibited when we shook Hoover's.

"See ya in Zaragoza!" yelled the men. "See ya in Oviedo! See ya in church!"

Logan was disappointed that he had not been called up. "I've been in this bloody hell-hole fifteen weeks," he said. We saw Joe Hecht, who had taught our first Spanish classes.

"No more Spanish lessons," the recruits moaned. "The teacher's going."

"Bring us Franco's balls!" the men shouted.

" 'e ain't got no bloody balls," a voice replied.

They were lined up at the crest of the hill, where they passed a table set in the middle of the road, and were checked off. Several men who had tried to get into the draft and been refused were turned back again when their names could not be found on the list. There were trucks waiting and the men climbed into the trucks, shouting and waving for the full half-hour they had to wait before the convoy could be assembled. The Spanish men and women waved; the women wept remembering the time their own men had marched away, remembering their dead; for there was not a family in the town that had not lost at least one man. The trucks moved off, and as we watched, a Government pursuit-plane soared over the town, its red wing-tips flashing in the sun. We heard them singing, and we knew from the number of stanzas they had already sung what the lines were . . . though we could not distinguish their words as the trucks moved into the distance.

"The earth shall rise on new founda-tions," they were singing,

"We have been naught; we shall be all!"

No sooner had the draft left than new men began to arrive; more Americans and British and Canadians, and they all had cigarettes with which they were more than generous, for the first day or so. Then they rapidly began to believe what they had been told in Paris, in the south of France, in Figueras—that there simply *was* no tobacco in Spain except for the weekly French issue and the occasional issue of a curious item that was labeled '*cigarillos finos*' but which we called 'anti-tanks' because they were both small and deadly. They tasted like cow-dung, they would not stay lit; they bit your throat and tore out your tongue.

Jack C—— had plenty of cigarettes at first, but no one liked him anyhow. He was gross in appearance; he was so loud you could hear him for blocks; he was self-assertive, and no matter how many cigarettes he gave away (until he had no more) he could not win the liking or the respect of the men. There are people like this, who want pathetic-ally to be liked, and whose every advance, stemming from a consuming desire to win affection, meets with a rebuff. The harder they try, the more they are disliked. Jack was a New York athletic director, but Irving N—— was a barber from California. By virtue of possessing a glib tongue he had talked himself into a job as political delegate of Company One; and then he talked himself into the N. C. O. school. The men would say, "How the hell did *he* get into N. C. O.?" and smile bitterly. I had other reasons for disliking him. He did not smoke, but he drew his issue anyhow. These cigarettes he offered judiciously, perhaps not consciously, to the right people. He also made an offer, before he went into the officers' school, of a pack of American cigarettes for the best article for the Company's wall-board newspaper ('The Song of the Maxim'). This was apple-pie for me, and I felt sort of ashamed to compete, but the lure was too compelling. When I went to collect the cigarettes, Irving denied that he had offered them. "Comrade," he said, "you must be misinformed." "Listen," I said, "I've got a hundred witnesses." "How *could* I have promised a pack of cigarettes when I haven't got one?" he asked. "You'll have to figure that out yourself," I said, "you did." "I offered *one* American cigarette," he said, and gave me two. Later that day he gave me two more he had "discovered," and for the next couple days he would un-obtrusively slip me a cigarette from time to time. But they never made up a pack—I counted them—there were only eight.

Jack was made a sergeant, but he shouted at the men so much and bullied them so often, in an effort to convince them of an authority he did not possess, that he was re-placed. Or rather, he resigned. "Keep your lousy sergeancy," he said. "I don't want it anyhow." They talked to him for this; he was C. B. for a day, and could not move out of the barracks. He sulked, and you could not help feeling sorry for him, and you could not help but be amazed by the lenient humanity of this army, and the consideration the officers displayed for the individuality of their men. Drunks —and they were relatively few—were generally fined thirty pesetas and got three days Confined to Barracks. Bad cases went to a little white house up on a hill, where they cooled off, but one man who tampered with a little boy just disappeared—we never saw him again.

Meantime the training went on and the life of the town rolled its slow and steady pace. These people were desperately poor; they had nothing but the governmental food ration and the little they could coax out of the soil. You could look into their windows and see that they had nothing, but they were looking forward to a better time to come. This much the Republic had done for them, that never had been done before: they were given the land they worked. No longer was there a sacred or profane landlord over them, to whom they paid more than they could earn in a lifetime. There was no well-fed Civil Guard to act as watchdog for the ruling classes and suppress with violence the slightest murmur of discontent. There was no self-constituted hierarchy of spiritual intermediaries to woo them into contentment with this life and promise a better one—after death. They had always known the Church was their enemy, but they were not enemies of God. They wore crucifixes, they hung them in their homes, and you knew, seeing them on the streets—the women in their black knitted shawls, felt slippers, cotton stockings (when they had any at all), and the men in their slippers and patched corduroy pants, their large or small berets, a blanket around their shoulders or a scarf around their faces—you knew that they were Christians, as Christ would have understood the word. And all over the Republican land the Government was building schools for their children—the new one in Tarrazona, built in the modern style of fine new brick, contrasted strangely with the medieval hovels in which the people lived—schools by the score, and child health-clinics and rest-homes, and even in the Army the men were being taught to read and write.

We had relatively little to read, but we did a lot of writing home. The war despatches in the papers, *Frente Rojo, La Vanguardia, Mundo Obrero,* were terse; you had to read between the lines: 'In the sector of X—— the forces at the service of the invasion succeeded, at the cost of many casualties, in taking Hill 601. Fighting with unusual brilliance, our troops retired to previously determined positions.' You knew what that meant, and it was repeated daily. Rumors floated into camp after the draft had left for the front, with Major Allan Johnson, the American base commander, accompanying them. The men treated them as such; yet even while they referred to any such bit of information as a "shit-house rumor" they spread it even farther. Major Johnson returned from the front and spoke to us.

"All I can tell you," he said, "is that I have been with the Brigade, and it is in action. It's cold as hell up there; I froze a couple toes." (He laughed and we laughed with him.) "The fighting is pretty stiff these days, and I want you all to be prepared to go into action, in support, at any time. I don't know when you will be called but it's your job to be ready *when* you're called."

Our maneuvers across the terrain outside of Tarrazona began to assume a more intensive form, but it is difficult for the most imaginative, engaged in such activities, to believe he is doing more than playing. You obey the whistle, drop onto your face; but your heart beats with regularity and precision. You get up and run like mad for five paces and drop again. Your heart begins to pound, but not with emotion, just fatigue. Your only wounds in maneuver might be a bruised knee, a twisted ligament, a scratched palm;

you can get up confidently and charge an imaginary machine-gun nest, knowing as you dodge from tree to tree
that the imaginary bullets will not hurt you. You need not
worry if your gas mask leaks; nothing but air will leak into
it. There seem, in training, to be only two major points of
contact with the front—the lice that you cannot avoid
(especially when there are no facilities for washing), and
guard duty at night in a war-time town.

Lice can be readily eliminated through the application
of vinegar and alcohol (they sting) and a hot bath. We
received one such ablution during the five weeks we were
in training. Your clothes, too, are placed in a huge machine,
where steam under great pressure, and disinfecting gases,
rid you of the beast. But when you are on guard duty a
half mile from the town, beside a water tank with a loaded
rifle, and with orders to shoot any one who does not answer
your challenge, you feel closer to the unreality of war. The
night is bitter cold and the charcoal burner has gone out.
The moon casts heavy shadows, and it is easy to see a tree
walking and to challenge it. You know that there are enemy
elements in town (they tried to poison the reservoir twice
before), and you know that quiet in your rifle lie deafening
sound and violent death. You touch the bolt and feel that
it is cold to your hand; you work it, and the first cartridge
leaps from the magazine, points into the chamber and slides
in. You remove it. You wonder if you could shoot if you
had to; if you would make a hit. (You feel these things even
when you know the reservoir is no longer used!) Somewhere on the other side of town a dog is howling in the
early morning, and you wait for your relief; alone, lonely,
numb with cold. Walking back and forth wrapped in the

blanket, you wonder what curious chain of circumstances has brought you to this point so many thousand miles from home and all the things that home can mean to you. You can think of your children and their mother, from whom you are divorced, and reality becomes confused with wishful thinking; the impossible (even the undesirable) becomes both possible and urgent, but you are a long way from home and you have entered upon another scene of action, where life is reduced to its fundamentals, bread is really the staff of life again and nothing takes supersedence over the requirements of food and shelter from the weather. . . .

. . . On the streets the Spanish barrel-organ plays and the little kids dance solemnly to the strains of *Pop-Eye the Sailor Man* and *The Music Goes 'Round and 'Round*. These incongruous tunes attract many men to the front of the barracks, where they watch the children dancing and smile embarrassedly at each other. One little kid, an orphan named Miguel, tougher than the rest, scorns to dance. He has gathered a group in the vine-covered patio, where he smokes a cigarette and demonstrates his thorough knowledge of the military commands to the soldiers. *"De frente, heh!"* the men say, and Miguel starts to march; *"Halto, oop!"* they cry, and he comes to a halt on the right foot, clicking his heels together. Miguel has a stick which he uses as a rifle. *"De frente, sobre el hombro, oop!"* the men say, and the child shoulders his arm and marches out of the doorway into the street, where he bayonets a little girl and runs away, laughing. His clothes are in rags, his nose runs, he is really dirty but as hard as nails. "Great kid," the men say, "a tough nut." We have seen him sleeping in the doorways; he's been given seven homes, but with his parents dead in an air raid on a southern city, he prefers independence to any of them. Watching him we thought of the hundreds of children killed by Fascist bombs in a children's home in Barcelona last month.

The rumors that Teruel has been retaken by the Fascists grow more persistent, but there is nothing about it in the papers. "Have you heard the news?" the men say to each other, and the answer is, "Yeh, they've taken Teruel." The men shake their heads, and gradually the rumor has gained such ground that an explanation is demanded of the former political delegate, George Watt, who is now adjutant-commander of Company One.

"It is true," says George, "that the Fascists have retaken Teruel. They took it on the twenty-second, after expending tremendous amounts of material and men in their offensive. We must realize the exact significance of this. And the point for us to emphasize is *not* that Teruel has been lost, but that when we took it from them, we took it in five days; it has taken them *two months,* using every resource of foreign intervention, to retake it. This fact should give us immense courage and determination, and it should give us confidence in the strength and morale of our Army. Teruel was taken by entirely Spanish troops; there was not an International soldier among them, though the Internationals were in reserve in case they should be needed. The loss of Teruel is not important when you take these facts into consideration."

Somehow this seemed like equivocation to most of us, though it was indisputably true; but from this point on the tension in the camp rose until it was almost unbearable. We knew that the Italian and German planes made almost daily raids over Barcelona, Valencia, Alicante and Madrid, killing hundreds. We knew that Sir Anthony Eden had resigned as Foreign Secretary of Great Britain in a protest against the capitulationist foreign policy of Prime Minister Chamberlain. We knew that King Carol of Rumania had abolished parliamentary government in his state, and replaced it by a Fascist régime. We knew that Hitler was consolidating his grip on Austria, that Chamberlain was playing the Fascist's game (he was no dupe); that some sort of deal was on foot between Germany and Italy, over the fate of Spain.

Things began to happen fast; we made guesses at when we would be called to the front, and figured it would be within a month and a half, to prepare for the spring offensive, which would be mutual and bloody. We tried hard to learn Spanish rapidly; we spent our off-hours learning our guns and tactics better, instead of sitting around chewing the fat. We had almost daily target practice (five shots a man), gas-mask drill (for gas was expected), musketry problems that involved combat formations in the field and firing at silhouette targets. We listened to lectures on first aid, and the company began to assume the appearance of an army. It was reorganized; some men were drafted out by the personnel office, to be trained in anti-aircraft and the anti-gas company. The food showed some improvement, though *garbanzos* (we call them chick-peas here) and rice were the staples, with dry bread, *burro* meat and oranges (mostly dry and woody at this season of the year) providing what variety there was. And Comrade Archer, the tall Negro cook, had little imagination.

But the second week in March we knew it was all over; Hitler had Austria as a price for giving Mussolini a free hand in Spain; and there were immediate reports of intensified intervention, with many new German and Italian planes, big guns, technicians, flowing into the country. We were told frankly that the situation looked serious; that at least another year of warfare was in prospect, and even an issue of *Twenty Grand* (union made) failed to sober us. A rumor went around that ten days would see us at the front, but we discounted it. It began to get really hot, a pretaste of the heat to come, and the camp was full again; there were nearly fifteen hundred men in training. We were convinced that a major war was in the offing, what with the uncorrelated news before us of Schuschnigg's arrest by the Nazis, the fall of the French cabinet, Blum's formation of a new one, the mobilization of French troops on the border and the clamor of the British population for the resignation of Neville Chamberlain, who continued to place the interests of his class above the interests of his country. There was enormous enthusiasm among the men, that mounted as the news became more threatening (a compound of elation and of fear); there was a zip to their marching that they never achieved again, and officers were lenient when entire companies paraded marking their time with loud cries of "*O*op, oh; *ee*p, oddo; *o*op, oh; *ee*p, oddo," and then sang

> Ser-en-os y aleg-res,
> Valientes y osa-dos,
> Cante-mos, sol-dad-os,
> El himno a la lid . . .

This was the Republican national anthem, and it never sounded less like the tinny jingle that it is, than it sounded at that moment. It borrowed a certain dignity and elation from our sense of responsibility and our enthusiasm. . . .

. . . We were sound asleep on the night of March 13 when the barrack lights suddenly went on, blinding us all. "Turn off those lights!" the men yelled. "Who the hell did that? Christ Jesus, put out the lights, you bastard!" the voices called, but no one answered.

"All up," George Watt said. "Every one stand by to answer to his name. When your name is called, come into the company office."

"What's up?"

"What the hell's going on?"

"Yow!" a voice yelled. "We're moving!"

"So's your bowels."

There was no need to tell us to dress; we slept in our clothes, most of us. Duffy and Mann, the cousins, looked bewildered; but then they always looked bewildered and nobody could figure out why they had requested a transfer from the cultural commission into the Company; they belonged in a Greenwich Village tea room. 'Maybe they just wanted to be with the boys,' some one had said. 'Such insinuations, tch, tch!' The men stood around scratching their heads.

"We're going to the front!"

"Ten to one we're not."

"I'll take you."

"It's a night maneuver."

"It's the front."

"That's another shit-house rumor."

"Whaddya think, they're gonna call the roll at five A.M.?"

One by one, as the names were called, the men went into the company office, where comrades from Personnel sat with a typewritten list of names and addresses.

"Are you fit to go to the front?" they asked; this, and nothing more.

No word had come from home, from the kids, from their mother, from my friends. I desperately wanted a letter from home, something to carry with me into . . . what? I was ashamed of what I felt because there was no letter.

4

SPANISH boxcars are only a third the size of American box-cars, and forty men crowd them to such an extent that it is impossible for any one man to stretch at full length. "You're in the ar-my now," the boys sang. "Passenger cars from the border to Tarrazona; freight cars from now on." We sat on the hard wooden floor, jounced and jarred by the banging of the wheels, cold, cramped and dirty. The door of the car was open only a crack, and the Canadian sergeant saw to it that no one opened it any farther. We lay in each other's arms, between each other's legs, trying to get warm. There was a baby-faced young Scots boy in my squad, whose name was Carroll. He dozed on my shoulder, propped against the corner of the car, his wet mouth open and drooling like an infant's. It felt good to have him there and I began to get sentimental about him; I decided to protect him, he looked so young and helpless.

What was it all about? the men asked. Where were we going in this rattling train of some two thousand men, Americans, Canadians, Cubans, Germans? Some said Teruel, some the Aragon. All we knew was that when the band stopped playing in Albacete (the same tune with which they had played us into town five weeks before), Major Johnson said, "You men are badly needed at the front. You haven't had as much training as you might have had, but what you lack in training you make up in enthusiasm and anti-Fascist conviction. The first Internationals, who helped to save Madrid, had no training at all. I wish I could be with you. Good luck."

We drew our rations—one pack of French cigarettes (*Atlantis*), three loaves of bread per man, a can of Argentine corned beef, a large can of apricot marmalade for each squad. And the train moved off toward Valencia. It was rumored we had lost Belchite as well as Teruel; it was said they were attacking all along the line; that we were starting an offensive ourselves. Everybody was cleaned out of camp; Merkel and Archer from the kitchen, Garfield (much to his chagrin) from the hospital, the whole Non-Commissioned Officers School (no longer N. C. O.'s), the Cultural Commission, the entire Personnel Office, every one was there. Allan Logan managed to escape from the hospital, where he had been confined with flu, and joined the draft. Diaz was in the Albacete hospital with pneumonia, that beautiful animal. Prieto was along. Proios, the Greek, was along (he had arrived in camp only a week before). The Duffy-Mann cousins were along (they had some cigarettes from home). Tabb had been released from the anti-gas school. And we sat in these small wooden boxes, deafened by the noise,

fatigued by the jolting and the crush, uncomfortable, cold.
There was no possibility of sleep.

On that journey no militant marching song was heard. In
the darkness of the car, lit occasionally by the sparks from
the rope trench-lighters we had bought in Tarrazona, you
could listen to the preferred songs of lonely men:

> Just a song at twi-light
> When the lights are low,
> And the flicker-ing shad-ows
> Softly come and go . . .

We were in Valencia by midnight, where we loaded more
bread, more canned corned beef, some marmalade, and lay
over for four or five hours, then moved again, northeast.
(We had expected *Lucky Strikes*—there were none.) Those
who had fallen asleep in their comrades' arms awoke again
with the slamming of the cars, the banging of the primitive
couplings. The song came to their lips again . . .

> Though the heart be wear-y
> Sad the day, and long,
> Still to us at twi-light
> Comes Love's old song,
> Co-omes Lo-ove's old, swee-eet, so-ong.

At such a time, in such a place, it was impossible to condescend to these songs, to regard them as other than an
authentic expression of man's persistent loneliness; and the
proof was that you *wanted* to sing them, and you sang them,
with intensity, with passion.

A railroad map glimpsed at Segorbe at seven in the morning showed that we were on the line to Teruel! And we

kept moving, the train climbing now into rugged country, where the mountains once again were terraced from root to peak for the cultivation of vegetables and olive groves. There were many irrigation ditches made of concrete, to save and channel the scanty rain that fell only during the rainy season, now overdue. The land seemed more fertile and more flourishing, but there were the same towns, unchanged in their feudal aspect of centuries past. Two structures dominated these crowded towns, the church and the manor house, and their significance needed no political exegesis. The soil was red; everything you saw was beautiful; the very erosion of the soil revealed new aspects of unexpected, sculptured loveliness, as the train, pushed and pulled by two engines, climbed into the mountains. Palm and cactus grew everywhere, and there were the everlasting olives and the figs.

At ten-thirty we detrained at a junction some fifty kilometers behind Teruel, where the hills lay low and bare on every side, and where George Watt, now wearing lieutenant's stripes and in command of our Company 1, gave orders for the men to take cover in the hills against the possibility of air raids. We ate our corned beef and poured our marmalade onto huge slabs of bread, and then, at the command, ran for the hills, scattering as we ran. The countryside was bleak; the hills were an agglomeration of broken stone, crushed to small sharp fragments and tangled with a growth of low dry shrubs with thorns and olive-green leaves. There were occasional bomb holes on these hills, and we whistled as we looked at them. They were the first bomb holes we had ever seen, and they put the fear of God into us, but even so, that fear did not become immediate; it merely lay in our minds waiting, quiet and alert like a coiled snake. The faces of the men were sober now; they were not so inclined to horse around; the weeks of discipline, lax as it was, were having an effect.

By mid-afternoon we had received further orders and climbed into a long convoy of slow Russian trucks that started back in the direction of Valencia. This was bewildering, but we were no longer in a mood to question anything. We were tired, we were cold, and if the box-cars had been uncomfortable and cramped, they were as large and comfortable as Grand Central Station compared to the open trucks. There was not room enough for all the thirty-six men in each truck to sit down; they sat on the edges, on the tail-gate, on the cab roof, numbed by the biting wind, fighting to keep their balance even when they were half asleep. They sat or knelt, jammed into the truck bodies so tightly that it was impossible to shift an arm or leg to rest it. Men sat on each other's legs, could not reach their own pockets. We pulled our blankets up around our faces against the cold wet wind and nodded, only to wake with an arm or leg paralyzed with pain. All night the trucks wound back down around the mountain roads without their headlights, stopping and starting. A few men beefed and there were continual plaintive cries of 'Get off my leg,' 'Move a bit, can't ya?' 'I can't,' 'Jesus, what a ride!' but generally they showed amazing discipline and generosity to each other. The driver, we learned, had not slept in five nights, and he took only two fifteen-minute periods out of the long night to catch a nap on the side of the road. But we were in no mood to be considerate of the driver.

At midnight we were in Tortosa, and the town was full

of the sea fog and hundreds of trucks that seemed to be converging from all directions. There was a traffic jam, which had to be disentangled in the dark, no truck daring to show a light. And when we finally got out of the mess, we started rolling north along the Mediterranean shore. We were dead from fatigue, beaten into a pulp, our minds detached from our bodies, our bodies one continuous ache from head to foot. From under the poor shelter of our thin blankets, early in the morning, we could watch the wild mountain scenery through which we were passing once again—cliffs of bare, precipitous rock that shot straight up from the roadside, a tumbled landscape such as I imagine the Rockies must present, or the moon. Despite the agony of hunger and discomfort and the cold, we slept, nodding awake at intervals to catch a glimpse of the moon scudding behind wet clouds or cliff-faces, disappearing again. This was ultimate loneliness and desolation; it made no sense; it had no meaning, but it was impossible to summon the energy even to wish that you were some place else, far away, in a comfortable bed in a steam-heated room. You accepted it as one of the facts of life, wondering a bit perhaps that it was possible to accept such enormity as normal.

At dawn we pulled off the main road under the olive trees and shivered in the early light. There was still some marmalade, and we ate it, spoonfuls of it, or spread it on our remaining bread. We could not make a fire to keep warm; smoke can be seen a long way from the air. No one knew where we were; we were tired, filthy, stiff, hungry, thirsty. And so we slept in the growing warmth of the rising sun, lying under the olives. That afternoon there was word that the Fascist offensive had been temporarily halted; that a great offensive was going on (ours or theirs?); that mobilization had been decreed all over Spain. We stayed in the same olive field, divided into squads that were each assigned to a tree, and we stood guard in squads all night to 'prevent pilfering,' as there were known to be deserters in the neighborhood. We had met some that afternoon; ragged, unarmed soldiers, sitting on the stone walls near by, their faces streaked with dirt, their beards long, a look of desperation in their eyes.

We had been warned against them; we had been told that certain "weak elements" had broken, so when these men talked to us we smiled with the superiority of ignorance. "You go Fifteen Brigada," one Finn said. "No more Fifteen Brigada; all killed; all dead; you got to smoke?" "What happened?" we asked, and he said, "You no believe? Fifteen Brigada all dead; I get away, lose gun and ammo; everybody dead; you no believe? Hell up there; we no do anything, no can. You got to smoke? Everybody blow to pieces; everybody kill." We chided him. "You ran away." "Sure I run; you run too; all over; all gone, no use no more, Brigada gone, only a couple get away. Me." He saw that we did not believe him, that we despised him, and he wandered away from us. He did not actually walk away from us, but suddenly he was far away and we returned to stand guard in the camp all night, cold, cold.

Morning brought the fourth day on cold rations (aptly called iron rations), the fourth day on our way toward the front. Trucks were scheduled to call for us, but no trucks came, so we scattered over the fields for cover and lay there sleeping in the sun. Some of us found an abandoned house below the hill, with a crumbled concrete tank full of stagnant dirty water; we washed our faces and our feet, our clothes. Reports kept coming in; I don't know from where. We heard that the French border had been suddenly opened, that a hundred new airplanes had come over, many big guns. But the rumor could not be confirmed. We gathered that Belchite had really been lost, that a section of the XVth International Brigade (which comprised the Americans, Canadians, the British and a mixed battalion of Spanish and Cubans) had given way, been routed. We saw more of these "weak elements," tattered and demoralized, wandering in the vicinity like scarecrows, not daring to come near our camp. They had no clothes, no food, no equipment of any kind.

At two-thirty the following morning we were waked and started a forced march of fifteen kilometers to the headquarters of our Brigade. I do not know what we expected to find at the end of this exhausting march over the hills, but what we found shocked us beyond any possibility of easy acceptance of the facts. Early in the morning, before dawn, we saw hundreds of lights, camp-fire lights in a valley below us, on a hill ahead, and we commented on this. It seemed to us a foolhardy thing to do, to light campfires only a short distance behind the front. And in the early morning we arrived at headquarters, which was under a tree on a low hill beside the road. We stood around until we were separated from each other, Americans together, Canadians together, British together; we shook hands with each other and parted company, and the hundred and fifty-odd Americans marched a kilometer back in the direction from which we had come, and then up the side of a wooded hill on which we were told we would find the Lincoln Battalion.

Every soldier in every army is taught first off to be neat and clean, to keep his clothes in good repair, his buttons sewed on and his shoes polished, his face and hands and body washed, his beard shaved. He is respectful to his officers and stands at attention when he is addressed; he moves with precision about his business, walking as a soldier should, head up, chin in, arms at his sides. All of us had blankets neatly rolled and slung over our shoulders; all of us had pack-sacks stuffed with the things that soldiers accumulate —writing-paper, envelopes and pencil, thread and needle, tooth brush, soap and razor, a towel, extra buttons, shoe polish and a brush. In addition, we had dictionaries, pamphlets, books, newspapers. Some had harmonicas, knives, mirrors, combs and brushes. We were proud of our army. It was a People's Army, drawing its strength from the people's will to resist oppression, their determination to maintain their liberties at whatever cost. We were determined to show the 'foreign military observers' that we, whom the finance-controlled newspapers of the world chose to call a Moscow horde, a rabble in arms, were not only better fighters than the superbly drilled automaton armies supported by the people's taxes (and serving their masters), but were just as well disciplined.

Scattered over the side of this wooded hill that commanded a magnificent view of the mountain scenery near Gandesa and Batea, we found a little over a hundred men, disorganized, sitting, lying, sprawling on the ground. They had week-old beards; they were filthy and lousy; they

stank; their clothes were in rags; they had no rifles, no
blankets, no ammunition, no mess kits, no pack-sacks. They
had nothing but the rags in which they were dressed and
the filth with which they were covered. They were not interested in us. They did not greet us; but rather, they looked
at us with obvious cynicism. They did not speak to us at
first; they ignored us; they did not answer our questions
except in grunts or with expletives. We did not know what
to say; what to do. We did not *want* to ask questions; we
were in awe of them. But after we were assigned to companies—which were hard to find because no one knew just
where they were—we reported to a ragged man who admitted to being in command, and sat down, listening to
these men talk.

Here was apparent total demoralization, utter fatigue,
rampant individualism. The men criticized their command
mercilessly; it sounded like treason to us. The men of Company 4, to which I was assigned, were largely seamen. I
had known seamen before, during the 1936 East Coast strike,
when some of us in the Newspaper Guild wrote publicity
for them, and my home in Brooklyn was a headquarters for
the Citizens' Committee organized by my former wife.
They were good guys, scrappers, tough as nails. But these
men seemed to be licked; if they had had tails, they would
have been between their legs. They barked at each other
and at us; they cursed continuously, making accusations
that horrified the new replacements. They thought less than
nothing of the Battalion Command (most of it had been
killed off in the action out of which they just had come),
the Brigade Commander Cópic, his chief-of-staff Merriman,
his commissar, Dave Doran. Through them I learned of the

death, his first day in action, of Richard Tynan, a young seaman whose overcoat buttons my former wife had sewed on the night he sailed for Spain. Some one said that both Earl and Hoover had been killed at Belchite ("Cut in half with machine-gun bullets; I was right next to him.")

We asked about food; when it came up? They laughed. There *was* no food. The Battalion kitchen had been blown up; the Brigade kitchen was going to feed us if it ever got around to it. There had been no food for five days. We learned that the Brigade had been on the run for five days, through Belchite, Caspe, Alcaniz (where Lister's outfit finally stopped the rout). It had been cut off five times and had had to fight its way out each time and run again. Irving N——was shocked, but not beyond speech.

"Comrades," he said. "Do I understand you retreated and threw your guns away?"

"Yeh," they said.

"But comrades," he said, "that's cowardice. Don't you realize how difficult it is for the Government to get arms? Don't you realize that it's impossible to retreat from Fascism; that unless we lick Fascism all over the world it won't be long before——"

"Shit," some one said; they looked at him and spat. I expected them to tear him to pieces.

A youngish-looking man, who did not seem to be a seaman, and whose dirty face was streaked where perspiration (or tears) had run down it, said, "Comrade, we've been through hell the last few days, and do I understand you're accusing us of being cowards?"

"Well," said Irving, "I don't want to be misunderstood——"

"Haul your ashes," said an Italian-American with an amusing handle-bar mustache. His name was Joe Bianca. He spat too. . . .

. . . Rarely have I seen such beautiful country; the soil was sandy and baked hard by centuries of sun; it was rough, dry and rugged, with many hills, outcropping of rock, and grown with sage, scrub pine, oak. The days were hot, the nights cold, just as in Tarrazona, but respectively more excessive. There we slept in barracks on straw ticks; here we slept on the ground. There was nothing to do; we lay on the hill waiting for the days to pass, the orders to come. There were no rifles yet; there were no orders. Every day the Italian and German airplanes flew overhead in formation, V's and echelons, and some one shouted, *"Avión!"* and the men lay flat on the ground, close in to the trunks of the trees, but the planes either did not see us or they had other fish to fry.

As the days passed we learned more of what had happened; Mel Ofsink, the Commander of Company 1, into which I had transferred to be with Tabb, described the retreat to us. Major Merriman, tall, scholarly, wearing horn-rimmed glasses, spoke to us: "We will go into action again soon," he said. "In this action we will be expected to retake terrain lost previously, and the sacrifice of every life may be asked." We gathered that there had been sabotage during the early part of the retreat; that outfits on either flank of the Internationals had withdrawn without the formality of notifying them. One Spanish major, two lieutenants and a sergeant had been shot, we were told. "Any man seen mistreating a rifle or machine-gun, or throwing it away," said

Commissar Doran, "is to be shot on sight." But no arms had come for us.

In the course of the slow days the Battalion began to be reorganized. It was under the command of Captain Milton Wolff, twenty-two-year-old Brooklyn commercial art-student, who looked like Lincoln, wore a handle-bar mustache like Joe Bianca and a long black cape that made him seem even taller than he was. He was fantastic. My section-leader was Dick Rusciano; he was a printer from Queens, had been teaching in the N. C. O. school, and came up with us from Tarrazona after a long stretch behind the lines. The food situation began to improve slightly, but the men were ravenous. Coffee came up at ten A.M. instead of dawn; the noon meal at five; the evening meal anywhere from ten to midnight. The men fought to get in line for a piece of bread, a spoonful of rice, a little salad, that were eaten from tin cans if you could 'organize' one for yourself, or off of leaves with your fingers. You were always hungry. There was no water on the hill, and as it had to be fetched from far down the valley, no one cared to go for it.

Months in the line had reduced these men to a truly animal level, or so it seemed to Tabb and me. They growled at each other, they were surly, selfish and curt, although they could also be capable of astonishing generosity, considering the circumstances. (One man who received two cartons of *Camels* gave them all away.) The strain, however, was apparent, and they were not to be taunted or kidded about anything. They seemed to care for nothing; many men had run away during the course of the retreat and had been found at the French border, or in Barcelona where, they explained, they "heard the Brigade was being reorganized."

Some obviously wanted to get out of an intolerable situation; swore they would not go into action again; would desert at the first opportunity. (I recalled the man with the gloved artificial hand in Paris. 'Oh,' he had said. 'More suckers.')

In the course of the days, news filtered in from the outside world. Lister was still holding them at Alcaniz. "Hope to Christ he keeps holding 'em," the men said. "The longer he holds 'em, the longer we rest." There was talk of the many who had died; of previous actions; of union fights back home. "Boy," one seaman said, "when I saw Joe Ryan's goon-squad coming down the line, was I scared pissless!" Failure to fortify Teruel and Belchite during the months we held them, we were told, accounted for their loss. This seemed plainly like sabotage; we had been taught by Major Johnson that "what he takes with the rifle, the soldier holds with the spade." The Fascists were launching terrific counter-attacks; we could hear the rumble of artillery, like summer thunder in the distance. The situation in Spain was changing rapidly as a result of recent Government defeats. The U. G. T. and C. N. T. of Catalonia, great trade-unions, had finally settled their ideological difficulties and were united in the prosecution of the war. The Unified Socialist Youth were organizing divisions for the front. The trade-unions were sending labor-battalions to fortify. The French Government, scared again, had opened the Pyrenees frontier to relatively large quantities of war materials, desperately needed by the Loyalists to counterbalance the heavy Fascist mechanization openly supplied by Hitler and Mussolini, who did not intend to see their stake in Spain go glimmering. A new phase in the war had apparently been reached. There was a rumor that Mussolini would attempt to land 40,000 more troops on the Mediterranean shore. The XIIIth Brigade (Slavs, Czechs and Poles) went back up to support Lister. The French Government grew bold and its Minister for Foreign Affairs, Paul-Boncour, loudly announced that France would not 'tolerate' temporary or permanent occupation of her frontiers by any foreign power. Even back home Roosevelt and Hull declared for revision of our Neutrality Resolution, under pressure of popular feeling about Spain and China; and it appeared for a moment that this cynical piece of legislation might be replaced by the O'Connell Bill. The Fascists started an offensive at Huesca, using a smoke-screen for the first time, and all-German troops. A large-scale Government counter-attack was imminent, we were told, with our own Brigade 'leading the way.' But we had no arms.

We had no arms; at the most there were about fifteen rifles in the Battalion. But there *was* a truck, and it took those of us who had the gumption down to a river about six kilometers away, to bathe. Here we lay flat in the ice-cold mountain water, while a squadron of Fascist bombers pulsed over our shivering white bodies. There was soap, new socks, anti-lice salve for pubis and armpits. We lay around and chewed the fat; Tabb said he had fifty dollars back home waiting for him, didn't need it and would lend it to me. I wrote to the mother of my kids to get this money, but she never did. An emaciated comrade who had the deep eye-sockets and the bone-like face of a skull, said, "Didn't you used to work on *The Brooklyn Eagle?* I helped your wife on the Citizens' Committee during the Seamen's Strike." "My former wife," I said. "Oh," he said. "How are your kids?" This was Joe Hecht, but I did not recognize our first Spanish teacher back in Tarrazona; he had changed in the four weeks since he left the training-base.

Ten men were 'decorated' for bravery in action; they received wrist-watches and pocketbooks. (I remember one— Sam Grant; he wore a tin hat day and night.) I swapped a new Spanish dictionary for a fine brass spoon and organized a large marmalade tin for a mess-kit, poked a hole in it, threaded in a string and hung it on my belt. I was made a corporal under Dick Rusciano and spent morbid hours wondering how it would be possible for a man of my training and habit of idiosyncratic isolation to lead other men in battle, even five other men. Hoover suddenly appeared, coming up the hill like a ghost from the grave. Yes, he said, Earl was dead at Belchite, cut to pieces by machine-gun bullets, "I was right next to him." Hoover himself had been slightly wounded, but was determined to transfer into a motorcycle unit. This was a different man from him we had known before. He was quiet, he was shaken, he was scared. When the planes came over on their regular reconnaissance flights, he flattened onto the ground and shook like a leaf; his face was a dead white; he bit his lips. He said he was going back to Barcelona, and he certainly left the Brigade; no one ever saw him again. He 'fucked off' over the border, as the men expressed it, and his name is not Hoover.

Now began a period of a few days which reduced the new replacements to a standard of living and a mental attitude somewhat on a par with the veterans. We formed a habit (that made no sense to us) of moving every night, marching fifteen to twenty kilometers, first south, then back north, camping a day, moving back again. The rainy season came on, suddenly and with a vengeance. The *'chavolas'* or lean-tos we had prepared at our original camp-site were inadequate to shield us from the cold rain and the wind, and we had been told that there were houses about a kilometer out of Batea; about three kilometers away. In driving rain we marched out of camp on a search for these houses, and they existed, but there were not enough of them. We sat hours by the side of the road, waiting for our scouts to find shelter for the various companies and sections, wet to the skin, shivering, sneezing. We just sat. Then we marched again, our feet sucking and squelching in the mud, our faces streaming with rain, our blankets, draped over our heads, heavy with water. And late at night we met the kitchen-truck on a side road, and in the light of its headlights we were fed cold coffee, cold *garbanzos,* standing there in a downpour that limited visibility to three feet in front of your face. Then still later we marched into Batea and took over a theatre, built a fire on its concrete floor, a fire that filled the place with smoke, and tried to dry out. "Whoever heard of the XVth Brigade doing anything right?" the men said.

By dawn we were up again and marched back to our original camp; the rain had lifted but it was cold, cloudy, damp. The food truck gave us coffee, jam and bread, and a ration of Spanish cognac. The camp was soaked. We were wretched and demoralized, dead for lack of sleep, suffering from colds, fever and rheumatic pains in the muscles. The cold and damp continued, and we were sent on patrol far beyond the camp to watch the valleys that led down from the front. Any successful Fascist push would come down these valleys, and the old instructions obtained: shoot on sight any non-civilian who refuses to answer a challenge, who takes cover when challenged. My particular patrol was not relieved for over twelve hours; nobody knew why, but it occasioned a terrific argument among the men. "God *damn* this lousy outfit!" men would say. "They don't know their ass from a hot rock. Is it any wonder we get licked; is it any wonder we get cut off and surrounded? Look at the officers we got; look at the phony bunch of bastards on top—" "Comrade," a voice would invariably reply, "you're talking through your hat." "Fuck off," the answer came to that.

On a rocky hilltop I was posted to watch for the invisible enemy. Grand spaces of air lay between me and the far hills, and a sense of cosmic intelligence made itself felt and manifested itself in the smallest ways. It was an edifying sight to watch the dung beetles rolling your manure away, laying their eggs in it. A beetle with a ball of dung about three-quarters of an inch in circumference would be attacked by a beetle without a ball. You could feel that even in so small a way you were contributing to the balance and economy of nature. You could again contemplate, but not for long, your death in action. But you could not contemplate it with equanimity. You could wonder about your kids, and take out of your pocket the first letter the older had written, dictated to his mother and hand-illustrated. Delivered on a mountain-top in Spain, almost four thousand miles from home, it was shattering; it killed you with excitement and with longing:

We are writing this letter on Tuesday night.
Some day we are going to make a strawberry pie with baked apples in it.
And dear Poppy, Mommy told me that you were in Spain.

*We're just going to tell Frankie and Emilio and Morton that
you're in Spain.*

*I brought four papers with colors home from school today.
And Poppy I love you. The loyalist hats haven't come yet. I
can draw a picture of you with one on. We have a new table-
cloth. Mommy bought some new pencils. Mommy bought
a new pair of stockings and she wouldn't buy silk ones because of Japan.*

*I haven't any new books, Poppy. Maybe when you come
back if you have any money you'll buy me only one and I'll
show it to David and I'll look at it.*

We're right near the pier.

*Just a minute. In our new house we have a little room, me
and Davie, and Mommy never lies down in it. We don't
have to go to a store across the street. We have a store right
next door.*

*I want you to know dear Poppy that I'm going tonight on
Tuesday send a picture and it will be a tent and you will
have it in about one month. Pooh! pooh! pooh! (That'll be
funny, just Pooh!) (When Poppy gets the letter will it be
Pooh! pooh! pooh! Write Pooh! all over the whole page but
don't tell him it says Pooh! And he'll laugh.)*

Do you have this Indian tent in Spain?"

And their mother wrote *When you think of me and the kids,
you must think of us as we are . . . cheerful, comfortable,
nourished and busy. I wish it were possible to say as much
for every human being alive. Our Relief investigator is a
middle-aged man with common-sense. . . . Rent is low (22),
we shop at market, and go without none of the necessities,
as you and millions of others are doing.*

Here's to reality . . . and if my heart is momentarily heavy, I still have intelligence and spirit to keep it pumping good red blood. This is no time for sorrow, no time to look back, no time to think back, no time to make complications. For you, my dear, I hope you are one of the lucky ones. . . .

[*March 31st*]

Two nights before there had been a *fiesta* around a huge bonfire, and singing and a cheap French "champagne" that tasted more like sour hard cider, and there were *avellanos* to eat and shells to toss in the fire, and there were speeches. Young girls had come up from Barcelona to visit us, representatives of the Unified Socialist Youth, and though at that time we knew little enough Spanish, one of them, a small plain girl, was able to fire us with immense enthusiasm. There was also a young man, every inch a man, who had been impressed into Franco's army in the north and had managed to escape to us with a Fiat machine-gun and three other armed men. "We must be moving," the older men said. "When they throw a *fiesta* for you, it never fails."

At five in the morning of the 30th we were up and lined up and marched down toward the road, where there were cases and cases of unused Russian rifles, packed in grease. These were issued to the men, and as we had no rags with which to clean them (they had been packed since they were manufactured), we tore wide strips off our underwear, wiped barrel, stock and bolt, ran strips through the bore. My rifle, whose metal-work bore the stamp of the Russian Imperial Eagle, was numbered 59034. Under the partly obliterated Imperial emblem was a new stamp, the hammer-and-sickle of the Soviet Union.

There was no time to clean the arms adequately; we cleaned and wiped them as we marched. We halted for a moment to receive little paper packs of cartridges (165 rounds a man) which the men stuffed in their pockets, packed into their blanket-rolls. We halted again to take on a load of hand-grenades, a modification of the World War Mills bomb, made of segmented cast iron and provided with a lever and a pin. None of us had ever tossed a live grenade. We went onto the main road and marched in artillery formation on either side of the road, the scouts going ahead at the point and on the flanks, the main body moving slowly along. Every fifteen minutes there were *avion* warnings, and we scattered off the road into the ditches and the fields, lying on our faces till the whistle blew.

It was hot, and the day ground us down. The pack-straps cut into our shoulders. The Fascist *avion* was overhead and the dust of the road bit into our lungs. The more experienced men shed what little equipment they had; tin cans and blankets, plates and spoons, extra underwear, placing the shining objects carefully under bushes so they could not be seen from the air. We marched and flopped all that day, feeling the sweat in our armpits, the dust on our faces, our feet swelling in our bad shoes. There was artillery and the sound, deeper, more rumbling, more menacing, of air-bombs in the distance.

We marched most of that night and before dawn of the 31st we made camp in an olive field. The men dropped under the gnarled trees and slept heavily; some did not even wrap in their blankets; they were too tired to unroll them. They lay with their legs stretched stiffly out, snoring. There was a moon and there were heavy clouds that blacked it out

from time to time. It was cold. The guards stood at some
distance from the sleeping men, lonely with their rifles,
wrapped in blankets like Indians. The night wore you down
with its eternal vigilance; you could hear the night listening, as you were listening, for something you had no way
of knowing till you met it.

In those long hours before dawn it was almost impossible
to think of what was coming with the day; impossible to
realize that the training-period was really over, and that
within a few hours you would meet what you had come
four thousand miles to meet. There was no fear in me, standing with my blanket wrapped around me, the rifle cold
under the blanket, hugged to my body; you could feel no
fear when all you wanted was to sleep. It made me sore;
technically I was still a *cabo,* a squad-leader, but Rusciano,
the section-leader, had made me stand the first guard. Or
was I a *cabo?* I'd been a *cabo,* a machine-gun loader under
Tabb, a scout under Luke Hinman, all in quick succession.
Tabb was dead to the world, his clown's face with the wide
nose, the thick lips, staring at the moon, his mouth open. I
wished I were asleep beside him again, rolled in the same
pair of blankets, as we had been for the past week or so. I
yawned and, against my better judgment, sat down on a rock
in the low brush and let my head droop. The nod woke me
and I reached for the pack of *Twenty Grand* we had been
issued, carefully lit one under the protection of the blanket,
took deep drags and stuck my head out like a turtle to ex-
hale the smoke. There was no pleasure in smoking like this;
I pinched the butt and put it in my pocket.

But within the hour there was a stir in the camp; Milt
Wolff's Brooklyn voice could be heard saying, *"Aténtos;*

en pie!" The men, reluctant to be wakened, grumbled in half-sleep, moaning like women in childbirth. There was mist over the ground and the sage-brush was fragrant in the damp pre-morning air. I wondered whether I was supposed to stand my ground till I was relieved, and loneliness was intensified by the possibility that the Battalion might move off without me. Then I heard Tabb's voice calling and came into camp, stumbling over the low brush, catching the dangling blanket on the twigs. The Battalion was forming up; the men were grunting, pushing each other, adjusting their equipment. I rounded up my squad and moved off with the rest. Where was the enemy? I don't remember who was in that squad.

We were moving in extended order up and down hill, wild, wooded country, rough to the feet, exhausting. There would be no stopping now. Dick Rusciano sent me ahead as a scout and I moved in a dream of heightened consciousness, somewhat ahead of the rest, off to the left, back to the right, making contact with outfits on the flanks. Where were the Fascists? It was going to be a hot day; the artillery we had been hearing the past few days, back of the lines, was silent now; the sky was clean of *avion,* silent with heavy white clouds hanging suspended, burning up in the brightening sun. You could feel the sweat trickling in your armpits, down your back. You shifted the blanket-roll, the pack-sack, wishing you had the courage to discard them as the others had, grumbling when the long needle-bayonet caught in the branches of the fig trees. Then we approached an open piece of terrain—an olive field with a wooded hill beyond. Where was the enemy? Dick said, "I want you to go ahead as a feeler."

I wasn't exactly sure of the meaning of the word, but as I moved off into the olive field, taking cover automatically behind each tree, feeling the weight of the heavy sweater and the leather jacket in the pack-sack, it became clear. It was something like a combat-scout; I was expected to 'contact' the enemy; if the enemy was there. I was expected to draw his fire, and as I moved forward, seeing the other men taking cover at the far edge of the grove, there was a painful sensation in my chest and I automatically turned my body to present less surface to the front. It was difficult to maintain the mind at its present pitch of awareness; to take in everything, to see clearly. Your eyes misted with perspiration; your throat was dry.

There was nothing on the hill and the Battalion moved into position, took cover and waited. Tabb and I were sent ahead to the next hill; there was nothing there, so we moved onto the next. "This is going to be apple-pie," Dick said when he came up to us, sitting on the rock panting in the sun.

A whip cracked overhead and we ducked. We looked at our section-leader and said, "What's that?" "That," said Dick, "was a bullet. *Sección!*" he shouted to the sweating men lying in the lee of the hill, *"en posición! A tierra!"* Automatically the men obeyed, moving cautiously forward onto the crest of the hill, dropping their blankets and pack-sacks behind. *"Abajo!"* Dick shouted, but he didn't get down himself, I noted, as I crouched idiotically behind a bush. "I can't see anything," I said. "Well, get farther forward," Dick answered. "Get down, you dumb fool!"

We lay on our bellies on the crest of the hill, straining for sight of the enemy. The crackling overhead intensified; twigs and leaves floated down onto us. I couldn't see a damned thing. *"Fuego!"* yelled Dick.

"Where?" I said, feeling close to tears.

"They're on the hill opposite," Dick said. "Give 'em hell, *chicos!"* he yelled, moving up and down on the ridge, placing his *cabos.* "Dick!" I shouted "You're exposing yourself!" His thin body, his fine Italian face was suddenly very dear to me.

"There's lots of room between bullets," he said. . . .

. . . We had one section of Spanish boys attached to each company, and lying there in the line I caught a glimpse of one of them crawling through the underbrush, his mountainous pack-sack swaying like the howdah on an elephant's back. He came from behind me and to the right and was crawling toward Tabb's machine-gun squad, saying, "I want to see the machine-gun working." I heard Tabb shout to him to get down, that he was in the line of fire, but the boy kept coming at him, smiling, saying, "I want to see the machine-gun," and then he rolled onto his side, his hands seeking his groin, shouting, *"Mama mia! Aï! Mama mia!"* Tabb's gun let a burst fly at the rough crest opposite, and I looked across, could see where the bullets hit the stone, but there were no men in sight. You never seemed to see them; they kept their heads down. The phrase, *Superiority of fire,* kept running through my head, superiority of fire. If you could get it first, they kept their heads down; if they got it, you kept yours down. If you got it, you could advance; if they got it——

Dick sent me on patrol alone, and when I got back the Spanish boy was still lying in front of our lines, groaning.

Dick told me to get a stretcher-bearer and I went back down the hill, sweating and grunting to myself, but momentarily relieved by being out of the line of fire. Below there was a first-aid man, but no stretcher-bearer was available and the *practicante* (whatever his name was) was reluctant to come back up the hill. "Bring him down," he said, and I said, "We can't; you'll have to go up," and all the way back up the hill he kept saying, "Keep down, be careful, look out, the fire's pretty hot up here, where is he?" It got on my nerves and I felt good thinking of him alone out there, dressing the wound, while I could drop back behind the hill and sit down and light a cigarette. The Spanish boy was still moaning, over and over, *"Mama mia! Ayúdame!"* and it was a nice feeling, hearing the bullets cracking overhead (you never hear the one that hits you), knowing they couldn't get you. But I began to shake the way I had been shaking before when, after three hours of firing from that position behind the bush, I'd rolled out and come back of the hill the first time. In the line itself you fired till the rifle got too hot to handle; then you opened the bolt and blew down the barrel and let it cool, resting your face on your extended arm, waiting. You got so you were afraid to lift your head again to fire, certain that the moment you lifted it, the bullet you wouldn't hear would catch you smack in the middle of the forehead. And then you suddenly awoke to the fact that you had been asleep in the line itself, dead to the world under the drilling of the rifle and machine-gun bullets, any one of which might have— You awoke with a jerk and a pounding heart, and fired conscientiously, compensating by the intensity of your fire for the lapse of consciousness. The metal work blistered your hand; the sun blistered your neck; your shoulder was sore as a boil; your throat was dry and working.

Then there had been the sudden animal cry of the Spanish boy and the female screaming, the pleading voice over and over and over, and Dick behind, saying, "Roll over and come back here." When I got back he wasn't in sight, so I sat down and tried to roll a cigarette with the little tin machine, but the tobacco wouldn't stay in the roller and the paper got crumpled and my hands shook, remembering the bullet that had kicked up the dirt in the hollow where I had been lying, just after I rolled over on my side. Dick said, "Look over there; there's a mountain over there. Well, there are a lot of troops behind that hill, but we don't know who they are, ours or theirs. Go over and find out and try to get back by dark." The body felt light; the head detached from the body; the feet a long way below and carrying the detached body along by their own independent effort.

There was a sniper who followed me along through the edge of the woods and across the open space, and I kept thinking. This is too close for comfort, you bastard, you god-damned son-of-a-bitch, and then I entered the woods and promptly lost my way. (I wonder what it's like in Brooklyn now, I thought, and how much do they get on relief, and do the kids get enough orange juice and corn-flakes and does she get enough to eat or does she scrimp on her own chow to line the kids' bellies?) I looked back but the hill on which the Battalion had taken up positions was hidden, and I stood there thinking. When I left I was going due west into the sun, and the mountain was somewhat north of west, and now the sun is on my left when it should be on my right and what is it like in Brooklyn? I sat down and rolled a cigarette, letting my mind play with the compass directions, and then Luke Hinman came along. He was a Battalion scout and had given me a few simple lessons in scouting a few days before, and so I asked him about the directions, watching his hard, kind face with the broken nose, the firm lips, the blue eyes. He didn't talk much.

Moving through the woods quietly with your rifle at the ready was good; it was good to be on your own, not attempting to command a squad (what had become of the squad anyhow?), responsible for no one but yourself. Then I came across a guy we can call Hal, another Battalion scout, who was sitting in the woods, or rather lying on his back with his eyes closed. He had blue eyes too, I noticed, but they were different; he had a soft wet mouth and a face that looked somewhat out of focus. "What're you up to?" I asked, and he said, smiling, "I'm on patrol," so I moved on and found the hill and came cautiously behind it. There was another company of the Lincolns there, the third, "But we're pulling right out," said Blackie Mapralian, the Commander, so I started back through the woods and located Hal again, who was still lying on his back. "How's the patrol going?" I said, and he said, "Couldn't be better." Goldbrick was the word that came into my mind, and I laughed to myself as I went along, thinking, Would they shoot him for that if I said anything which I won't, but would they? On the hill behind ours I met Hank Wentworth. "Dick's worried about you," Hank said. "Where you been all this time?" "Well, to tell you the truth," I said, "when I started out I saw the kitchen truck at Headquarters, and I got something to eat." "What'd they have?" he said. "Nothing came up to the line yet." "Oh, salad and steak and rice and French fried potatoes and wine and cookies and nuts and coffee—" "No crap," Hank said. . . .

. . . But just before dark Dick received a message from Battalion which read, "Advise that enemy is expected to attack on your right flank; place a light machine-gun out on your right with instructions not to fire till they are 50 meters from you." And because I'd been over the terrain he sent me out with Sid, who was Tabb's gunner, and kept Tabb on the hill.

Sid had received a glancing blow in the head earlier that afternoon, and he had a handkerchief around his forehead that kept slipping over his eyes as we doubled down the back side of our hill and along through the woods that bordered the olive field. He was short and slim. But the sniper had seen us moving and he followed us through the woods as we went ducking around and under the low spruces, caught in the brambles, scratching our hands and faces. I was praying for the sun to set, but it was still high over the western hill.

When we reached the point where we would have to cross the open space, we looked at one another. There was Sid, small and scared, and the black wet face of the Negro, Johnson (my God, I thought, he must be fifty years old!), and Moish Taubman, who used to say he was the laziest man in the Battalion, but had guts of cast iron. We crouched near the opening, waiting for each other to suggest some way of getting across. The bullets were hissing high or cracking low, and Moish said, "That son-of-a-bitch is going to hurt somebody if he ain't careful," and Sid said to me, "You're stronger than I am; suppose you take the gun, and go across first."

I took the light Dikterov in my arms like an infant (and I remember thinking of Dave, who had just turned three a week before) and faced the hundred meters of ploughed earth ahead. I took a deep breath and crouching low, started to run. I was crouched too low, felt myself falling, stumbling, lifted my head and shoulders so I could take longer strides, and zigzagged stumbling over the heavy clods of plowed earth, thinking, Fifty meters is awful close; if we wait till they get that close— Dick had said, "Bring the gun back, and come back yourselves."

The Fascist machine-gun spoke and the dirt kicked up around me; I ran, seeing the little wooded clump ahead swaying and bobbing toward me, wondering if the others were right behind. When I reached the poor shelter of the wood I fell flat on the gun and dug my face into the hard ground. The machine-gun bullets were snarling overhead and I lay there waiting, counting in my head one two three four five, holding my breath for them to stop. Twigs and leaves kept dropping, and looking behind I could see where the slugs were kicking up the dirt, whining off the stones like a plucked piano string. No one had followed, so I lay face downward on the gun, trying consciously to go to sleep. Then they came panting, almost grunting with the effort, and threw themselves down all around, Johnson dropping the little shovel and the machine-gun pans, that clattered on a stone. And after awhile the Fascist gun stopped firing.

We sat in the heavy darkness, tending the gun that faced

up the valley, waiting. There really wasn't a good spot for that gun at all. It was so quiet that for a time we whispered about the possibility of the Battalion moving off without us, but there was no reason for the Battalion to move. We had taken two hills that day (was it really only one day!) and there was nothing to worry about. We scouted about individually in the dark, and I found a fine white blanket that Sid said I'd have to leave. We couldn't smoke; we couldn't talk. There was a mongrel dog that kept following us around, sitting down when we sat down and occasionally barking. That was the only sound in all that darkness and it gave us the creeps. Sid said we ought to kill it and we talked it over, decided that it would not be wise to shoot it, and no one had the nerve to stab it with a bayonet. "That damn hound'll give us all away," Johnson said (you couldn't see him in the dark), and mumbled quietly to himself. "He's probably just lonesome," Moish said, "what the hell." But no one came; we listened till our ears hurt and no one came.

"I'll lead the way back," Sid said, and started confidently off. "Wrong way," I said, but Sid didn't answer. "You're going the wrong way," I said, and Sid stopped, waited for me to come up close and then said, *"I'm* in command of this squad." "O. K." I said, "but you're going the wrong way anyhow."

We picked our way up the side of a hill, slipping on the exposed stone, dead tired and aching with the long day's tension. Johnson was carrying the gun, moaning quietly to himself. When we reached a halt on the side of the hill, he said, "Comrade, this comrade says you're going the wrong way, comrade. He brought us out here; maybe he ought to know the way back. Maybe you better let him take us back, comrade. I'm done in," he said and sat down with the gun cradled in his lap. . . .

. . . I was put on guard for an hour after we got back, and sat with my blanket wrapped around me, yawning and nodding. Tabb said, "Bessie's gone to sleep on guard," and I said, "The hell I have," and Dick said, "Go to sleep." I remembered us plodding along home (home!) stopping in the darkness and listening, moving carefully around the shrubs and over the rocks. The smell of sage-brush was strong, sweet in the night. Then we heard the voice, Tabb's voice, saying quietly, "Sid . . . Bess . . . Sid . . . Bess . . . Sid . . . Bess," and we came up to him, sitting there alone on a stone in the moonless dark, waiting for us. "Dick was worried about you," he said. "He sent me out to find you, but I didn't know where you were."

We were asleep, and then suddenly the night was loud with sound; the machine-gun bullets were whacking and whining all around and the curious echo was sounding that sounds across an empty space when guns are firing. It was like water washing on a cliff below. We lifted our heads cautiously and looked out from under our blankets; the ridge opposite was bright with rifle fire, pink electric stars going on and off, and there were many bursts of grenades falling like roman candles off the Fascists' hill, plopping, plopping. They seemed to be holding a *fiesta,* but Tabb, who was sleeping with me, said, "They got the jitters; they think we're attacking." *"Halto fuego!"* Dick yelled in the dark. I had my rifle in my hand, had pulled it in under the blanket, which gave me the illusion that I was somewhat protected, and working the bolt, stiff with the cold and wet with dew, I held it to my shoulder and fired. The flash and the roar startled me, and I put the rifle down, lying with my head cradled in my arms, hoping I wouldn't get hit in the darkness; it seemed somehow that it would be worse to get hit at night than in the day.

[*April Fools' Day*]

It was still dark when Tabb woke me, saying, "We're moving to another position; Dick wants to talk to you." It didn't exactly make sense, but Dick said, "Manuel here'll take you and Hank to a hill. I want you both to sit on that hill and look up the valley; you'll be rearguard scouts. Watch for anything that turns up; there'll be other comrades on the other hills; if you see anything, let us know."

The group of us moved off in the dim light, down off our hill and back up the valley to a point where the juxtaposition of four hills made a right-angled crossing of the valley, and Hank and I climbed the one that was indicated to us, found a sheltered spot under a young pine and with our rifles propped between our knees stared fixedly up and down the valley. There was nothing to be seen.

The sun came up and the clouds burned up in its flame; the sun stood high over the quiet hills and it was good to sit in the sun after the chill of the long, exhausting night. We both knew that soon we would go to sleep and we talked idly about whether it were really possible to prop your eyelids with toothpicks. We shook ourselves and turned our heads slowly from side to side, our eyes looking but seeing nothing. It required a concentration almost beyond our powers to focus our eyes on any given point and watch that point; we nodded. We agreed to sleep in turns and keep watch in turns, and we slept sitting up. We both awoke, hearing the Battalion truck moving up the valley toward Headquarters, the *responsable* standing on the running-board of the cab, a rifle in his hand. We thought and spoke of the coffee, the bread and marmalade in the truck and our stomachs started to clench and unclench like a fist. We watched till the truck came back down the valley an hour later, and the dust cloud behind it had settled. In the distance there was a little artillery and there was the throbbing of airplane motors, but no plane came over. Hank fell sound asleep.

But I really don't know any of them, I thought; nothing about them. Here was Hank Wentworth, thin and rangy, from some place in the Middle West; an excellent woodsman, a good union man, an anti-Fascist. He had spent a lot of time in the woods; he spoke with a dry sort of humor and he had a tendency to get tight a bit too often; he never spoke of himself. There was Milton Wolff, tall, wearing a fantastic black cape and a wool hat and long mustachios; there was Rusciano, a printer; Tabb, a printer too; Luke Hinman from the West Coast, a labor organizer, and Hal from the West Coast, and the Spanish boy calling for his mother, and Sid from Ohio and Johnson from the South, and a multitude of other Americans from the West, New England, from Chicago and Florida, from Philadelphia and Minnesota, Texas. They did not know each other but here they were, together closer than men who have known each other a lifetime; separate but bound, sharing what they had and didn't have, knowing nothing of each other. What brought them? (I saw Luke, tall, thin, moving down the valley alone, looking right and left.) Conviction and certainty, what were they? What had they left? Their past lives, their future quite possibly, carrying their own unhappiness within them, their own uncertainties. They were no iron men, but they were heroes. Seamen and clothing workers, clerks and artists, students and fathers of families. The phrase you heard so many times—'united in a common cause'—meant everything, and it meant nothing. For you could not hold an abstract idea in your mind at the front. You became aware at moments that the idea had never disappeared; that it was behind everything you did, behind the necessity you felt to do the job and do it well. It was something you did not talk about; it was something you took for granted. Hank stirred in his sleep and said, quite plainly, "Hamburger on rye with onions on the side."

All that day we sat under the pine tree, nodding and sleeping, waking and watching, our stomachs a dull ache within us, alone but surrounded by unseen comrades. The sun declined over the western hills, and we thought again, despite exhaustion and hunger and discomfort, of the beauty of this country; of the people we had seen with their lean, eager faces; the children begging for bread in Barcelona, Valencia, in the small towns; people we had come thousands of miles to help as best we could, but of whom we rarely spoke out of embarrassment and fear of appearing sentimental. These people stood behind us all. (I saw Luke coming back from his patrol, every line of his body, tiny in the distance, drooping with fatigue, but alert, still alert.) There was the smell of pine pitch and the hot sage-brush and the sight of the terraced hills and the tumbled rocks and the theatrical cloud formations. The war seemed very far away and it was difficult to think of what might be happening in other sectors of the same front; the artillery was summer thunder in the distance, musical and harmless; the distant airplanes droned but did not appear; there was a rare burst of machine-gun fire far away, innocuous, pleasant to hear. . . .

. . . Late that afternoon of the endless afternoon we saw Manuel coming down the valley fast, carrying something in his hand, and when he got to the intersection of the valley he waved. We could spot the other comrades coming down off the near-by hills, and we unbent our rigid limbs and started sliding down. Manuel was waiting patiently for us and when we reached him he put his hand into the newspaper he was carrying and gave a handful of *avellanos* to each of us. We started to crack the nuts between our teeth. "Come," he said, "we are going," and we fell in behind him, moving off down the valley till we came to the dirt road.

We kept looking to the right, the left, behind; there was a feeling of suspense; a feeling that something was going to happen any minute. Further ahead, down the road, we could see a large body of men, standing, sitting, lying near the great lime-washed stone house that was being used as the Brigade first-aid post. No one said anything; no one asked any questions, but we knew we were moving, moving fast. Tabb was seated beside the road, the light Russian machine-gun at his side. His funny face was unshaved, his hands were dirty; he said nothing. But the place was loud with commands; small groups of men moving forward and back, threading their way between the tired men, seeking their units. "Company One this way!" "Scouts and machine-guns up ahead." *"Cola! cola!"* the tired men joked, leaning on their rifles. "Who ever saw the XVth Brigade do anything right?" some one said.

I went to the head of the disorganized column, found Luke and Hal sitting beside the road, sat down beside them. I looked at the tiny butt in Luke's long, stained fingers, and he handed it to me. Hal was staring at his feet; Milt Wolff was down the road, conferring with Merriman and Doran of the Brigade, looking twice as tall as normal in his long black cape, stained with red dirt. They were looking at a map. He turned to the men, raised his hand and said, *"Batallón! A formár!"* It was growing dark. He waved his arm, said, "Let's *go*," and the men who had been sitting, lying beside the road, picked themselves and their equipment up and shuffled along in the dust of the eroded path, moving downhill. The head of the column halted, and men bumped each other. Angry voices said, "Watch that bayonet; pick up your feet; get the lead outta your ass," and the column moved on again, stumbling down the hill toward the main road.

When we reached the hard surface we fell in again, covering off with weary arms, dropping our arms again. Men were too tired to lift their wooden ammo boxes from their shoulders. Apprehensive of *avion*—for we felt exposed on the open road—we glanced up and around. Hal called me to the head of the column, saying, "The Battalion Command will be a few meters behind you; I'm going ahead; maintain contact between us." His blue eyes were watery, red around the edges. I was glad I hadn't been put out on the flank, like Luke, for I was so tired I knew I could not have maintained the extra speed required to move up and down

the hills that skirted the road, while the Battalion marched
on the even surface. We were moving south, toward Gandesa, away from the lines we had taken the morning before. Were we retreating? Why? It was dark now, and in
the direction of the town the sky was lit momentarily by
wide bright flashes and the rumble of the summer thunder
sounded from directly ahead.

"Contact!" Hal said, and I trotted forward, feeling the
cartridge packs bouncing in my pockets. "We're passing the
place where we entered the lines yesterday morning," Hal
said, and I trotted back down the road toward Wolff, wishing I could have waited at the side of the road till he came
up. When his tall figure appeared in the dark, I said,
"Wolff?" "Yeh." "Bessie at point. We're passing the place
where we entered the lines yesterday morning," and turning on my heel, started moving back toward Hal. On the
way I passed Tabb, trudging with the Dikterov over his
shoulder, Sid and Moish Taubman and Johnson behind him,
carrying the pans. There were other gunners from the
Brigade machine-gun company, packing the detachable parts
of their heavy Maxims, the metal cartridge boxes, bent to
their loads. It would have been easy, in the dark, to have
abandoned the scouting job, fallen in with the main column.

"Contact!" Hal said. "Contact, God damn it to hell, where
are you?" . . .

. . . The Battalion turned off the main road to the left,
onto a dirt road, and then halted. The men flung themselves
down, falling asleep instantly. Tabb was lying down with
the gun in the crook of his arm like a sleeping child, when
I passed him, and he called to me.

"Listen, Bess," he said. "Why don't you join this machine-gun squad?"

"I'm a scout. You can't change jobs like that."

"It won't make any difference," he said. "I'll tell Dick when I see him that I asked for you. I'll take the responsibility."

It was plain that he wanted some one to carry ammunition for him, but even that was better than running back and forth all night. There were half a dozen scouts anyhow; I could do it for the rest of the night. "All right," I said, and we lay by the side of the road in the black night sharing a small butt under cover of his poncho. Around us the other scouts and machine-gunners were sleeping; it was quiet except for the distant gunfire; it was black, except for the distant flashes that were not bright enough to light the surrounding fields. I had a feeling something had gone wrong. I had a feeling that we were retreating; that the same thing had happened to us that had happened before we joined the Brigade.

"What's up?" I said. "Where are we going?"

"I don't know." (I knew he felt the same.)

"I'm pooped," I said.

"*Yo también.*"

"Maybe we're retreating."

"Nonsense," Tabb said. (I knew he was lying.)

We lay there a long time and we must have been asleep, for we both awoke, hearing Hal's voice saying, "A fine bunch of scouts you are. The Battalion's moved off without us; you've lost the Battalion."

Other voices spoke. "How could it?" "Where's it gone?"

"Nobody gave us any orders." "You said to stay here and we stayed."

"Skip it," Hal said, and we saw him move off the road into the shelter of a roofless stone hut, where he consulted with some other scouts over a map held in the dim glow of a flashlight. They were in there a long time, but neither Tabb nor I could summon the curiosity to overcome our great fatigue. We rose out of sleep deliberately at the word of command and started off behind the leading men, Tabb carrying the pans he had taken from the Negro, Johnson, I the gun. We were content to be led; we did not question the command or even wonder where we were going. We were only intent on keeping up with Luke and Hal, who cut off the dirt road and into a field that led uphill. The artillery sounded in the distance and we picked up our feet and put them down, aching in every muscle, yawning from moment to moment, changing our loads from shoulder to shoulder.

It's true, I thought; it's happened again and I don't care. No excitement stirred in me at the prospect of the struggle that must come when this band of perhaps eighty men had to make a run for it through the Fascist lines. The idea, the image would not form in the mind. I only knew that every lagging step was carrying us nearer to a point at which we'd have to succeed or fail for good. Johnson took the Dikterov from me; I was right behind Tabb, grunting at his heels, sighing. There was a comrade ahead of Tabb I knew only as Swede, who was walking in his sleep, his feet carrying him to the right, away from the straggling line of men. Tabb would quicken his pace for a moment, grasp the Swede by the arm and bring him back in line. He said nothing, but soon started moving steadily toward the right again. The leaders called a halt. . . . It must have been late as hell; it must have been almost morning, and we had been marching, walking, stopping, marching, walking since just before dark. The weight of the three machine-gun pans in the sack at my side was noticeable; they bumped and swung around to the front, and I adjusted the strap again. My shoulder was sore where the rifle-strap cut into it. It was bruised from the firing. Johnson was gone; I'd called him an hour before; and so was Sid. I wondered what we could do with the pans now that there was no gun for them. I supposed Johnson would show up sooner or later, but if we needed the gun——

You could smell yourself; it was funny, when you were hot and sweaty in the day, you couldn't smell yourself, but at night you could. Then I became aware that my mouth was open, my tongue hanging out, and I started to giggle. My mind spoke to me, saying, I've read somewhere that you can get so tired your tongue will hang out, but I never believed it. Yet it was definitely open; it was easier to let it hang open than to close it, and when I did close it I soon found it open again. A long way from home, my mind kept saying, be it ev-er so hum-ble it's a long way from home, be it ev-er so hum-ble a long way from home. What are they doing? I thought, and what are they doing? If it's three o'clock now it's ten o'clock there and the kids are in bed asleep and are they sick and are they well and is she sitting there with a cup of coffee, she always drank coffee at night after the kids had been washed and put to bed and she took a bath and put on the red-flowered pajamas

and made the coffee and sat curled in a chair and read a
book, wetting her thumb before she turned a page and
that always annoyed me I don't know why and maybe she
is reading about the war in Spain and it's a long way from
home and won't they ever stop and let us sleep. . . .

[*April 2d*]

We were moving up a narrow dirt road in the hour before dawn and we were really lost but it didn't make much
difference if you kept moving in the right direction; northeast was where the lines should have been. There were a
few lights ahead, a town, and the column of eighty men was
strung out for over half a kilometer, the men picking up
their feet and putting them down. Even when a halt was
called some of them kept on walking automatically until
the thought entered their minds that the others had stopped,
and they stopped too, standing still in the middle of the
road, undecided whether to flop on one side of the road or
the other; it was a difficult decision to make. It did not
occur to us to wonder what town it was or who held it (at
least it did not occur to me), but suddenly the sides of the
road were strewn with equipment; we saw the stuff lying
there and bent to examine it.

There were rifles and blankets, pack-sacks crammed with
the articles soldiers collect (underwear and socks, a pipe,
a notebook, a toothbrush and an extra pair of *alpargatas,* a
jacket). There were burlap bags with a few cans of bully-
beef or fish; there was a stinking codfish in a bag, heavy
and stiff. There were mess tins and knives, forks, spoons,
and we began to re-equip ourselves with the articles we had
lost in action. The men slung the blanket-rolls over their

shoulders, rummaged in the pack-sacks, walking all the time, opening the cans with a dull knife, shoving the food into their mouths. There was bread, sardines, cartridge-belts and ammo.

It did not occur to me to wonder whose stuff this was; it might have belonged to the Fascists or it might have been abandoned by another outfit. I picked up a plate, a spoon, a long kitchen knife, three cans of Argentine corned beef which I stuck in my pockets, hanging the plate on the snap on my belt, sticking the knife in the belt itself. It was beginning to get light, but that did not concern us. I decided not to eat till we rested again; it was too much of an effort to think of opening one of the cans.

Then there was a truck standing abandoned in the middle of the narrow road; there were rifles (Russian rifles) leaning against the tail-gate, and there were some blankets (I took two) and a cartridge-belt that Tabb took. "Do you think this is better than my own rifle?" he said, and I said, "How should I know?" so he slung both of them over his shoulder. Some one said, "I wonder if the damned thing will run," and climbing in, started the engine and switched on the lights. I was standing on the running-board of the cab, but as the truck started to roll I got off; I didn't want to be ahead of the others. The truck moved slowly down the road through the few men in advance, and the men turned their faces in the truck's lights, and their faces were pale and lined. The red tail-light disappeared into the distance.

Then the left side of the road rose and there was an embankment skirting the road. We saw the men but did not wonder who they were. They stood there, wrapped in blankets, holding rifles, and they didn't say anything and we didn't say anything either. Tabb was in front of me; I couldn't see him, but then I heard the men ahead start to run and they jumped onto the embankment and I followed them. Taubman was right behind me.

Tabb dropped the extra rifle and the blankets and lit out after Luke and Hal. I started to shout. "Tabb!" I yelled. "Where are you? I can't see you," and he turned his head, said, "Shut up!" and kept running. We were in a field now, and the field was full of sleeping men; men sleeping in blankets on the ground, and officers sleeping in pup-tents under the olive trees. *We* didn't have any pup-tents, even for our officers. There were horses tethered among the trees, restless in the dark. I tripped over a sleeping man and he sat up and said, *"Coño!"* "Tabb!" I shouted, "stop a minute, will you? I can't keep up!" but he didn't answer and so I just kept running, tripping, falling and running. I strained to see ahead, and then I heard the voices behind, crying *"Halto! Los Rojos! Halto los Rojos!"* and lengthened my stride. There was a terrace just ahead and Tabb was climbing it; he reached down to help me up and I said, "What's the idea?" and he said, "Drop your stuff, get rid of it," and started for the next terrace. I slipped off the two blankets, threw away the knife and plate, but decided to keep the rifle and the machine-gun pans. I could hear the voices plain now and the rifles and pistols and the bullets snapping overhead. We made a dash for the next terrace and went up it; and then there was another, and another. Oh, I thought; I'll *die;* I'm at the end of my rope, I can't do it I can't do it I can't do it. I could hear the others running ahead of me, moaning as they ran, and I knew I had to keep up with them, or rather my legs knew it; they would not stop although my body was getting heavier by the minute; it wanted to sink; it wanted to drop onto the ground, but my legs kept going.

It was light when we entered the woods on top of the hill and moved into the thick underbrush. We sat down suddenly, panting; we lay on our backs gasping for air, hearing the rifles in the distance and weird singing over to the left. "Moors," Hal said. We sat up and looked at one another. There were only the four of us, Luke and Hal and Tabb and I. I brought out a can of corned beef; there was a key on the bottom of the can and I opened it, cut the meat into four pieces and handed it around.

"You better take that red star off your cap," Hal said, and Tabb looked at me. We both took off the Republican star pinned at the peak of our caps.

"I think it would be a good idea if we left the rifles," Hal said. "Travel faster." No one said anything. We were silent awhile, listening to the strange singing far off to the left; watching the sun filter through the heavy underbrush. We were embarrassed.

"You dope," Tabb said. "What made you keep yelling like that?"

"I didn't know," I said.

"We were in their camp."

"I didn't know."

Luke and Hal were looking at me. Then we heard the footsteps, the crackling of dry leaves and snapping twigs, but they were right close to us; they were right on top of us and even though we held our rifles in our hands we were still sitting on the ground when the two soldiers stepped into the brush and covered us with their guns.

"*Qué Brigada?*" one of them said, his lips firm, his eyes frightened but hard. There was a pause.

"*Qué Brigada, tu?*" we said. It was all right.

"*La Trece,*" they said.

"*Quince,*" we said, and they sighed. I guess we all sighed. They sat down and they had some tobacco in their pockets. . . .

. . . The land was folded like an accordion, hill after parallel hill, grown with pine and oak, dark with sage, rugged with stone. Down below us in the *baranco* there was a family of peasants evacuating, a large family streaming from a small stone hut, piling their mattresses and household goods into the *burro* cart (a bed is the first thing to think of taking when you are forced out of your home). They were terrified when they saw the six soldiers slanting down the hill with rifles, and they replied to the *Salud!* with obvious relief. They gave us water and a bag of hazelnuts; they thought that Mora de Ebro was still in Loyal hands and they said that the main road was a short distance down the valley to the left.

By common consent we avoided the beaten paths, climbed up and down the hills, moving always toward the northeast. The sun was high and hot on our faces and we shed our remaining equipment as we went—the machine-gun pans in the sack, the little paper packs of cartridges (except for a clip or two); our extra clothing.

"Where are we going?" I said.

"To Mora," said Luke.

"How do you know it's still ours?"

"I don't.'

"Don't you think we ought to sleep now and travel at night?"

"You ask the damnedest stupid questions."

From the hill we could see the white hard-surfaced road that twisted between the mountains. It shimmered in the distance, waves of heat rising from its surface. Nothing was moving on it, and we watched as long as we dared, but nothing moved. The land was deserted; there was no living thing in sight; for as far as we could see there was no evidence, except the road, of man's habitation in this place. We were lonesome as we moved down off the hill toward the road, and when we reached it we sat down in the shade of a tree and looked at it. Bare, hard, white, silent; there was something sinister about it; we could not bring ourselves to move along its surface.

"Reminds me of California," Luke said to Hal. "You remember Dot. We used to burn up the roads something fierce; had a bottle of gin in the side-pocket."

"There's something weird about this road," I said, and Luke laughed and said, "Yeh." (I have a talent for saying the obvious.) We crossed it and slid down the steep embankment to the drying river bed and steeped our hot heads in the water. We washed our hands and faces, drank, soaked our caps in the water but decided not to take off our shoes, for we weren't sure we could get them on again. Our feet were swollen, bleeding. The other side of the river the heights rose again, almost perpendicular, heartbreaking. When did we sleep last? I thought, days and days ago. It wasn't like the old days gone by when you could sit all night and talk and go to work the next day and sit all the next night and talk and go to work the next day and sit all . . . It was astounding that even in this state of extenuation you could notice the beauty of the place; the theatrical hills were arranged like a stage-set and I remembered how, just before dawn, before we walked into the Fascist camp on the outskirts of Villalba, I had listened, stopping to hear better, to the liquid song of a bird, pure and crystal in the night.

Mora de Ebro, the peasants had said, was sixteen kilometers by road. And if it wasn't ours? Tabb moved along, his comical face hanging almost onto his chest. We were all dead, moving in a dream of exhaustion, carried along by nothing that could be called will or a decision; our bodies carried us and not our minds, and we would go on until we had to stop.

Luke was in front when we reached the top of the hill and saw the men below, moving through the deep *baranco*. Hal was behind him and then came Tabb and I. The two men from the XIIIth were fresh; they'd gone on ahead. We found a can of bully-beef, bright and shining in the sun, and opened it; it was salty, but I carried it for another hour rather than throw it away. (We were too tired to eat.) But below us now there were straggling columns of men, moving through the mountains, climbing the hills ahead, winding toward the Ebro. "They're ours," Luke said, and we moved down the hill and joined the men. They were the German, the French and the Italian volunteers; they spoke no English and were fresher than we were. Short and squarely built, blond, the Germans were packing their heavy Maxims up and down the hills, sweating and silent, and we sat and let them pass in wonderment. Their faces were streaming; their breath escaped their lips with a hoarse, rasp-

ing sound, but they moved steadily along, looking at the
ground ahead of their feet, changing off their heavy loads.
They moved on ahead of us and up the next mountain
side, and Hal said, "To hell with it; let's go back down to
the road," and so we did. In single file we dragged ourselves along the silent road, Luke in advance, looking neither
right nor left. I watched the sky for *avion,* turning to look
at Tabb whose head was bowed onto his chest, his arms
hanging at his sides, and Hal, far behind, his soft mouth wet
and open, his red-rimmed eyes half closed by the brilliant
white light that lay over the road. He was limping. Far
behind we could hear the thunder of artillery (at Gandesa?)
and the high whine of the diving airplanes. . . .

. . . The suburbs of the small city on the Ebro were
jammed with ragged and demoralized men, wandering idly
about in the utmost confusion. "Where's the Mac-Paps?"
they said. "Where's the British?" *"Où est la Quatorzième?"*
"Wo ist die Elfte?" "Seen the XVth Brigade?" They
were sitting or sleeping in the fields on the edge of town;
they stormed an *intendencia* in a warehouse near by, begging for food that was distributed immediately and had
just run out when we reached the town. They were filling
their faces with condensed milk, chocolate, tinned sardines
and tuna fish, bully-beef, bread. I spotted a truck that belonged to some unknown outfit and asked for food. They
refused. I spoke the few words I knew of three or four
languages, begged and threatened, until I was given a large
earthen crock of cold coffee, a couple cans of beef, a piece
of chocolate and three packs of *Gaulois bleu.* (I couldn't
resist putting one pack in my pocket for future reference,

and divided the other two equally.) We lay in a small fenced-in enclosure that was practically covered with human excrement, and slept heavily for about two hours, until dusk. They said the Fascists were on their way, but we didn't care. They said tanks were coming up, but no one paid any attention. There was no command, there was no authority, there was not even a point to which you could report.

There was a *peloton* of men from the Mackenzie-Papineau Battalion camped across the road, and as we were hunting for English voices we soon discovered them. They suggested that we stick to them until we could find our outfit, and they said, "Where's the Lincoln?" "We're the Lincoln," we said, and they said, "Pleased to know you." We lay on the ground and slept a few hours, until it was almost dawn. We had heard that the Lincolns had been cut to pieces; that they were holding the lines above Gandesa; that they were surrounded at Gandesa; that they had cut south and reached Tortosa on the Mediterranean. We spent an hour just before dawn trying to learn, in the dark, how to operate a light Czech machine-gun, for the energetic Canadian *peloton*-leader had decided that we were going to make an observation patrol from a mountain top a few kilometers back of Mora.

[*April 3d*]

When the sun rose and beat on that hill we could not stay awake any longer, and we slept. Tabb was a few meters below me and to the right. Hinman and Hal were somewhere on the hill; all of us were supposed to be watching the Mora road for the approach of tanks. We did not see any tanks, but far beyond we did see the signs of a terrific artillery barrage and air bombardment. It seemed to be around Gandesa; great clouds of black smoke were rising from a valley between the hills, billowing thousands of feet into the air. We could hear the airplanes, but we could not see them; the roar and rumble, though almost twenty-five kilometers away, was terrifying. But we could not watch it; propped against the trees, we were asleep.

Then we were awake and scrambling down the hill toward the road where we had left the truck the Mac-Pap *peloton* had commandeered. Word had come from another patrol that tanks were on their way—Fascist tanks rattling up the road toward Mora. We got down that hill and into the truck, laughing and shouting, half-hysterical with exhaustion and excitement, and the truck ran toward Mora at a speed of over seventy miles an hour, almost colliding with a new barricade that had been built in the suburbs. Here we got out and started to follow the crowds of soldiers moving toward the river. We came into the town, that had been evacuated of civilians, and moved through its paved streets. House doors were open; houses had been looted. Soldiers were seen emerging from these houses with live rabbits, pigeons, chickens, geese, bottles of wine and *coñac*. Soldiers were sitting on the pavement, too exhausted to go on. It was strange to see men, in the streets of a civilized town, urinating on the pavement. A soldier came down the street, carrying an enormous bowl of freshly mixed salad, dishing out spoonfuls to the men standing, sitting, walking.

An ambulance came through town, and Hal, who could not walk any longer, got into it; the ambulance disappeared. In front of a house where a temporary telephone connection had been set up we saw Garfield, who was hopelessly plastered and flourishing a bottle of *coñac*. He saw us and came running to us, tears streaming from his eyes. He kissed us all and pounded us on the back and kept saying over and over, "Oh my God, am I glad to see you; oh sweet Jesus, am I glad to see you! Isn't it awful; isn't it terrible? I never hoped to live to see anything like it."

"Where have you been all this time?" we said.

"With the Brigade *sanidad*," he said. "I was in a classification post. Do you know what a classification post is? It's a butcher shop; they come in and you send them out and they come in and you send them out; blood all over the place. Blood and guts. We got bombed. The first-aid post got bombed. It was wonderful; it was terrible. Here," he said, reaching in his pocket. He gave me a fine little Swiss first-aid pack. "I've been saving this for you." He threw his arms around me and kissed me and cried on my shoulder. "I never expected to see you alive again," he said. "How are you, Al? How are you? Didn't you get hurt? You're wonderful," he said. "I knew on the ship coming over you were wonderful. You'll be all right," he said.

"I know," I said.

"Sure," he said, "they can't kill you. You have a rendezvous with fate."

"Sure," I said.

"Have a drink. I'm drunk. I'm cockeyed."

"I know," I said.

In the big room under the house where the telephone exchange had been set up, men were sitting, drinking, eating. The telephonist was listening. *"Oiga!"* he said. *"Oiga! Diga! diga!"* Garfield produced wine, *coñac,* candles, which he insisted we needed and that he had organized for us, hazelnuts, walnuts, marmalade, *Chesterfields.* "I got more," he said.

"*Tanques?*" the telephonist was saying, "*Tanques, verdad? Tanques qúe vienen? Fascistas? Si, si. Comprendido. Ter-minado.*"

We went out into the street again; hundreds of men, speaking half a dozen languages, were walking toward the bridge over the Ebro; some were dog-trotting, their faces gray with exhaustion, their equipment rattling as they ran. Cars and trucks were threading their way through the crowds. There was a little truck standing near the bridge, with a little Spanish boy sitting on the tail-gate, crying. He was about five years old. We talked to him, but all he would say was "Mama, mama, mama." We couldn't speak Spanish; we offered to take him along (no one was in the driver's seat), but he pulled away from us. "*Mama perdita?*" he said. We started over the bridge, a great iron structure guarded by soldiers. At the shore line and at the junctures of the spans, boxes of dynamite were piled and stacked; wires ran along the iron roadway of the bridge. The soldiers were smiling, and we smiled and said, "*Salud!*"

There was a small town on the other shore, Mora la Nueva, and we walked through it and stayed on the road that wound uphill. We looked back at Mora across the broad, swift and shallow stream, swollen and muddy now in the spring freshets. As we watched, the great iron bridge rose slowly and majestically into the air and slumped into the river, and the earth shook with the delayed sound of the explosion. We looked at each other, and back across the river. There were explosions in the town itself now; the first

Fascist shells were landing in the city and there was the smoke of fires. From directly over our heads, on the crest of the hill, there came swift, violent reply that deafened us and we dropped onto the ground. Our own artillery was answering. "Nice to know we got a couple pop-guns of our own," I said. "This is no place to be," said Luke. "They'll be throwing the stuff over here in a minute."

II

TRAINING GROUND

5

THE NORTH bank of the Ebro back of Mora la Nueva slopes gently upward in a series of stone-walled terraces holding olive fields, gnarled trees that have been growing many years. There are narrow irrigation ditches traversing the fields, and it was said that these ditches were vestiges of ancient fortifications built by the Catalan people at some time in the past. Among these fields and in these ditches there were hundreds of straggling men of the various units of the International Brigades—French, German, Czech, American, Canadian, British, Cuban, Polish, Spanish, Rumanian, Italian. They had nothing to do, so they wandered idly about; they had nothing to eat, and so they slept. *"Qui dort, dine."*

A small group of us searched the hillside for the temporary headquarters of the XVth Brigade. It was said that Brigade Commander Vladimir Cópic was somewhere about; but no one had heard any news of Merriman, the California professor who was Chief of Staff, nor of Doran, the Commissar. It was expected that the Fascists would cross the Ebro, and it was said that we would shortly go into trenches along the river bank. Neither happened. We met a few men we knew, but they were just as bewildered as we. We came across Dick Rusciano, who was followed by a handful of Spanish comrades. He was walking with the aid of an enormous cavalry sabre he had picked up somewhere. He was cheerful, and with his usual passion for organization, he immediately took us in tow, started to form a section of us. Then he too marched us up and down the hillside, searching for the *estado mayor* of the XVth.

We went down the hill into Mora la Nueva, but they were starting to shell it; the few civilians left were hurriedly quitting town, and so did we. Tabb and I kept grumbling about having to climb the hill, and Dick reprimanded us. We climbed the hill again, sat under the olive trees, slept or wrote letters. Our artillery on top of the hill banged away at Mora de Ebro across the river, and we thought it might be a good idea to move into a ditch lower down. We sat in the ditch, that was filled with men and their excrement, and the shells began to come over. One smashed the tree under which we had been sitting; it rose into the air and came down in splinters. And so we moved along the ditch with the rest of the men, until we arrived on top of the hill, and went around behind it.

There was a nasty cold wind and it was getting dark. In the semi-gloom I found a blanket and wrapped myself in it; it was wet and sticky. We met Irving N——, who was wandering all alone across the hill, and attached him to our group. Dick sent him down the hill to hunt for the Brigade; then we all went down the hill again into the streets of Mora la Nueva, where we slept the night on the asphalt pavements of the town. Asphalt isn't bad to sleep on, if you're tired enough. But it was cold; the wind seeped through the blanket and the cold rose from the pavement, yet we slept. Before dawn Tabb and I were routed out by Dick to serve as guards on a pair of trucks that were going out to hunt for other men of the XVth. We were heading for Tortosa, on the sea, and the drivers were nervous and exhausted.

"Crazy detail," my driver said. "Don't know if we're going to run into their territory or not; don't know where the lines *are;* don't even know if there's any men to round up. Keep that rifle ready." It was so cramped in the cab that I wondered how the hell I could be expected to lift the rifle and aim it at any one who stopped us on the road. Or how we could get out if we were challenged; or what good it would do anyhow. I had lost all my hand-grenades.

"You know what I got half a mind to do?" the driver said.

"What?"

"Head this damn junk for the border."

"Have a cigarette," I said. I wondered if he would head for the border and what I would do if he did, but he didn't.

"The detail's all fucked-up," he said. "Where's the Lincoln? Where's the Macpap? the British? the Franco-Belge? the Thaelmann? the Garibaldis? the Dombrowskis? Nobody's seen fuck-all of 'em. The bastards are driving to the sea," he said. "Maybe they've got to Tortosa already; we'll find out. If France don't come in now, we're fucked ducks. *Mucho malo,*" he said. *"Mucho* fuckin' *malo."*

We wound down the mountain roads to the coastal plain, and in the early morning light I could see that the blanket I had picked up was soaked in blood; there were great congealed scabs stuck full of hairs, and I picked some of them off, but it would take a couple days for it all to dry out. I showed it to my driver and he nodded. We watched the road ahead, the hills beside the road, the sky; nothing showed. We were silent for hours at a time, and I asked the *chofer* if he wanted to change off; that I'd had a good night's sleep the night before, but he said No, it was against the rules. He was driving in his sleep half the time, and we shaved a dozen trucks before we reached the straight main highway to Tortosa. Every town along the Mediterranean shore was empty and deserted. The road was jam-packed with peasants evacuating toward the north, on mule-back, in donkey-carts, afoot. They looked at us in the cab of the truck, moving against the stream they made, and they kept moving. Hundreds were camped along the roads; hundreds were plodding north toward Barcelona, their few possessions, mattresses, blankets, household utensils, domestic stock, on their backs, in wheelbarrows or on their *burros'* backs. Little children were walking, holding onto their mothers' skirts; women carried babies; older children were driving goats, sheep; old men were helping their old women along the road; their faces were impassive, dark with the dust of the roads and fields, lined and worn. Their eyes alone were bright but there was no expression in their eyes. Looking at them you knew what they were thinking: 'Franco is coming; Franco is coming.' That was all they could have been thinking; that explained why they were moving north. It must be that they did not want to wait for Franco and his liberating forces, and I thought of the exodus from Almeria about a year before, when the refugees had been bombed and machine-gunned on the road—old men, old women, women, children. There was not a town that was inhabited, but the Mediterranean was blue and beautiful, calm as far as you could see.

Tortosa was full of soldiers, and we moved through the town, through the streets filled with the tumbled rubbish of the latest bombing, back inland and west, up the mountain roads. We stopped and questioned soldiers. *"Quince Brigada? Hay visto la Quince?"* They had not seen any one from the XVth Brigade. High in the mountains behind Tortosa we heard the guns and the reverberating echoes; we passed other soldiers moving back up into the hills, toward the lines. The Fascists were driving toward the sea, toward Tortosa; they were perhaps sixteen kilometers behind the town. We were told the road was under fire, but we had to go on and so we did. No shells fell near us. The country was so mountainous it looked as though a few machine-guns could have held off a million men. We came back down, went up side roads, crossroads, through small towns, and on a hillside near Rasquera we found three of our men: George Watt and John Gates (then adjutant Brigade Commissar), Joe Hecht. They were lying on the ground wrapped in blankets; under the blankets they were naked. They told us they had swum the Ebro early that morning; that other men had swum and drowned; that they did not know anything of Merriman or Doran, thought they had been captured. They had been to Gandesa, had been cut off there, had fought their way out, travelled at night, been sniped at by artillery. You could see they were reluctant to talk, and so we just sat down with them. Joe looked dead.

Below us there were hundreds of men from the British, the Canadian Battalions; a food truck had come up, and they were being fed. A new *Matford* roadster drove around the hill and stopped near us, and two men got out we recognized. One was tall, thin, dressed in brown corduroy, wearing horn-shelled glasses. He had a long, ascetic face, firm lips, a gloomy look about him. The other was taller, heavy, red-faced, one of the largest men you will ever see; he wore steel-rimmed glasses and a bushy mustache. These were Herbert Matthews of *The New York Times* and Ernest Hemingway, and they were just as relieved to see us as we were to see them. We in-

troducd ourselves and they asked questions. They had cigarettes; they gave us *Lucky Strikes* and *Chesterfields*. Matthews seemed to be bitter; permanently so. Hemingway was
eager as a child, and I smiled remembering the first time I
had seen him, at a Writers' Congress in New York. He was
making his maiden public speech, and when it didn't read
right, he got mad at it, repeating the sentences he had fumbled,
with exceptional vehemence. Now he was like a big kid,
and you liked him. He asked questions like a kid: "What
then? What happened then? And what did *you* do? And
what did *he* say? And *then* what did you do?" Matthews said
nothing, but he took notes on a folded sheet of paper. "What's
your name?" said Hemingway; I told him. "Oh," he said,
"I'm awful glad to see you; I've read your stuff." I knew he
was glad to see me; it made me feel good, and I felt sorry
about the times I had lambasted him in print; I hoped he had
forgotten them, or never read them. "Here," he said, reaching in his pocket. "I've got more." He handed me a full pack
of *Lucky Strikes.*

　A convoy of trucks and buses roared back up the Mediterranean road toward Mora, honking furiously for the peasants,
the people on the road to get out of the way. The men laughed and sang; British, Canadian, Americans. I remember seeing *Teniente* Gregory, the Scot who had commanded the recruits in Tarrazona; his peaches-and-cream complexion was
soiled with dirt; he was laughing, singing with his men.
They swapped stories of the action, tales of hair-raising escape, courageous with the memory of fear. Where was so-
and-so? He was gone. Where was so-and-so? Nobody knew.
Mitchell, the handsome Negro, was gone; Logan of the British was gone; Jack C——, the loud-mouth, had stopped an

anti-tank shell at Gandesa, took it full in the chest; 'Lopez' was gone; Proios the Greek was gone, many men whose faces I remembered but whose names I can't recall were dead or captured or left wounded behind the Fascist lines, which amounted to the same thing. When you are behind the enemy's lines and must keep moving, you cannot carry wounded men. One man had been left propped against a tree with a bullet through his neck. They laughed when they described the way he whistled when he breathed, and I remember his face but not his name. The Swede who walked in his sleep—he had not been wounded. Before we went into Batea he was in our *peloton* with Tabb and Moish Taubman and Johnson and Sid. (Moish was gone and Sid was gone and Johnson.) He seemed to be stupid, but he wasn't. He never spoke, he never asked questions, but he had a face like a snake—he had the attentive expression of a reptile, pale, hard, unmoving eyes, a wide thin mouth, an impassive face. They said he had refused to retreat; had set up his machine-gun on a hill, and told the others he was with, "Go on, I cover you." They left him there on the hill alone, his machine-gun banging away as the tanks came up.

Hemingway did not seem to be discouraged, but Matthews was. Hemingway said, Sure they would get to the sea, but that was nothing to worry about. It had been foreseen; it would be taken care of; methods had already been worked out for communication between Catalonia and the rest of Spain; by ship, by plane, everything would be all right. Roosevelt, he said, had made an unofficial offer—or so he had been told—to ship two hundred planes to France, if France would ship two hundred planes to Spain. That was one of the best things we had ever heard of Roosevelt, but where were they? The war will enter a new phase now, Hemingway said; the Government's resistance will redouble; the people of Spain and Catalonia were fighting mad; the political organizations and trade-unions were rounding up new replacements; the people were anxious to put a stop to Franco's drive to the sea; the people wanted to counter-attack. France had refused a new plea for assistance by Negrin; in mid-March Barcelona had been bombed eighteen times within forty-eight hours, and 1300 had been killed, 2000 wounded. The Fascists were dopes; the Fascists were dumb if they thought they could get away with that. The more women and children and old men they killed—deliberately, cold-bloodedly—the madder the Spanish people got, the madder the democratic people of the world became. The Pope expressed his horror and his Christian indignation. Lerida was reported taken, and reported not taken. Indalecio Prieto was out as Defense Minister; he did not like the Internationals; he violently hated and feared the Communists whose example, unceasing agitation and unquestioned loyalty had helped create a unified army—and to him the Internationals were all Communists. Miaja was going to create a diversion farther south. All over the world popular sentiment, always for the Loyalists from the start, and despite floods of Catholic and fascist propaganda, was growing stronger with every defeat the Government had suffered. There were huge demonstrations in London, Paris, Prague, Moscow and New York; the decent people everywhere were putting pressure on their governments to come to the assistance of Spain, but what can the decent people do? They do not own the press, the radio, the news-reels. They do not own the governments they help elect . . .

. . . What could be found of the XVth Brigade had been rounded up on the hills back of Mora la Nueva. The Lincolns lay on the side of a gently sloping hill where the grapevines were just beginning to turn green. There were deep eroded gulleys in this hill, where water had once cut sharply through the sandy soil, and in these *barancos* the men were resting. That was a crazy time. We had no shelter from the intermittent rain or the beating sun, but we were issued *coñac* and cases of bad French 'champagne.' We were lousy, dirty, ragged; food was scarce and poor in quality, *garbanzos,* beans, rice—but we were issued *Dairy Maid* chocolate every day for five days, Canadian tobacco every day for almost two weeks, the last time we saw tobacco in any quantity. We had so much tobacco we didn't know what to do with it. We had no clothes, no soap, no razors, no socks, but the canteen came up with gloves, pocketbooks and wallets, pen and ink, notebooks, envelopes and paper, razor-blades and shaving-brushes, shoelaces, pins and needles. And there were floods of newspapers, magazines and books.

We began to be aware of exactly how bad the situation was. The Brigade went in with about two thousand men, came out with thirteen hundred; the Lincoln Battalion went in with about five hundred, and now we had about a hundred twenty. Most of the men who had come up from Tarrazona with me for their first action were gone, though many old-timers too had not yet appeared. Sam Grant, decorated just before the action, was gone—steel helmet and all. Joe Bianca, the Italian-American seaman from the machine-gun section, was with us, but half his men were gone, including the social-worker who had reprimanded Irving N—— that day. We lost the commanders of Companies 1, 2 and 3, the only companies we had. We lost the commissars of Companies 1, 2 and 3. Wolff had not yet returned, nor Leonard Lamb of the Brigade staff. Undoubtedly many were still behind the Fascist lines, wandering through the hills toward the Ebro; or so we thought, for they never came. Mail came up with Harry Hakam, the mailman; and we sat crouched around a lighted match under a blanket in a deep ditch, while he went through the mail. He read hundreds of names, but only about fifteen men claimed letters. It took him half an hour to read all the names on the letters, and after the first few times nobody would say, "Dead" or "Missing"; we just kept silent.

. . . We got slightly stewed on *coñac* and 'champagne' that night—Tabb and Wentworth and Hinman and I—lying in the lee of a terrace, and I told them how, many years before when I had been married and living in Vermont, we had been broke and undernourished, unable to pay the rent, the grocers, with scarcely any clothes to cover us, and a sailor-friend had sent us a $15 quart of champagne, that we drank warm out of mustard jars. We laughed. We carefully stood our rifles by our sides, for we had been warned that there were men eager to get to the border who wanted them, or men who had abandoned their arms in action and did not want to be found without them. And during the night I remember hearing a voice saying, "Here's a rifle," and automatically putting my hand out, grasping mine. I was half-asleep. Some one else had hold of it too, but I was too sleepy to wake up and I merely said, "You can't have my rifle," and the voice said, "Let go, comrade," and I said, "Comrade, I can't let you have my rifle," and the voice said, "You'll get it back in the morning." "Who are you?" I said. "None of your business, comrade," and I mumbled a protest and fell back to sleep. But in the morning the rifle was gone, and I was panic-stricken. So were Tabb's and Wentworth's. I asked who was in charge, who had taken the rifles, and some one said, "Lopoff will know," and I said, "Who the hell is Lopoff?" and they said, "He's in command now," and I looked for him.

He was siting in a hole; he had a broad Oriental face, a week's growth of black beard and a sullen expression. "Comrade," I said, "some one took three rifles last night." "*I* did," he said. "We put out a guard and needed rifles." I didn't like him. . . .

They set up a bath machine under the trees on top of the hill among the camouflaged artillery pieces, and we took showers, were issued clean clothes. The Fascist planes were overhead, but at 15,000 feet, so I felt no anxiety; but you could not convince the men that planes at 15,000 feet could not see men moving on the ground. "They got us with our pants down," the men said. "That would be a hot one," but the planes were flying west, across the Ebro and they did not bother us. I met Prieto, who had grown a beard, and he embraced me in the Latin manner. Diaz, he said, had died of pneumonia in the Albacete hospital; he, Prieto, was attached to our Spanish-Cuban Battalion, the 24th. He shook his head about Diaz; he said he was a good guy, but dumb, and I realized as we talked that he was stunned by the fact that Diaz, magnificent animal, should have kicked off in bed while he, Prieto, frail and none too strong, should have come successfully through the retreat. It really didn't make much sense at that.

We took shelter in the *barancos* on the downward slope of the hill; long, deep and narrow clefts that had been washed out by the rains. We dug into the sides of these gulleys and tried to make ourselves at home. Dick Rusciano organized the section into *pelotons,* and the first replacements began to appear, Americans routed out of jobs behind the lines, from the auto-parks, the hospitals, transmissions. We talked calmly of the Fascist drive toward the sea, of the possibility of our being cut off from all escape both north and south, for they were pressing on Balaguer in the north as well, and they would have liked to close the French frontier. "Well, I can sail a boat," or "I can swim," the men would say, or, "Well, maybe it's time we started for the border." We spoke speculatively of how we could get to the border and across it without being caught, and we laughed a good deal, Dick joining in with us. That was a crazy time and we were not much reassured by proclamations from the Government about the diversion Miaja had started near Madrid, about the reorganization of the cabinet, about the new 'Government of National Union,' about the assurances that separatist Catalonia had given, assurances of adhesion to the rest of Spain. The Blum cabinet in France had fallen and Daladier was asked to form another. The Fascists did not try to cross the Ebro, and they had not reached the sea. The Communist Party of Spain promised that if the army could hold out for 'two weeks' there would be adequate materiel, airplanes and guns, not only to hold the enemy but even to start a counter-offensive. We had no way of knowing when this two-week period had started—for news was always late in getting to us—and we speculated on which 'foreign power' was going to supply this stuff—France or the Soviet Union. We were pretty bitter about France.

But these reports received substantiation from Vincent

Sheean, who came up from Barcelona to see us. He reported having seen French materiel on the Valencia road and heavy guns coming over the border, men hastily scraping off the French colors on their barrels with pocket-knives. We saw a large fleet of our own planes about this time (*"Nuestros! nuestros!"* the men shouted, and others invariably answered, "Get down you dope; all planes are Fascists," or, "Famous last words of famous men—'They're ours!'"). Sheean was a good guy, large, gentle, kind; he seemed diffident and ill at ease among the men, who frankly admired him and his work, and he handed out the few cigarettes he had. "Do you remember," I said, "about nine years ago, I wrote you a letter?" "No," he said. "I was in Paris. I used your name to get a job on the *Paris Times,* and got the job." "Did you?" he said. "And I wrote and said 'thanks,' and you answered and said you didn't know your name pulled any weight?" "No," he said, "I don't remember." I couldn't understand how he could forget; it was the sort of thing that I would have remembered.

But the demoralization continued and the pep-talks delivered by the new acting commissars failed to lift the spirits of the men. They took everything that was said with a bucketful of salt and smiled privately to themselves. Because there was plenty of alcohol about, they drank the alcohol and resisted the authority, which was lax enough anyhow. I remember one afternoon when a comrade we may as well call Winston, who lived in our particular hole in the ground, came in stewed to the ears and raving mad. "Gimme my fuscel," he said, hunting for the fine Czech rifle he had organized somewhere. "Gimme my gun, I'm gonna kill somebody." "Who you gonna kill?" we said, and he said, "Don't make no dif-

ference who." Dick ordered the rifle taken up, and said he
would give it back when Winston sobered up. He was a good
guy, Winston, a fine soldier, a crack shot.

"Where's my fuseel?" he said. "I want my fuseel God
damn the sonsabitches they took my fuseel." Then suddenly
he sat down on the ground and started to cry. "The bastards,"
he said. "The goddamn c... s...... bastards. I seen guys
die had more room between the eyes than they got across the
shoulders. Gimme my fuseel."

"Take it easy," we said. "Everything's gonna be O.K."

Tears streamed down his face; he was broken-hearted.
"They killed all the good guys," he said. "They're all dead
and gone with their guts hanging out. I seen guys die had
more room between the eyes than they got across the
shoulders."

There was an ulcerated tooth that had to be extracted, and
as I went in the ambulance to the 35th Division *sanidad* some
thirty-odd kilometers away, I could remember Winston,
whose direct expression seemed in some way typical of what
many felt but still had the strength to suppress; many who
felt trapped now that the odds were against us, many who
were determined never to go into action again; many who
were determined, or at least said they were determined, to
make for the border at the first opportunity. I could remember Wolff, who had come back without his long black cape
and long black mustache; and Lamb, who had come back,
and a westerner named Ray Ticer, a skeleton of a man who
returned dressed in the most amazing agglomeration of rags
and patches that was ever seen off a vaudeville stage. All
three had swum the Ebro, been housed and clothed and fed,

after a fashion, by the peasants. And I could remember Hinman and Frank Stout (also a Battalion scout), lying on their sides in our *baranco* interminably chewing the fat, talking of California and Nevada where they had done organizational work, of previous actions and the retreat from Belchite where Hinman's closest friend, Fritz Orton, had been killed. "Christ," Hinman said, "I couldn't figure you out at first; you asked so many damn-fool questions."

Then there was Emiliano Marin, the Puerto Rican with his dark flat face and the stick of wood he held between his teeth to prevent them from chattering, to prevent him from biting his tongue when the planes came over. He said that he was sick, but no one believed him; he had been wounded, had lain in hospital and been bombed, and now he dragged himself about the camp like a sick dog, silent, his Pekingese eyes accusing us. He said he was sick but no one seemed to care, and he began to annoy us. Then there was the news that Tarrazona and Albacete were no longer the headquarters of the I.B., and the removal of the British and 24th Battalions to secondary positions in the lines down by the river. And there was the *fiesta* in the near-by tiny hamlet of Darmos, which the men took as a token of swift return to the front, and where we got a fairly decent meal of fried rice and *burro* meat and wine and nuts—and candy and cigarettes that had come from packages sent to men who now were dead or missing—ten cigarettes a man and a small bit of chocolate. Full of food and half-drunk we marched five kilometers down to the river and spent the night digging trenches in the rocky soil till morning, grumbling at the stupidity that had held the *fiesta* on that night, filled us with food and drink and made us work. It was the anniversary of the Republic. . . .

. . . The 35th Division *sanidad* was housed in a beautiful mansion that once had been a wealthy man's estate, near the coast between Reus and Tarragona. There were clipped hedges, tall canes and landscaped grounds, where men were already digging *refugios*. There was a bathroom with a marble bathtub; there were English and American nurses, fine food, real beds with springs and mattresses, and real coffee with milk was served four times a day—at breakfast, at ten in the morning, at four in the afternoon and before you went to sleep; good coffee served in clean tin cans. Sleep; a hot bath; clean clothes; a shave; rest—and epsom salts that were obligatory. It made you wish that you were really ill or slightly wounded.

Then near-by Tarragona was bombed; the Spanish, British and American nurses went about their work as the window-panes rattled and the hideous drumming reverberated through the house. We all ran out onto the flagstone terrace to watch the black smoke rise over Tarragona, and by morning of the next day the word had come that the Italian Fascist troops had reached the sea at Vinaroz, below Tortosa, cutting Loyalist Spain away from Catalonia, and all traffic had been cut between Barcelona and Valencia. (In Rome, the Pope gave his apostolic benediction to the sacred cause of General Franco.) Ambulances drove up, nurses hastily gathered mattresses and linen and medical supplies, the patients were all hustled out onto the gravelled driveway and we were evacuated about twenty kilometers north along the Mediterranean highway to Cambrils and the Fifth Army Corps Hospital. This time the refugees were all moving south; Barcelona was overcrowded and they had been turned back. Their faces were bewildered and grim, but they moved with determination back in the direction from which they had come two weeks before, the mattresses, the household goods, the crates of chickens, flocks of goats and sheep, the children and the babies and the old men and the women.

The town of Cambrils was not much to look at but the hospital, set back in its magnificent grounds and gardens looking over the sea, the modern stone building with its many wings was impressive. The place was electrified, there was running water, heat. A former convent, it impressed you with the discrepancy of such enormous sums of money spent for such a purpose while the population lived in rags and hovels. (The Pope had given apostolic benediction . . .) The food here was even better than it had been at the *sanidad* (fried rice, beef, stuffed *pimientos,* good wine), the beds were more comfortable and there were sheets! There were many wounded here, tended by Spanish nurses, and the meals for those who could get about were served in the enormous refectory of the place, at long tables waited on by pretty girls. . . .

When I returned the Battalion had moved into a deep *baranco* closer to the river, and the work of reorganization had been begun. The *estado mayor* of the Battalion was housed in a little stone shack and farther up the ravine the Spanish and Americans were divided into two nominal companies, the Americans under the command of Rusciano, with Joe Taylor, a Negro comrade, as his adjutant. Here the men were building *chavolas* made of pineboughs, the cane that looked like bamboo, anything that could afford them shelter. Occasional shells from across the river fell on the brink of the *baranco;* none fell in. New men had come in from the auto-parks, from soft jobs in Barcelona, from hospitals, jails and labor-battalions, and altogether we were a crummy bunch. There was little discipline and less morale. Many of the men were definitely unfit for military service, either physically or psychologically. I remember one, who became the butt of the camp's jokes; a huge hulking youngster we may call John Henry, of good American family, but weak as water. He had come from the auto-park where his work was relatively safe; he had seen action earlier and it had broken him. He had given up; his mouth was wet and open; he never washed; he stank; his clothes were rags and he seemed proud of it. He introduced himself to me (I was now company clerk) by saying, "I'm dumb, yellow and worthless." He talked a lot; he was eighteen years old. He was not dumb.

There was old Elmer Amidon, whom I remembered from Tarrazona; he owned to being thirty-eight but he was nearer fifty. An old-time miner, his body and his mind had been broken by a lifetime of grueling work; he seemed, as a consequence, to be simple-minded and the men laughed at him. With him there had come Rod Wergles, an American sailor who had exophthalmic eyes (blue eyes) and had discovered, in the training camp, that he had a weak heart. His blue stare disconcerted us, and later he grew an enormous beard. There was Jones, whose magnificent physique afforded a startling contrast to his gold-brickism, of an 18-karat kind; he had been a Jack-of-all-trades, a college student, miner, sailor, lumberman and mechanic; there was nothing he had not done at one time or another. Here he seemed completely out of place; he bummed every one for cigarettes at every hour of the day; he spent a lot of time sleeping and he got out of every detail he could possibly avoid. And there were others, men who had been in action previously and then been transferred behind the lines, but who had been so demoralized by action as to be worthless. You knew they would fuck off if they had the opportunity and the guts—as it was, they talked of it continuously. There were a few others who had come for adventure and had found it was not quite what they expected; they had deserted, spent some time in jail or labor groups, and were now, in this emergency, sent back.

These men and their attitude ('They killed all the good guys . . .') convinced you for the moment that our situation was truly desperate—or so it seemed; it seemed that the International Brigades had been practically annihilated, that at least 75 per cent of our fighting strength was gone, and few new recruits were coming over the Pyrenees these days. But for the benefit of the folks at home the Lincoln Battalion was always intact, and the constant figure of thirty-two hundred Americans were fighting in Spain. We understood why this was necessary, but it did not prevent us from becoming cynical. Now, the Government was rounding up all available men; the call was out for volunteers and we heard that our Brigade would be rebuilt again, with young Spanish replacements. The Internationals had been permanently broken up through their losses in action, through definite sabotage by high-ranking officials who were either jealous of the I.B.'s reputation, or regarded them as the minions of Moscow (which they were not), by a certain amount of incompetence and inexperience, by a small amount of desertion, very small.

We issued rifles, ammo, hand-grenades; I checked on these details and met a new recruit. He said his name was Rolfe; I looked at him. "Edwin Rolfe?" I said, and he said, "Yes." "*The* Edwin Rolfe? The poet?" "The same," he said.

"Christ!" I said, "You know Carnovsky of the Group Theater, and Phoebe Brand." "Sure," he said. "Christ!" I said,
"they told me you were here in Spain; that I should look you
up and say hello." We laughed. "Hello," he said. He had been
editing the *Volunteer for Liberty,* our publication, first edited
by Ralph Bates. He was frail; he resembled a bird; he had a
fine, delicate bone structure and he did not look as though he
should be in an army. I asked him what he was doing here
and how he liked it, and he said it was pretty tough at first,
but that he liked it fine. He had volunteered to quit the desk
job when the call came after the Fascists reached the sea. I do
not think I have ever met a gentler guy, a less pugnacious
guy, less of a soldier. But he had the iron of conviction in him
just the same. He had a tiny automatic pistol some one had
given him, and it became him, though I could not imagine
him ever using it. I felt better to have another writer on the
spot. Writers will understand just what I mean.

It rained; the rain came down in torrents and we took
shelter in small stone houses that were near by. They said that
trucks would come, and late at night we marched down to
the main road, but no trucks came, and so we marched back
again and spent the night in our soaking clothes. It dried and
the sun beat at you like a fist, and every night after dark we
marched down the long ravine to the road and along the road
that skirted the Ebro, walking as though we were treading on
eggs, for the Fascist machine-guns were just across the river,
and the river was not very wide. We followed the river,
turned off the road and climbed the bluffs that faced the other
shore, where trenches were in process of construction, and all
night we dug in soft sand, throwing up a shovel and having
three shovelfuls fall back again. It seemed pointless; it seemed

hopeless; it seemed indicative of our position in this war. Have you ever shovelled sand?

Ed Rolfe and I lay down on the floor of the trench and shared half of one of his *Chesterfields* under cover of a blanket. Far down the stream toward Mora we heard a machine-gun chatter in the night and the echoes sounded up and down the stream. Then it was silent and we went to sleep.

6

[May–June]

THE SPANISH replacements arrived in Darmos in a convoy of *camiones,* and stood huddled together. We looked at them with some amusement, which we were at pains to conceal, for we had been advised in a speech by George Watt, Commissar of the Battalion, that our task was to win their confidence, to instill in them the convictions that we felt ourselves, to impart to them (insofar as it was possible) the benefit of our experience as 'veterans.' They were a funny-looking crew; they had no arms; they were dressed in the same sort of nondescript uniforms we had; but each was provided with a pack-sack that bulged to the bursting point, and in addition almost every one had one or two cardboard suitcases. We were curious to know what they had in these suitcases, and we soon found out.

All were young, between sixteen and twenty; many had never shaved; most were conscripts from farm, factory, and office, and had received their little training in Villasecca. Many were from the province of Alicante in the south, and

all seemed to be at that stage of adolescence where they were
more girls than they were men; their complexion, naturally
pale olive, bloomed with youth; they had down on their
upper lips and on their cheeks; their eyes were the dark and
beautiful liquid eyes of Spanish girls. They were ill at ease;
they seemed unhappy; certainly few held any convictions
about the war and now had left their homes, their parents,
for the first time in their lives. To go to war.

Into the pack-sacks and the suitcases their mothers and
fathers, their sisters and relatives and *novias* had crammed
the poor comforts that the Spanish people were able to provide. They had innumerable changes of poor clothing they
would never be able to use; they had knitted sweaters and
caps, heavy socks made of poor quality wool; they had books
(those who could read); they had reams of writing paper,
envelopes, bottles of ink (colored) and pen points. Some had
guitars. They had mirrors (some with wooden frames around
them), hoarded bars of evil-smelling soap and talcum powder; all had the inevitable bottles of toilet-water without
which the Spanish soldier, even in the front-line trenches,
feels unfit to meet the enemy. In addition they had food-
stuffs—the poor quality chocolate that was so hard to find,
cakes and cookies, loaves of coarse bread and tins of meat and
fish that their parents had managed to obtain, enormous bags
of walnuts, almonds, hazelnuts, dried figs, dried apples. ripe
apples, oranges. Some even brought live rabbits.

"The Internationals," George Watt had said, "are about to
assume the rôle for which they were originally intended; in-
structors and examples for the Spanish soldiers. Our Battalion and all the battalions of the International Brigades are
being rebuilt with Spanish replacements. Before, we had a

few Spanish sections attached to our battalions; now the Spanish will be mixed in, in the companies, in the sections, in the *pelotons* and in the squads. There will be International squads with Spanish *cabos;* Spanish squads with an American *cabo.* We must work to show these men (few of whom have ever been in action before) exactly why we're here in Spain; that we're not foreign invaders in the sense that Franco's German and Italian 'volunteers' are foreign invaders. We're here solely to help the Spanish people perpetuate the democracy which they voted into power. Few of these boys have any political convictions—how could they have? They're very young; they've been carefully denied the opportunity for education. We will be their comrades, their brothers, their teachers and their friends."

I imagine most of us were skeptical of the success of this arrangement, but we did our best. The Spaniard is inherently nationalistic; but no more so than other national groups. Most people, trained from birth to distrust the foreigner, are nationalistic. Most people, trained from birth to feel an innate superiority to any one who was not born in his own God's country, especially dislikes to be given orders by a man of foreign birth, who cannot even speak his own God-given superior language properly. Chauvinism is a curious and vicious thing, and it rarely occurred to those Americans who always felt superior and condescending to the Spanish (and there were some) that perhaps their own inability to speak Spanish lowered them somewhat in Spanish eyes. But if you cannot speak a foreign language, you can always condescend to those who do. And resentment on the part of one begets resentment in the other. There was always, therefore, a certain amount of friction between the Americans and the Spanish, which, superficially, would seem to be a paradox when you consider that these Americans had abandoned everything in life to come to the assistance of the Spanish people. But a small, persisting snobbism on the part of the Americans, and a residue of distrust on the part of the Spanish (few clearly understood the issues at stake), contributed to the persistence of this friction. (Franco's propaganda also helped.)

But at first the spontaneity of the friendship between them was unquestioned. At the May Day celebration, held in the open fields near Darmos, the new men and the old took to each other like ducks to water. Spanish and Americans competed in athletic contests—foot-racing, boxing, the variety of soccer they call *futbol,* grenade throwing, rifle competitions, an 'infiltration' race, jumping and skipping, a three-legged race—with boyish enthusiasm and fraternity. They roared with laughter at the infiltration race, when soldiers crawled, using only their elbows, across the field; they pounded each other on the back as the wheelbarrow teams competed and the three-legged contestants fell on their faces. They sang together. Prizes were won and shared between them—a box of *Sunshine* crackers, a bar of soap or *Hershey's* chocolate, a pack of *Loo-ky Streek.* They definitely liked each other; the new recruits looked on us as seasoned warriors; they listened with invariable politeness to our efforts to explain the previous actions in our atrocious Spanish; they listened as we told them of America and of the international sympathy that existed for the Spanish people. They knew nothing of America, less of international working-class feeling. They told us, simply, speaking slowly and with infinite pains, of their homes in Alicante, of their work, of their brothers who were at other fronts down south. They tried to understand us and we tried to understand them.

They greeted the reorganization of the Battalion with enthusiasm. They greeted their American commanders with enthusiasm, and the Americans accepted Spanish *cabos* and *peloton* leaders with good grace. Certain Negro Americans, such as Marcus Ransom, squad leader in our company, were the most popular among the Spanish boys. The Negroes in our outfit loved Spain with a deep and abiding love they could not quite achieve for America—for here there was no prejudice against them because of their color; they were curiosities to the Spanish, but they were invariably liked for themselves. Marcus, who could not learn a word of Spanish, commanded a squad of Spanish boys with complete success. He developed the fine art of pantomime to a spectacular level; to us, it looked something like clowning, but the boys laughed with him and obeyed his orders; what is more, they loved him, called him 'Mar-koos' and followed him around like dogs.

After three days as a *peloton* leader, which I did not enjoy, Aaron Lopoff, Commander of Company 2, chose me to be his adjutant. "I'm not much of a military man," I said, and he said, "That's bad; but you're about the only man in the company who speaks my language, and I think I can teach you the job." The company adjutant was not second in command; but he was the commander's right-hand man, responsible for the details of the company's operation, mouthpiece for its commander, responsible for anything that went wrong. The job at first seemed to be a cinch (Tabb took over my *peloton* with a certain amount of reluctance), and I was still enough of a snob to get some satisfaction from living in the same hole with the commander and enjoying the perquisites that pertained to the job. (For one thing, the commander managed to find more American cigarettes than the average soldier; when such cigarettes were available at all). In our particular hole, wide enough for three men to sleep side by side in the small cave some other outfit had dug into the side of the *baranco,* we had (for a short time) a carton of *Chesterfields,* the gift of some Greek comrades in the company, who had received them from the Greek Sailors' Club in New York.

The composition of that company command was interesting. There was *Teniente* Lopoff, New York Jew, pulp-magazine writer. Commissar was Nicholas Kurculiotis, a Greek dock worker who could not speak a word of English, but had improved his time in hospital when previously wounded, to learn Spanish fluently. (I stand corrected; Nick did learn some English—'You got seegaret for me?') Company secretary and interpreter was Harry Curtis (not his name), previously wounded and now returned to the front after a long stay behind the lines as transmissionist and electrical expert. *Practicante* was Garfield, WPA actor from the west coast. We had six Spanish runners, three Spanish observers, a Spanish barber. Commanding the three sections were Pavlos Fortis, Greek sailor and machine-gun expert (and second in command of the company), who was also a pantomimist of considerable talent and spoke English the way he spoke Spanish. For Section Two there was Jack Hoshooley, Canadian-Ukranian hat maker, long in Spain. For Section Three there was Juan Lopez Martinez, eighteen-year-old *campesino* from Cadiz, a genuine hero and a fair singer of *flamenco.* Certain of our runners and observers rejoiced in the names of

Eleuterio Martinez Belda (eighteen, with the complexion and the eyes of a beautiful girl), Angel Hernandez Gallego (barber, four feet, three inches tall, with the squeaky voice of a ten-year-old), Emeterio Vicente Macia (he stuttered), Joaquin Vicente Garcia (no relation; peasant boy with long legs who we thought would make a perfect runner); Antonio Anton Pastor (short and plump, who turned out to *be* the perfect runner); Jose Virgili Argilaga and his friend Francisco Albareda Gracia (from Barcelona), and this business of all Spaniards having three names drove us nearly crazy.

Aaron, Nick and I lived in one hole; Curtis and the quartermaster Mike Washuk (who spoke of himself as 'Dayton, Ohio's Only Boy in Spain') shared another; all the others were out in the rain, and it rained plenty. When it rained they ran for a near-by tunnel that housed a railroad gun, an enormous ancient piece that was brought out onto the track regularly every day, fiddled with, and run back into the tunnel every night. It had a crew of about fifteen men, and they fired it once in awhile—or so I think—for the planes came over looking for it. And when the planes came over the new Spanish replacements dived for the ground like woodchucks, and stayed put. And this was about the only military training they got with us for some weeks, for it rained almost very day, and every day it was not raining Aaron had them working on their *chavolas,* to the despair of Wolff and the Battalion command, which issued beautifully typewritten *ordenes del dia* every day, with a detailed program of instruction that did not get carried out. In addition to the rain, flies began to appear—a peculiarly vicious little virus that gave us a foretaste of what the broiling Spanish summer would be like. They had none of the timidity of our American flies; you could wave your hand and they would sit quite calmly on your skin, and they had a penchant for your eyes, nose and mouth. . . .

But the rainy season petered out and the sun was steady in the Spanish sky, which is bluer than any other sky. There were no clouds. The vines were growing in the fields; the olives achieved their greenest hues; the almond trees had lost their shell-pink blossoms that were trampled in the mud, and the war seemed far away although there was an occasional Fascist battery speaking in the distance, and the observation planes were a regular phenomenon that we could watch with astonishing impersonality. But it was not so easy to be impersonal about the Spanish kids, who played *futbol* in the *baranco* every evening after maneuvers and target-practice, with the abandon and enthusiasm of colts. They were children and you could not help feeling badly about them. You looked at their unshaved cheeks and it did not take much imagination to see them mangled by shells, dead before they had really begun to live. They seemed to have no conception of what they'd gotten into, or if they did, they put on a good act, for kids. They wrote innumerable letters home, letters decorated with sentimental designs—a dove carrying a letter was the commonest—and illuminated with colored inks. (They sent their few cigarettes and all their money home to their parents.) They resisted the assumption of authority; it was a common thing to have a newly appointed *cabo,* a youth who seemed to possess some authority among the others, come to you and ask to be relieved of the rank. "Why do you want to be relieved?" Lopoff would say, and they would answer, "Well, *señor—*" "*Camarada,*" Aaron would prompt. "Well, *señor* comrade, I have known these comrades all my life, and it does not please me to be in authority over them." "You have been chosen," Aaron said, with a straight face, "because you possess the ability to lead—" "*Por favor, Señor Capitán,* it does not please me——"

If childhood friends were transferred from one squad or section to another, they frequently would sulk, or even weep. One youngster who fell asleep on guard had to be taken before Captain Wolff, who dutifully impressed him with the enormity of his crime. Wolff had a tremendous voice and I think he enjoyed using it. Speaking through an interpreter, he roared at the kid and told him that he really should be shot. "*Si, señor,*" the kid replied, shaking from head to foot, "I know it." "By sleeping on guard," said Wolff, "you jeopardized the lives of your comrades, who trusted you to keep watch. No punishment is too severe for that, even though we are not in the front lines, but only in reserve." I never saw a human being so frightened in my life, and I think Wolff rubbed it in a bit too much, but perhaps it was all right—the youngster never fell asleep on guard again. But I think we all felt that we were going to be in a tough spot with these kids, when we got into action again; we did not expect too much of them, for although Kurculiotis pounded away at them during the daily political meetings, explaining and illustrating and elaborating on the causes of the war and the nature of Fascism, and although they enjoyed listening to his oratory (and he was a born orator), and although they greeted his talks with cheers and gave the responses, *Viva la República!* and *Viva el Ejercito Populár! Viva! Viva!* and even added *Viva el Comisario!* they seemed to be in a trance while he was speaking, and when he asked them questions their uninspired replies were politically naïve. The only realities they accepted at that time were the reality of daily discomfort and poor food, the reality of homesickness, the reality of fear and bewilderment. It was impossible for them to connect what they were expected to do, with the fact that Czechoslovakia, a country they had never seen, was at the moment standing fast against the threat of Hitler's imminent invasion. Most of them knew hunger and unemployment at first hand from long experience, but their rudimentary 'education' and the perversion of the education they had received had made them accept these daily facts as their irrevocable portion in life.

And from thinking of these children, just grown out of puberty and still tied to their homes by every bond of long association and dependence, you returned to your own children again, and there came a sudden, final and crystalized realization of how dear they were to you, how deeply you could feel their absence. For it was again difficult to think of them as they should be thought of—just one pair of kids of the millions suffering daily throughout the world, and suffering less than many thousands and hundreds of thousands. You could think of them saying, 'When is Pop coming back?' and 'Is Pop *ever* coming back?' and you realized with shame that it was largely self-pity that brought tears to your eyes at the thought of never seeing them again. This possibility would rise to consciousness again and again, and yet it was too appalling for long or steady contemplation. And you wondered wherein lay the horror of such contemplation, such possibility. Was it the thought of your own end (which has little enough significance)? Or was it the pity you would naturally feel for fatherless children, if it were possible for you to imagine your own death? And there was no answer to this, but you knew deeply how much you wanted to see them again, how much you wanted to watch them grow into independent, decent manhood, how deep was the need they filled in you, and how much you wanted to give them, of guidance, of tenderness and unpossessive love. And the thought of how far off was the time when you *would* see them again—if you ever saw them—was full of pain; and it was not alleviated by the certain knowledge that their mother would do her best to make up to them for your absence, or your loss. . . .

Lopoff went to the hospital at about this time to have a cyst removed from his foot, and Pavlos Fortis moved into the hole in the bank with Nick and me. Many people have the curious idea that two men of the same nationality ought to get along together, but Pavlos and Kurculiotis were each other's poison. With Lopoff gone, Nick began to reveal certain traits he had concealed before, possibly out of deference to the authority Aaron exercised with such an easy grace, or perhaps he was just beginning to feel his oats. Theoretically, the commissar of the company or battalion shared equal responsibility with the military commander for the functioning of the unit, but this was not enough for Nick. He began to order Pavlos around; he began to demonstrate his ability as a military man. He moved around the camp with the air of a division-commander, issuing orders to the soldiers, the corporals and sergeants. "Fort-*is!*" he would shout, coming into our dugout, and launch into a welter of language that was Greek to me. Fortis responded in kind, and they had interminable arguments.

Pavlos was a brute of a man; as strong as an ox. His nose had once been broken, and was plastered to his face; his hands were hams and his thighs bulged through his trousers. (Yet he was curiously handsome; his eyes were beautiful.) Drinking or smoking, he always held his little finger out stiffly from the others, and this used to amuse us until we learned that it had been broken and could not be flexed. But it gave him an air of great gentility. With Nick he would argue in an extremely gentle but forceful manner. He was eloquence itself, and although I could not understand a word he said, he always convinced me that he was right. His eyes flashed, his hands and fingers made gestures; he widened his eyes like an actor and thrust out his lower lip. He was the toughest human being I have ever met, and the gentlest. (They seem to go together.) A deadly shot with the light Maxim—he lay down to it as a man lies down to a woman—he was like a child in other ways; he definitely loved his fellow man and while I was his adjutant he found innumerable ways for me to avoid the jobs I was supposed to do. "Baby," he would say, "you don't need maneuvers today. I go maneuvers; you sleep, *chico*." Sometimes I did, but sometimes my sense of guilt overcame me and I went along with him. But nothing was right unless he did it himself, and he could not bear to see another man do a job that he might have done himself. If there was no work to do, he would invent some for himself, sweeping the camp grounds (scarcely becoming of a company commander), wiping off the ammunition, cleaning the spare rifles or machine-guns, enlarging the *chavola* or building one for another comrade. He was loved and respected, but he did not possess the attribute of authority. About Kurculiotis he would say, "That man—ah! He got beeg head." He taught me two words of Greek—one sounded like 'popsa' and meant shut up; the other sounded like 'mun-*ee'* and was the Greek equivalent of the Spanish *coño;* together I could use them on Kurculiotis when he got too obstreperous, and be sure to receive the reply from him (in English), "Gunt!" . . .

. . . They had issued rifles and ammo, and at three in the morning one day of mid-May they marched us ten kilometers and piled us into trucks. The kids, despite orders to the contrary, still were carrying over-stuffed packsacks and their cardboard suitcases, and they displayed a sudden nervousness that did not make us feel any too good. This might be action, or it might mean a maneuver on a larger scale than we had held before. Pavlos showed me a slip of paper with the itinerary, which ended with the curious name of Uldemollins. This town, we knew, was on the road to Lerida, which the Fascists had held for some time, so the feeling became general that we were going to see some action. But despite this nervousness, or perhaps because of it, the Spanish kids were especially enthusiastic in their shouted greetings to the girls, ugly or handsome, that we passed in the small towns on the way. *"Ai, guappa!"* they would cry, which is the Spanish equivalent for 'Hi, toots!' or 'Hello, beautiful,' and the girls would peek out of their balcony windows from behind Venetian blinds drawn against the strong morning sun. We camped in pine woods all that day, and we were all nervous and jumpy. The order came to dig in, make *chavolas* against the possibility of a long stay or sudden rain, and then the order was countermanded. The kids alternated all that day between a nervous jumpiness and an extravagant display of good spirits. The most trivial incident became the pretext for an elaborate and noisy quarrel.

A squirrel was sighted on a tree-top, was frightened out of its refuge by rifle-fire (7.65 mm.) and ran from tree to tree with a howling troop of about seventy-five delighted youngsters behind it.

We slept in the pine woods that night; an order came to prepare to march the next morning, and was countermanded within the hour. It had been cold the night before and no fires were permitted, but we were soon warm enough—a combination of sunshine and nervous tension. We felt secure from the Fascist *avion,* for we were in deep woods, high in the mountains. Kurculiotis was everywhere in the camp, a bright blue satin quilt, that had originally been pilfered from the town of Darmos, rolled and tied around his shoulder with a string. That was his entire equipment, but he wore it like the insignia of a lieutenant-colonel, and was making a nuisance of himself in a well-intentioned desire to see that everything was prepared for anything that might happen. Clearly he regarded Pavlos as incompetent, and felt that the burden of the company's administration fell on his narrow Greek shoulders. "Ach," Pavlos said, "He got beeg head. We go in action, you see different." I wasn't exactly sure of what he meant, but I had a hunch.

It was cold and rainy all night, and in the morning we marched into the town of Uldemollins—some one had finally decided we ought to have some shelter from the rain. Here, in the middle of the road, we met Joe Hecht, who after the retreat through the Aragon had been transferred into the auto-park 'for a rest.' He took me aside, saying, "I've got something for you," and reached into a box he kept in the cab of his truck. From it he produced: one pack of *Old Gold,* three packages of powdered chocolate (*Nestlé's*), a piece of Gruyère cheese, three cans of *Lion Brand* condensed milk, one bar of *Palmolive* soap and half a bar of milk-chocolate. Suddenly there seemed to be some sense in life again, and these items, which lasted less than half an hour (except that we did not eat the soap), plus a swig of a fair Spanish cognac taken to keep out the rain, made the cold and dampness bearable and sleep possible on the concrete floor of the abandoned school into which we had been packed while waiting orders. (School had been 'out' for many months, for fear of air-raids.) The top of living depended on just such small things as this, which occasionally came to the men through the good offices of the Friends of the Lincoln Brigade, back in New York.

Through his connection with Transport (and good connections with the Commissariat—he'd once been a commissar himself, and became one again later) Joe said he knew the Brigade was moving again within a couple days, but where he did not know, nor for what purpose. We spent the whole morning and afternoon in the large bare rooms of the schoolhouse, trying to dry out and keep warm with little success, and watching the Spanish youngsters working off their excess energy and nervous tension. They were more like children than soldiers; they shouted, danced and sang in the rooms and played interminable childish games on one another. Watching them the older men wondered whether they could be held in the event of a good hot action and its attendant panic. Luke Hinman and I got so depressed watching them and speculating silently on the lousiness of such children—of *any one*—having to go through a mess like this, that we profited by a small cask of good wine we found to get rather drunk and silly ourselves.

The *camions* came up again in the late afternoon and we rode stiff and cold for 150 kilometers into the outskirts of a fairly large town called Tarrega, a short distance behind Lerida. We were housed in a series of stone outbuildings and stone-walled enclosures floored with clean straw, fed some beans and went to sleep. Our hunches seemed about to be confirmed; we were either going to support the troops in the Lerida-Balaguer sector, or initiate a counter-offensive in this district that would be designed to take from the Fascists the hydroelectric stations near Tremp that supplied the majority of Catalonia's electricity. I wished that Aaron Lopoff would turn up, and if I could have prayed I would have prayed.

Kurculiotis was becoming more impossible every day; much as Pavlos resented him, he could not hold him in leash. Nick had, peculiarly enough, taken a dislike to the American comrades, and they returned the compliment. In all his political talks he favored the Spanish, 'sucked up to them' the men would say. He allowed Curtis, the translator, the most infinitesimal amount of time to interpret what he'd said, and interrupted him constantly. He treated Fortis as an acknowledged inferior, barked at him and consequently minimized his prestige in the eyes of the men. Things were not so hot anyway; the food reached a new low. For ever since we had been cut off from the South we had had no oranges, no *marmalada* (bad as it was), no rice, and the 'coffee' became undrinkable. The 'garbage' the next night consisted of a few marblelike *garbanzos,* a few shreds of green matter and salty canned beef. There was no wine ration; there were no almonds; there was no bread. We knew that the country was sacrificing a good deal and suffering a great deal more to supply us with arms, and that a serious situation prevailed. The brilliant Non-Intervention scheme that was to localize the conflict worked perfectly—arms could not be sold to Franco or to the legitimate Government, but nothing prevented arms being sold to Germany or Italy who shipped them (with their men) into Spain. German planes flew across Switzerland into Spain every night; Italian troops disembarked on Franco's shores weekly, and the coastal blockade starved men, women and children with beautiful impartiality.

But there were certain compensations. All indications pointed to a large-scale Government offensive, which we thought would be 'definitive' one way or another. By day we scattered over the surrounding fields, and all day long the artillery thundered from across the plain that led to Lerida, forty kilometers away. We knew there had been vast movements of troops and artillery during the past week; we had seen them. The artillery rumbled all day and all night, and all day long from dawn to dusk we saw airplanes —*nuestros,* finally and definitely. Their red wing-tips flashed in the sun; we saw them landing and taking off from a near-by airport, climbing straight into the sky, almost hanging by their props. All day they came and went in flights of twelve, twenty-four, thirty-six and sixty! They flew toward the front and we heard the bombs and saw the smoke rising like a sea-fog rolling in toward land. Tri-motors, *Moscas* and *Chattos* wheeled over the town of Tarrega, came and went. Wolff called a meeting of officers and non-coms and told us that our offensive had begun; that we had every prospect of success; that we had adequate materiel in the form of artillery and airplanes and munitions to initiate and carry

out a long offensive. Our part in it was reassuring, in view of
the nature of our personnel—80 per cent untried troops. We
were to await the breaking of the Fascist lines, then enter
through the breaches and 'mop up.' It was good to know
the youngsters would not be used as shock-troops; we
laughed and cheered; we were anxious to get going, and
even young Jim Lardner, Ring's son, who had come to us
as a foreign correspondent and remained as a soldier, smiled.

The order to stand by came, and we formed in the barnyard of the enclosures where we slept (and where there was
a refugee family living), rifles slung, blankets rolled, pack-
sacks emptied of a few more non-essentials. (Gradually the
kids were getting the idea.) We stood for over an hour, then
sat down in place; then we were told to go into the pens and
barns and sleep, but not unroll our blankets. We slept all
night in full equipment, waiting for the order to move which
did not come. All over the country, we learned, the Government's offensive was going off as planned, and headway was
being made in the East (the Pyrenees), the Levante (Teruel
to the sea) and in the south. We had tanks, heavy artillery,
motorized divisions to counterbalance the enormous Fascist
mechanization. (France was scared again, it seemed, and let
a little materiel come in.) You had the intimation of a great
and decisive victory, and you could not tell how much of that
intimation depended upon the knowledge of new materiel,
upon unbreakable morale and conviction of justice, and how
much was wishful thinking, rationalization. We knew that
there was well-substantiated evidence of dissension in the
Fascist ranks. Their General Yague had made a radio speech,
it seemed, in which he said that certainly the 'Reds' were
brave—of course—because 'they are Spaniards.' For even the

fanatical *Falangistas* (Spanish Fascists) could not tolerate the military occupation of their country by the Italians and the Germans, who had taken over the civil and industrial administration of the 'liberated' land. They frequently murdered each other; nationalism is a curious thing, at best.

And the order to move finally came after three days and nights of constant shelling in the distance and the roar of airplane propellors. Tarrega was full of prisoners, twelve hundred of them, Spanish. Two complete battalions of Franco's troops had been taken with all equipment, including trucks, *sanidad,* kitchens and all—and without firing a shot. It was rumored that the front lines had been pushed far back (the shelling grew less insistent and seemed farther off; but you cannot tell yours from theirs, at a distance). It was rumored that Lerida and Tremp were in our hands again and the Fascist rearguard was demoralized. A Falangist radio speaker made the ill-advised remark that it would be better to join forces with the 'Reds' than to submit to Italo-German domination. And the order came and we marched—but not directly to the front, to a small town called Fondarella, twenty kilometers from Lerida. At any rate we were getting there, and our eagerness to get wherever we were going may have accounted for what Pavlos Fortis did, but I don't think so. On the fifteen-kilometer march to Fondarella I suddenly noticed that two Spanish comrades who had been carrying a box of ammunition had become tired and put it down. That's the way they were at times; they were tired, so they put it down. No one else was fresh, so no one picked it up. But Pavlos noticed it, swung it onto his shoulder and marched at the head of the column, the company commander carrying his company's ammunition.

"Put it down," I said.

"Nah!" he said. "*Chicos* tired; I take."

"Put it down," I said. "I'll get some one to carry it."

"Is no matter," he said. "I strong; is no matter."

"Put it down, you dope," I said. "That's not your job." He put it down.

Our aviation was active; our artillery rumbled day and night and our admiration for the Government grew by leaps and bounds, for in less than two months it had recuperated from the crushing defeats of Teruel, Belchite, Caspe, Batea, Gandesa and the Aragon, and it had launched a major offensive. Artillery was moving up; troops could be heard marching on the roads all night, and the brittle sounds of hundreds of horse. We heard—a shithouse rumor?—that we dominated the heights surrounding Lerida and Balaguer (this was different); the newspapers reported that the offensive was gaining ground everywhere; the Non-Intervention Committee met again and issued another of its 'decisions.' This time it decided once more to withdraw all foreign 'volunteers' from Spain, but England's perfidious hand could be seen as plain as day, for wasn't Mr. Chamberlain interested in concluding an agreement with Banjo-Eyes? And wasn't the 'withdrawal' contingent upon British and French concession of belligerent rights to Franco, which would tip the scales even farther in his favor by legalizing what already existed—the shipment of arms, munitions, planes and tanks and men into his territory? We sat and wished that Lopoff would come back. "You like this job?" said Fortis, who resembled Chapayev in many ways. "You like? I give. I give it anybody. *No me gusta.*" "*Yo tampoco,*" I said. And so we walked to Battalion headquarters where we found Vincent

Sheean and Joe North (*Daily Worker* correspondent) and Captain Wolff and Captain Leonard Lamb and Commissar George Watt and Ed Rolfe (attached to Lamb's company as a 'runner') all slightly stewed on good *vino* and singing 'Sweet Adeline' in the most distant sort of harmony. They were trying to drink from the spigotted glass container the Catalonians call a *chorro*. You hold it up and the wine spouts in a fine stream from the long glass nozzle . . . into your eye.

That was at four o'clock in the afternoon. At eight that night we were in trucks moving back to where we'd started from. There was no sense in this and it was weeks before we knew what had happened; that the offensive which had been so carefully prepared, in which we had every expectation of success and ample material to sustain a long job, had been called off. It was cold and cramped in the trucks, and we arrived outside Falset, in the general region of Darmos and Mora la Nueva and the Ebro, in the early morning, and made camp (Company 2) in a grove of nut trees; short, stunted trees that grew not much taller than your head. The nuts were green on the trees.

Kurculiotis looked like a small-time opera company's Mephisto. "Gunt," he said, "you got seegaret for me?" It had become difficult for me to look at the guy, and he knew it. "Everytheeng for me, pliss," he said, grinning like a death's-head. "Go on, roll your hoop," I said. *"Qué dices?"* he said, and I repeated it. He asked Pavlos to translate for him, but Pavlos could not get the idea. He did say something, and I asked him what he'd said, for Nick had started to glare at me again. "I tell him," he said. "I tell him you say Go fuck yourself." Well, he wasn't so far wrong at that. . . .

. . . We built *chavolas* between and under the nut trees, and we read the daily papers. The Americans were excited about the proposed scheme of the cynical Non-Intervention Committee, and they offered as beautiful an example of wishful thinking as you will ever see. Not one of them believed in any single thing the Committee had ever said or done, but the combination of fatigue and fear and the knowledge that the Internationals no longer represented an effective military force tipped the balance of reason in the direction of desire. And any straw is strong enough for a drowning man. The men were tired; many had been in Spain a long time; many actions had narrowed, in their minds, their chances of surviving the next; they felt that, in this respect, the law of averages was working against them. And some few had felt their original convictions falter. But even when they learned that the Soviet Union would not adhere to the new 'plan' for the withdrawal of volunteers, their certainty that that withdrawal would soon take place was not shaken. For hadn't the Committee even particularized the machinery of withdrawal; wasn't it going to appoint a commission to count noses? They gave a multitude of reasons why we *should* be withdrawn; they adduced the sudden stoppage of the Lerida offensive as evidence that the Government *was* going to replace its few foreign fighters. They pointed to the replacement of the last two International Divisional commanders as evidence that the Brigade's day was shortening. (These two men, both Communists and able leaders, were replaced by the Government as a slap to British criticism of 'Moscow' interference in Spain.) And we knew that our own Brigade Commander Cópic would shortly be replaced by a Spanish commander. Bets were laid that the

Internationals would never go into action again, but they were dictated more by hope than by conviction.

And the war went on; and the only consolation and balm for nerves strained by the abortive trip to Tarrega and the long period of waiting was the fact that the fronts must have been satisfactory, or the Government would have called us in. We were a full battalion again, almost seven hundred men. And every day a Fascist observation plane flew at 10,000 feet above the camouflaged camp and the men lay under the nut trees waiting for the all-clear signal (a single shot) from the observers posted on the near-by hills. That plane was a bomber, and it did not lay its eggs on us. But other bombers, on one day, raided Granollers, the industrial suburb of Barcelona, and Alicante, the city in the south. In Granollers they killed 300 women, children and old men; in Alicante they blew 250 into bloody rags and wounded 300 more. In Rome, the Pope again deplored the bombing of civilian populations; but he was naïve—civilians are military objectives in our time.

Lopoff's whereabouts were finally discovered; he had been diverted from the hospital to a training-camp in Montblanch —then he returned. "How's the foot?" we said, and he said, "Hurts." Pavlos sighed and moved out of the *chavola* under the nut tree, reassuming command of the first section. He was delighted. Aaron and Nick (in his blue satin quilt) and Curtis and I occupied the shelter, which made three men to share the few cigarettes that came to Aaron and to me, in letters. (We generally waited till Nick was somewhere else.)

Dear Pop, the letter said, *The Loyalist hats and slippers came this afternoon. We wore them out, and everything and*

I didn't let anybody touch it. I'm wearing the slippers.
David's feet are too big for his. You're a good Poppy to send
them. Please send David some more slippers.

We got another table. We traded ours with a man named
Willie. He is our coal man. Yesterday Mom sorted all our
clothes and we took a big bundle over to the place where
they will be sent to the Spanish children. Mommy's writing
this with a pencil. Look on the other side. My finger is sore
so I can't draw a boat very well. Some day David and I are
going to Spain. Dan. In addition to the ship, there was a
drawing of a plane, dropping bombs. It was a good drawing
and the wing-tips had swastikas.

(The kids were furious about Alicante; they went around
with drawn faces, talked together in small groups, rushed
the new mailman, Ed Fliegel, when he came at breakfast
time in the truck. They either received no mail, or their
letters told them of the death of parents, relatives and
friends. Many wept in their *chavolas,* and they wrote innumerable letters. There was a new firmness in their faces,
in the lines of their jaws; Fascism had come home with a
vengeance and because they knew their city, their people,
explanation of abstract ideas was no longer quite so necessary. They had caught one glimpse of their enemy; they
would catch many more.)

"Stop telling me about your God-damned kids," Aaron
said. "I'm getting sick of them. I don't like kids."

"You bastard."

He looked at me, "Christ, but you're an ugly son-of-a-
bitch," he said, "How'd you ever get close enough to a
woman to get kids?"

7

OUR CAMP in the nut grove lay in a shallow *baranco* beside the dirt road. On the one side there was the road, dusty and broken, on the other, a steep wooded hill. Across the road the *estado-mayor* of the Battalion (a small stone house) sheltered Wolff and Watt and the Spanish battalion-adjutant; the assorted runners, observers, transmissionists and scouts had dug or built *chavolas* on the hill behind the headquarters. There was not a level stretch of ground within a radius of many kilometers; the terrain was impossible to maneuver over, steep terraced hills with deep clefts and ravines, heavily overgrown *barancos* treacherous with undergrowth and loose stones. Within three kilometers the British, the 24th and the Canadian battalions had dug in beside the road that ran, in one direction toward Tarragona through a small town whose name I can't remember; in the other to Marsa, Falset and the river. Behind us were precipitous hills, wooded part-way up and crowned with dizzy light-gray bluffs of sheer stone. When there was sun, the whole countryside shimmered with a white light against which you could barely open your eyes; the leaves were covered with dust, the rocks were hot to touch and small lizards ran in among the rocks. On cloudy days, the mist would bank up behind the higher hills, and then pour slowly and majestically over the cliff-faces, more slowly, more majestically than any waterfall. We used to watch them.

The early summer heat, the intermittent dampness and rain, the bad food and the flies, the strain of the deathly monotony of waiting, the scarcity of tobacco—perhaps all these were contributory causes of diarrhea, which is a mysterious disease and was known familiarly to us as 'the shits,' for man is the only animal who can afford to laugh at his bodily functions. But diarrhea, despite the jokes—'I could hit a dime at ten meters!'—is no laughing matter. It sapped our strength and our tempers; it augmented the dissatisfaction that was felt with the state of things—no matter what the state of things might be. Grub was lousy; there was no tobacco (where was the monthly shipment from the Friends? Whoever invented the idea that tobacco sent to the Americans should be lodged in the General Intendencia of the Army? That lousy censor in Barcelona is stealing butts again); medical supplies were almost non-existent; where was the mail and why didn't it come regularly? Where were the individual packages that individual men had been sent (I can show you the letter where they say they sent it in February!)? If we were going into action, why not go? If we were going to be repatriated, why wasn't something happening? The men sang:

> Wait-ing, wait-ing, wait-ing,
> Always fuckin' well wait-ing,
> Waiting in the morn-ing
> Waiting in the ni-i-i-ght . . . (descending scale)

It isn't as though we had nothing to do; every day the orders of the day arrived (late the night before), neatly typewritten and detailing a program of instruction worked out by the Brigade staff a couple kilometers up the road toward Marsa.

Target practice with rifle and machine-gun; company and battalion maneuvers over this impossible terrain. We marched and climbed, we spread out into combat-formation and infiltrated through the growing vines and the olive fields, up the terraces, to attack *en masse* and yelling with something less than enthusiasm, at the crest. We practised scouting, signalling, moving through enemy terrain; we attacked hills and houses, railroad tunnels; we attacked each other. The men marched up the road in a cloud of dust that could be seen for miles, stripped to the waist in the biting heat and sweating. At the rest-periods there were no *Camels* to afford the lift so badly needed; the water in our few canteens was tainted with chloride of lime or iodine. We sang:

> March-ing, march-ing, march-ing,
> Always fuckin' well march-ing,
> God send the—day when we'll—fuckin' well march no more!

"I hope you realize," said Aaron, "just how serious your charges are."

"Sure," we said, and we felt uneasy for a moment.

"You know how difficult it is to remove a commissar; what a bad thing it is all around."

"Yes."

"Will you back up these accusations you've made? Because if you will, I'll see what can be done about it."

After he had listened to what we had to say about Nick, after he had heard Curtis the secretary and Garfield the *practicante,* and Pavlos Fortis and another Greek beautifully named Hercules Arnaoutis, and Jack Hoshooley, leader of Section Two, and Nat Gross, Jack's pet machine-gunner, a handsome, hard-faced youngster who characterized him-

self as chief griper in the Lincoln-Washington, and after he
had called in Luke Hinman, who'd been in our company
for a short time after the retreat and then went back to the
Battalion scouts, he called in Kurculiotis himself. It wasn't
exactly pleasant to sit in the lean-to that day with Aaron
listening and Pavlos and Hercules translating into Greek,
and Curtis translating into Spanish and English, and make
accusations against a man who knew you didn't like him,
but the task was made easier by Kurculiotis' attitude. From
the start he assumed the air of a person of infinite patience
and forbearance with his inferiors, who were incapable of
understanding his motives anyhow, and he listened with an
assumed deference that irritated every one. Then he made a
long speech, which worked up into a majestic climax that
could have been heard a kilometer away, and he looked at
us all as much as to say, Nuts to you. After the hearing
Aaron said, "Now you can draw up a report to the Battalion
on the charges you guys have made. Do it in your finest style
and I'll back it up." The charges were, assumption of
authority the commissar did not possess; the issuance of
military commands over the head of the military commander; egotism, arrogance, chauvinism and incompetence,
and any one of them would have been enough in that
army, and all of them together were too much. Nick was
removed as commissar of Company 2, and to our con-
sternation he was made a common *soldado* . . . in Company 2. He was placed in a squad, issued a rifle, and instead of marching at the head of the company with the
demeanor of a lieutenant-colonel, he marched in the ranks
with the air of a general. He was a good soldier; one of the
finest; he gave the Spanish youngsters the benefit of his two

years' experience in Spain; he was quiet, friendly, efficient, unobtrusive. And we were flabbergasted. . . .

. . . In an unimpressive ceremony our Brigade Commander Vladimir Cópic, a Yugoslav with a fair baritone voice, was replaced by Major Valledor, a short wiry Asturian refugee who smiled continuously and gave the impression of tremendous energy. (He was liked better than Cópic ever was; he was more of a human being, less of an opera star.) In a very impressive offensive, the Fascist forces were trying to widen the sector they had driven to the sea at Vinaroz, and were moving toward Valencia. We got bad news; Castellon de la Plana had been evacuated under tremendous pressure; Villareal, twenty kilometers south of Castellon on the Valencia road, was seeing fighting in the streets. The drive was pursued with everything the Franco forces had, including fleets of Italian and Nazi bombers from the Balearic Islands, shelling from the sea, tanks and motorized divisions. This was difficult terrain to defend, for it was merely a narrow coastal plain, bounded on the one side by the sea, on the other by the mountains. Sagunto, still farther south, contained important munitions-works, airplane factories and the railhead of the line back up to Teruel. If they could take Sagunto, the going would be fairly easy to Valencia; if they could take Valencia, Madrid, which had held the enemy at its very gates since the first days of the rebellion, would be helpless. News came that the 43d Division, which had been fighting with its back to the Pyrenees for months, had been surrounded and forced over the border into France. News came of large troop-movements and heavy concentrations on the other side of the Ebro, and that was too close for comfort. More and more we felt that only a resolution of the European situation could save Spain, if Spain was to be saved. The Blum Government, at least, had recognized the importance of Spain to French security. The Daladier outfit was hand in glove, not only with its own brand of Fascists, but with the foreign gang as well. (Class is thicker than nationality.) "Why doesn't France do something?" became a cliché. "Don't they see that if Hitler and his little pal take over Spain, France will be strangled on three fronts?" Well, either they didn't see it or they didn't care, which was more likely. The French people were with us heart and soul; they had given thousands of their best sons, millions of their money; the French people's rulers were against us. They bore no ill-will toward the Fascists; they *were* Fascist.

We were low, and we were not cheered by the report that Villareal had been retaken. Tabb was low; now *peloton*-sergeant in the Third Section, we were not so friendly as before, as he had assumed a sarcastic attitude that was more directed at my holding the job of company adjutant, than at me personally. Garfield was low—he did not enjoy the job of company first-aid man, as he would have preferred to be in a hospital; he had found a pair of shorts somewhere, and wore them at all times, his hairy legs making merriment for the Spanish boys—and he had identified himself with the consistent malcontents. Jack Hoshooley was low; his wife in Canada kept writing to ask when he would be coming home. ('Don't you think you've done enough?' she wrote.) Nat Gross was sore because his steady stream of packages seemed to have dried up somewhere, and he was running out of *Camels*. The new company commissar, Harold Smith, made a fine pretense of good spirits; once wounded—his left hand was useless—he had insisted on returning to the front, but he could not make contact with the Spanish; for where Kurculiotis spoke the language fluently, Harold spoke it not at all. Ed Rolfe, attached to Leonard Lamb's company, was deathly sick with diarrhea, and dragged himself around the camp like a sick cat. He should never have been permitted to come up in the first place, but you could not help admiring the spirit that kept him smiling when his insides were tying themselves in knots. It was good to talk to him, or to sit silently with him and watch the mists pouring over the high bluffs on the mountainside; we had a common understanding that needed no words to make it plain. And I think we both felt that even if we had not made a mistake in coming to Spain, it had been wrong—for us. For there is more than one way of fighting Fascism, and a man should do what he knows best.

"You needn't think of going home," Aaron said to me, and there was a slight touch of sadistic pleasure in his smile. "Your future lies here in Spain, and perhaps in more than one sense at that. You started something when you joined the International Brigade, papa."

I did not remark on what I was feeling; that he had done the same. Day or night, I could hear him whistling in the dark, and it was a reassuring sound. For although by now I knew pretty well what had brought me to Spain, I was not sure yet of what had brought him. Men went to Spain for various reasons, but behind almost every man I met there was a common restlessness, a loneliness. In action these men would fight like devils, with the desperation of an iron-bound conscience; in private conversation there was something else again. I knew, about myself, that the historical event of Spain had coincided with a long-felt compulsion to complete the destruction of the training I had received all through my youth. There were two major reasons for my being there; to achieve self-integration, and to lend my individual strength (such as it was) to the fight against our eternal enemy—oppression; and the validity of the second reason was not impaired by the fact that it was a shade weaker than the first, for they were both a part of the same thing. It was necessary for me, at that stage of my development as a man, to work (for the first time) in a large body of men; to submerge myself in that mass, seeking neither distinction nor preferment (the reverse of my activities for the past several years) and in this way to achieve self-discipline, patience and unselfishness—the opposite of a long middle-class training—and the construction of a life that would be geared to other men and the world-events that circumscribed them. There is much truth in the old saws— for a desperate disease, a desperate cure.

Aaron and I had certain things in common. He was a fiction-writer and he was fascinated by airplanes. He had two brothers and a sister in New York, and had left home early to bum around the States. ("Those were the happiest days of my life," he said, as though he were not only twenty-four.) He had wanted to study aeronautical engineering, but there had not been enough money to finish the course, and he was not the sort of guy who could sit around and let the others do the work. He spoke of the airplane models he had made when he was a boy, with a gleam in his Oriental eyes. His hands moved when he spoke of them; the rubber-band models and the gasoline models that would fly and with which he won a schoolboy competition. He spoke of his father and mother with love, and I thought of how much I had missed in my own childhood. "You'll have to eat some of my Mom's *kreploch*," he would say. Or, "You'd like my Pop." He used to enjoy singing, if no one was around, and he sang many Russian cradle-songs that, he said, were the first songs he had learned. He had a small voice, but a sweet and true one, and it never failed to move me with its overtones of nostalgia and early memories. "My Mom thinks I'm working in a factory here," he said. "I write to Pop at another address. He's proud I've been made a *teniente*. Do you know," he said, "when we were going to Batea, a guy rode up on a big white horse; it really was a big white horse, and said, 'Congratulations, Loppy, you're a *teniente* now.' My Pop's an old revolutionary," he said. "He understands what I'm doing here."

Early in the evening, after the day's maneuvers, was a bad time for Aaron; he was low. Then we would either walk down the road to Company 1, and sit chewing the fat with Lamb (who was invariably cheerful) and Rolfe (who was occasionally glum), or with the two of them we would walk two kilometers up the road to the building that now housed the 35th Division Hospital. Here there was a remarkable character named John Kozar, a sailor I had met during the 1936 East Coast Seamen's strike. He was attached to the hospital as a *mecanico,* and he ran a small motor there that generated the power for the hospital's electric lights. He lived with the motor in what must once have been a small stable, and the place was unique in more than one way. He had a table spread with an embroidered cloth; he had vases of flowers, ash-trays, posters on the walls, a couple comfortable chairs and every sort of cooking utensil, including a Primus stove.

The boy had built up a legend about himself that was none the less entertaining for the fact that part of it might not have been exactly true. Of part Indian and part Russian stock, he came of a Pennsylvania mining family, and had been a coal-miner before he was a sailor. In New York he had worn octagonal eyeglasses, possibly because he thought they made him look genteel (there was nothing wrong with his eyes). But he was a tough nut, and frequently got into trouble because of the strength that lay behind his apparent gentleness. An ironclad anti-Fascist, he had come to Spain from France in the *Ciudad de Barcelona,* that had been torpedoed by a 'pirate' (Italian) submarine off the coast. He swam ashore towing a suitcase and a pound of *Maxwell House* coffee in his teeth (or so he said). He had driven a truck at Brunete (where his friend Richard Tynan had connected with a shell), and since then had held a variety of jobs behind the lines. But these were the least of his accomplishments, in our eyes. When we walked down in the evening there might have been two people there, or twenty. Soldiers and officers from the Mac-Paps, Spanish and British nurses from the hospital (there was a nice one named Joan, one of the few women who can wear trousers and not look ridiculous), doctors, chauffeurs frequented the joint. When we arrived Kozar (who liked to call himself Topsy) removed the key-ring from his finger, opened one of a number of locked wooden chests, and produced a pot. Then, in short order, we had—British tea, British orange marmalade, American coffee (when the tea was gone), French-fried

potatoes, bread—with butter!—chocolate, cigarettes, *Lorna
Doone* cookies, strawberry jam, eggs or chicken, cake, hot
chocolate. No one knew where he got these things; no one
was so indiscreet as to inquire. On two separate occasions
he gave me a fine leather coat and a waterproof sleeping
bag (it *was* waterproof; water could come in, but not get
out). He also gave me handkerchiefs, woollen socks, a small
leather brief case, underwear, soap and razor blades.

The motor putted all night and the night wore away
(most of us were there without permission), and these eve-
nings were interludes so precious in their faculty of breaking
the monotony that we could not imagine getting along
without them. During the course of the entire evening
Kozar rarely said a word; he was too busy serving tea,
coffee and cocoa alternately in tin cans; or sitting, listening
to what the boys and girls had to say. (It was good to hear
a female voice.) He was so unobtrusive in his job of host
that we rarely noticed he was there at all. So we kibitzed
the time away, had political arguments and sang. At least
once during the course of the evening Aaron, who was
generally too shy to take part in the conversation, could be
induced to sing. The single bulb cast our enormous shadows
on the field-stone walls, and the entrance to the room was
closed off with a mat made of bamboo. The worn-out rugs
on the earthen floor were soft to your feet, and we sat on the
cots and chairs and the bench as Aaron touched the guitar
that Kozar had produced. He sang:

> Give me a home, where the buf-falo roam,
> Where the deer and the ant-elope play,
> Where sel-dom is heard, a dis-couraging word,
> And the skies are not cloudy all day.

And this sentimental song invariably took us home to the America we loved all the more for being so far away from it; it cast a hush over us, although we were already silent, and we felt a little sad wondering if the folks back home realized what we were doing here, and how closely this struggle would affect them all in time to come. Or did they agree with Mr. Hearst that we were either bloodthirsty revolutionists, dupes of Moscow or 'bums' who deserved to have their citizenship revoked?

> Home, home on the ra-ange,
> Where the deer and the ant-elope play,
> Where sel-dom is heard . . .

There was an abstraction about his face when he sang; he looked at once years younger and years older; he had put everything he had (without trying), everything that was in him into the banal song; he might have sung *Boris Goudonov,* and it would not have moved me more. . . . It took him out of himself to sing, and if he had been silent all the way down the dark road to the little hospital, he opened up on the way back to camp.

"Wolff is after me to replace you with a Spanish adjutant," he said. "That's the policy, you know; but I've been stalling him." He laughed, and I could see his fine white teeth flash in the moonlight. "Why the hell I'm doing it, I don't know. You're no good to me; you might as well transfer into another company."

"Any time you say," I said. "Nothing could please me more."

We both laughed, but we did not laugh for very long, for it is difficult to laugh late at night on a road behind the lines in a country at war; the hills threw back our laughter, and the sentries we passed, standing alone by the side of the road, must have felt lonelier for our laughter. We came into the camp under the nut bushes, where the moon cast fantastic shadows on the packed ground in the open spaces, and it required a definite effort of the imagination to believe that there were about a hundred men sleeping under these trees, young men wrapped in blankets, sleeping on the inhospitable earth miles from their homes, waiting to oppose their weak flesh to the impersonality of hot steel. Out of respect for their sleep (and perhaps something else we could not speak of, for the sleeping and the dead look quite alike), we lowered our voices and sat at the mouth of our lean-to, where Harold Smith was, as usual, taking up more room than he should have, and Curtis was lying on his side wrapped in the canvas tarpaulin.

We sat side by side without speaking, our arms wrapped around our knees, looking at the moon, and at those moments I think we were closer than we ever were later (when we knew each other better)—with one exception. I felt like his father, but I could not tell him so, for he would only have laughed at me. I felt like his brother, but I could not tell him that either, because I had no words with which to express a literally fraternal emotion—my brother and I had never been very close. But it was good to hear him speak in low tones of his home, of his mother's cooking, his father's courage and integrity, his brother's illness, his sister's marriage. I was with him when he spoke of his model airplanes, and of a girl back in New York with whom he corresponded, but who rarely answered him.

"I hope we see one good hot action more before they send

us home," he said, "if they *do* send us." He said no more,
but I knew why he had said it. He had said before that he
hated the job of company commander (though he had not
as yet exercised it in action), but that the more he hated
it, the more determined he was to do a good job of it. You
felt, listening to this serious young man, who could be hard
as nails on the surface, that he needed to prove himself to
himself. That he wanted this 'one good hot action' as a company commander, to convince him that he was right about
what he felt about himself. I could feel him shudder at
my side, and I don't know whether it was the chill night air
or something else.

"Bess," he said, "why did you come to Spain? You have a
wife and kids."

"Had a wife," I said. "But I'd have to tell you the whole
story of my life."

"Well," he said, "don't tell me."

"I won't."

Dear Guys,

*Yours of May 22 (with Dan's and Dave's drawings) re-
ceived the other day, handed me a laugh. Grasp the image:
you say, 'You guys are marvellous. It is marvellous the things
you're all doing.' Well, I wish you'd been here to see us
the morning that letter arrived. We're living at the moment
in a grove of hazel-nut trees; wherever we go the guys 'dig-
in,' building themselves lean-tos or shelters out of any material available—boughs, poles, leaves and dirt. Well, we'd
been here awhile and we'd built 'shelters,' and then, the
night before your letter came it poured cats and dogs all
night, and we slept (?) in it. It cleared only slightly with*

dawn and the arrival of the coffee-truck, and it was still drizzling and bitter cold, and you never in your life saw so bedraggled a group of human beings—soaked to the skin, gray-faced from lack of sleep, shaking with cold, no tobacco to smoke, no dry wood to burn. Even the coffee was cold, and the bad Spanish cognac (paint-remover, we call it) could not warm us up. Nor have we been decently warm since—for there has been a nasty wind blowing. Either you freeze here, or you broil in the white sun. Ah, for the life of a soldier! And to top the climax, I am enjoying a bad case of diarrhea at the moment. Let it go——

For there are compensations—letters, an occasional pretty good meal and things like yesterday when Joe North showed up again and brought some presents: a fine steel knife (hard to get), a bar of French chocolate and four packs of Camels (almost gone). For a soldier's main preoccupations are food and tobacco and shelter, in that order.

Life is amusing, lady. A letter, with yours, from ——, who says, 'Be a good guy, and despite being busy with a war, try to write more frequently,' and then goes into a song and dance about his financial difficulties, mentioning that he had rented a 'swanky' new apartment, 'for reasons of economy.'

I'm tickled pink by your reports of the kids, and I feel a twinge when you say how anxious they are to see me. How you can do it I don't know, but you must prepare them for my long absence—and it may be very long, as you know. More than ever I'm sure I've left you a burden that, I know, you can carry, but which will take too heavy a toll of your strength. Forgive me if you can.

There is little to report; we wish we knew what was going on. Our period of training is getting longer and

longer and the kids are being welded into a disciplined unit
that should give a good account of itself if, as and when.

So long for the time being. I dreamed of you and the
kids the other night, the night it rained. It was the rain
that woke me up. I frequently dream of New York and
the kids, which can be understood. *Salud y Victoria!*

It was impossible to get used to the July heat; it kept
you in a state of constant enervation and flaccidity. The
training-schedule was reduced to a minimum, but it was almost better to be doing something in that heat than to lie
under its weight. Siestas lasted four hours, but you could
not sleep, for if you slept uncovered the flies would eat you
alive, and if you slept with a blanket over your bare arms
and face you suffocated and stewed in your own juice. For
it is not true that you can get used to anything; you can
stand pretty nearly anything, but there is no obligation to
get used to it.

The men's nerves were raw. There was no tobacco; for
weeks there had been no tobacco. Regular issues were a
thing of the past, and for weeks there had not even been an
issue of 'anti-tanks' or the curious items we called 'pillow-
slips,' which were tobacco (*sic*) rolled loosely in tissue-
paper, and which could be re-rolled. The shipment from
the Friends of the Lincoln Brigade did not appear (at the
July 4th *fiesta* every man got three cigarettes—dead men's
packages); individual packages were not arriving, and those
men fortunate enough to receive a few butts in an occasional
letter did not flaunt them abroad. Bad food was bad enough;
diarrhea was worse; an epidemic skin-disease called scabies,
which drove you wild with scratching, particularly at

night, plagued almost everybody (not to mention lice), but these could be borne. Bad tempers hung on a thread, and the fact that forty-eight-hour leaves were being granted to men with the longest service-records, to make a trip to Barcelona, its bath-houses and its Rambla de los Flores, meant little enough. For there were still many men who had been long in Spain, and this meant that the majority of the Americans might never get there. (Aaron awaited his turn with impatience while Fortis went and Kurculiotis went, Leonard Lamb and Wolff and Watt, and Jack Ho-shooley and Nat Gross and George Cady and half a dozen others.) For worse than the rumors of imminent action (the drive on the Valencia road had not abated) was the starvation for tobacco. The Spanish boys, who did not as a rule smoke very much, seemed relatively content to smoke dried *avellano* leaves, but we tried them and they were impossible.

The talk about the withdrawal of volunteers did not abate; it grew daily with an almost sinister insistence. There was nothing else that the men would talk about, and they speculated on it by the hour. The situation in Spain was bad; the international situation stank out loud; more than ever certain men felt trapped, for many had convinced themselves by arguments far more brilliant than they were sound, that our release from the I. B.s was not only probable, but certain. The camp was a hotbed of 'authentic' rumors 'right out of the horse's mouth.' Some one had come back from leave in Barcelona where he had heard thus-and-so from so-and-so who *knew*. (There were even supposed to be carloads of *Lucky Strikes* in Barcelona, locked in the vaults of the *Comisariado!*) No rumor was too fantastic for credence, and it took a good deal of time before the Battalion and

Brigade commissariats decided to accept the fact that 'Non-Intervention' was a problem with the men. Talk of it, of repatriation, had been discouraged; certain men received mild punishments for even mentioning it, for discontent grows by what it feeds on, even when its food is insubstantial. It was undoubtedly an error not to have recognized the problem before it was finally brought into the open, but the error was not fatal; for even if the weaker elements were very vocal, and had, to a certain extent, infected the stronger men, most of them, while weary and exhausted, had not and never did lose faith in the convictions that had brought them thus far. "These guys will gripe about everything," said Aaron, "the food, the officers, the commissars, the international situation—they will talk desertion, treason, they will talk of picking out a good hole and sticking in it when the time comes, but when the time comes they'll do nothing of the sort—they'll fight the way they've always fought, if not better." Well, some of us wondered.

A battalion political meeting was called and John Gates, Brigade Commissar, brought out the ghosts of withdrawal, Non-Intervention and repatriation and he laid them. He told us that if the Government did not need us, we would have been sent home. He flayed individuals who spread rumors and he refused to retract a particularly vile epithet he had hurled at one man. "If you can't call a c... s...... a c... s......," he said, "then we've got into a fine state of affairs." He attempted to point out the folly of believing in the London Non-Intervention Committee's pronouncements, and every man there knew he was talking the exact and bitter truth. Hitler and Mussolini never could afford to withdraw their 'volunteers'—ten times as many as we had—and it could no longer be denied that the British Government was a silent partner in the Fascist Powers' attempts to strangle Spain; that we were witnessing one of the most amazing and cynical displays of hypocrisy in world history. Gates pointed out that the earlier policy of repatriation after six months' service in the Brigades had been an error; that you could not build an efficient army or a body of foreign volunteers, you could not develop leadership by sending men in for six months and then retiring them. "I hear men say that the XVth Brigade will never go into action again," he said. "But I am here to tell you that it will—and possibly sooner than we expect—and that when it does, it will maintain its tradition of sacrifice and courage."

The men took these words and they said nothing at the meeting; there was no effective presentation of the 'case' some felt they had; that men of long service *had* been repatriated (aside from the wounded), and were being repatriated. That certain 'c...s' who had 'influence,' and had managed to dodge the front lines when their convictions wavered, had managed to get home. And they said nothing because there was a mixed emotion in their hearts—a realization that it would look strange for men who had come to Spain prepared to die, to get panicky now that things were going against us. And, too, there was the more practical knowledge that an army (even so genuinely democratic an army as ours) cannot well afford to consider individuals, and that a man who permits himself to crystallize discontent is quite certain to be 'marked lousy' by his superior officers, even though the discontent were justified. They had come to Spain because they believed in Spain and the necessity to save Spain so that America might not feel the weight of Fascist oppression; they still believed in Spain; they still felt that in fighting for her they were helping to stem the tide of international Fascism; and had they deserted they would never have been able to look themselves in the face again—but they were only human. They were tired; they were homesick; they were a bit afraid. And while they acknowledged the soundness of much that Gates said, they over-emphasized the 'bullshit' about sacrifice and courage and allowed their personal dislike for the commissar to color their criticism of what he had said. For like all complex personalities, Gates was liked only by those who knew him well, and his job was such that it was almost impossible for the men to know him. He was a short man, and like many short men he compensated by his personal courage and his erect physical bearing for his lack of stature. He was a young man with a burden of responsibility that could not easily have been carried by a man of many more years' experience, but within these limitations of youth and personality he did a terrific job and did it well. . . .

. . . Rumor assumed a concrete form. Training suddenly became intensified and a detailed program of instruction was drawn up that would carry down to the first week in August. "Aha!" the men said, "that means we won't move till then, if we move at all." Every afternoon the companies went out on maneuver, and sweated over the terraces and hills. Every morning there was machine-gun and rifle practice, and the firing echoed among the hills and the ravines like a regiment of rifles. But more significant was a Brigade maneuver, when the British, the Canadians, the Americans and the Cubans moved out of camp late at night with full equipment, marched to a town fifteen kilometers away, through the town and arrived on the shore of a dry river, just as dawn was rising. Here, as by prearrangement, the battalions split into companies, the companies into sections, the sections into *peletons* and the *pelotons* into squads, the men grouped into the pattern they would assume in small boats, and moved diagonally across the pebbled bottom to the other side. There we started to run uphill, spreading into combat-formation by battalions, attacking a terraced mountain that rose and rose and never seemed to achieve a crest. We attacked the mountain and we took it; there was simulated enemy fire from the peak, rifles and machine-guns firing into space; we used every artifice and tactic we had learned to capture the imaginary enemy's position. "Aha!" the men said, "we're going to cross a river. Now what river do you suppose *that* could be?" But I think we knew the river; we had crossed it once before, in the opposite direction.

So every day we practised crossing rivers (dry ones), large and small, and attacking exhausting hills that rose upon their other shores. The rumor crystallized; 'right out of the horse's mouth' we learned that when we came to cross that river it would mean penetrating the enemy's lines on the shore (naturally), marching deep into his territory with no facilities for possibly three days, to bring up food, water and munitions, to remove the wounded, with no communications with the rear. If the operation were successful (and certainly its daring weighed strongly in its favor), we might penetrate the entire sector he had driven to the sea, and come out on the other side—the Levante—taking his heavy guns by surprise. The heroic daring of the operation left us breathless and somewhat terrified. We'd have to move and move fast; stop for nothing, let nothing stop us, and quite possibly be surrounded and cut to pieces.

(We sat side by side in the shade of a fig tree and Aaron said, "Somehow I trust your judgment, but I don't know why."

"You flatten me," I said.

"Listen," he said. "We need tobacco."

"Claro."

"I happen to know Wolff has some pipe tobacco."

"No sooner said than done," I said, and taking out a piece of paper, wrote on it:

To: El Lobo, Cde., 58 Bon.
From: Teniente Lopoff, Cde. 2a Cia.
Re: Tobacco
Teniente Lopoff and his Sargento-Ayudante Bessie would like to know if El Capitan el Lobo could spare them the wherewithal to roll a few butts.

Aaron signed this and I reported to Wolff (who was reading Thomas Mann's *Joseph in Egypt*) and saluted. He frowned as he read it, then looked at me and shouted, "I thought I told Lopoff to get a Spanish adjutant!"

"You did."

"Why didn't he get one?"

"Am I my *comandante's* keeper?"

"Bessie," he said, reaching for his pouch, "you're a pain in the ass."

"Muy bien," said Aaron, "that's about all you're good for —here, let me roll that; you can't learn to roll a cigarette." We smoked in silence, drawing deep inhalations that left

us weak and dizzy. There was something on his mind, but I was startled when he said, "How do you know when a woman loves you?" I was so startled that I didn't answer, and he reached into his pocket and brought out a letter, one of the rare letters he got from the girl he wrote to so regularly, at such great length.

"Suppose you read this and tell me what you think," he said.

"You don't want me to read it, do you?"

"No," he said, and put it back in his pocket.)

We had a joke those days. "You heard the news?" and the answer was, "Sure, we're going to be withdrawn." "What's that?" "Sure, they're going to withdraw the volunteers from Spain." "No shit," you'd say, "and here I was planning to get married and grow up with the country." Then it was appropriate to sing,

> *Las chicas de Barcelona . . . ona,*
> *No saben fregar un plato . . . ato,*
> *Marchan para las calles . . . alles*
> *Vendan carne con pello . . . ello,*

which it would not be advisable to translate. But now when you said, "You heard the news?" they would say, "Now listen; what're they going through all this rigmarole for if they don't mean it? The Committee's met again and agreed on the plan. England, France, Germany and Italy even made a payment on the expenses of sending a commission. The Soviet Union's agreed—" "With important reservations," you'd say. "—Fuck the reservations. It's been sent to the Government and to Franco. A guy just told me that he had some dope, got it right out of the horse's mouth, that

within two weeks we'll be segregated from the Spanish
Army to wait and be counted. He even told me where the
concentration camps would be where they'll count us. On
the coast, so we can get ships right out."

They wanted desperately to believe in the withdrawal,
and I began to half-believe in it myself; and the more the
possibility of action presented itself to us, the more we
wanted it to happen before we went into action and got
killed off. "Hell's bells," they'd say, "we're not a fighting
force any more; we're not even good for propaganda. The
world knows we're all washed up." "Not *The Daily Worker,*
though," some one would say. "There's reasons for that—"
"Sure, but listen—it would be a smart move now for the
Government to repatriate us; they could say, 'See, we sent
home our volunteeers,' to Franco, 'now shit or get off the
pot.'" "Sure, it would be a smart move all right." "Ah, you
can't see the nose on your face; it's plain as mud; everything's shaping up that way. It's in the bag."

(Aaron came to the *chavola* with a paper in his hand. "I've
got it!" he shouted; "I've got it! Nuts to you all; you can
all go roll a hoop."

"What've you got, comrade?" said Harold Smith, "your
repatriation papers?"

"*Salvo conducto* to Barcelona."

"Any one'd think you were going to Europe," Harold
said, and Aaron looked at me with an indefinable expression
on his face that was, nevertheless, a definite cue.

"He doesn't understand," he said to me.

"No," I said. "He couldn't understand; he's only a
commissar."

"Commissars never forget, though," Aaron said.

"Once a commissar, always a c...."

"A bird in the bush," said Aaron, "is worth two in the commissar. You know, I think I should have been a commissar myself."

"No, no," I said. "Not *that;* anything but that!"

Joe Hecht, who was sitting around, having left his truck, as usual, in the middle of the road, laughed. He fished in his pocket and handed something to Aaron, saying,

"These'll keep you out of the rain."

"Are they any good?"

"Best American brand," said Joe, and Aaron carefully put them away in his wallet. Joe and Harold left, and I looked at my commander.

"You won't use them," I said. It was a question.

"Oh yes, I will."

"I thought you told me you could never patronize whores."

"I never could," he said, "but I'm going to. Hell, this may be the last chance I ever get to sleep with a woman.")

Garfield had definitely become a nuisance. With the imminent possibility of action, he was as nervous as a cat and did his best to get transferred back to a base hospital. "I'd be much more useful there," he said. "I really would. I know that stuff."

"We'll need a good first-aid man if we go up," I said.

"But you don't understand, Al."

Just before he left for Barcelona Aaron had bawled him out; he had become an agitator; it suited him, he drifted into it. When Mike Washuk (Dayton, Ohio's Only Boy in Spain) had been quartermaster, the Spanish boys com-

plained that he demonstrated favoritism to the Americans
when he dished out the chow. We watched him carefully,
and though we never saw any evidence of such culinary
chauvinism, we leaned over backwards and appointed a
Spanish quartermaster. Then the Americans began to claim
that Matias Lara gave the Spanish more grub than he dished
out to the Americans, and Garfield was one of the loudest
in the chorus. He complained of Lara, he complained of his
Spanish stretcher-bearers, he complained of the food, the
command, the heat, the Battalion doctor Simon (who had
his own complaints of Garfield), the conduct of the war,
the mail and packages he didn't get; he wanted repatriation.
Aaron said, "I'm worried about that kid; I think he's quite
likely to break in action," and he told him, "Listen, Garfield, you'll have to watch your step; I'm getting sick of you,
and if you keep this stuff up I'll take strong measures against
you for disruption."

Garfield was nothing if not articulate. He immediately
went into a song-and-dance about his guilt; he confessed it,
beat his breast and said he was a louse. Then he 'explained'
it; he said he wasn't the only one to complain, and why
pick on him; he said he was unhappy, that he hadn't heard
from his divorced wife Gloria since he left California; that
he loved her dearly and she was breaking his heart. He
began to feel pretty sorry for himself, and Aaron said, "Skip
it, you're breaking *my* heart; and let me see you get the lead
out of your ass. There's a job to be done and we have no
one else to do it." For Garfield played sick as well (he was
generally drunk), which saved him the trouble of going on
maneuvers, of escorting the daily 'sick, lame and lazy' to
young Doc Simon, and keeping a case-book on them. He

let his adjutant, Mike Pavlos, a cock-eyed Greek who was a swell guy, do all the work.

And it's true that he wasn't the only one to complain. The fine flower of international feeling between the Spanish and the Americans seemed to have withered; familiarity had bred distrust, if not contempt. We had had a Spanish *teniente* in charge of Section Three, who had had to be replaced; he was a menace. He corralled the Spanish and told them what he thought of the Internationals; he disliked being under Lopoff's orders (though company commander, Aaron was only a *teniente* himself); he distrusted foreigners on principle, and he did Franco's work beautifully. So specific was the case against him—chauvinism, agitation and disobedience of orders—that he was removed from the Battalion as well as from the company. But he had watered the persistent nationalism of the young Spanish, and the seed was flourishing. A language barrier is difficult to overcome in any event; most of us could not speak it fluently, could not mull over our ideas with our comrades. Hence, with notable exceptions, the two groups tended to drift apart, to stick together in national units, to distrust one another. My replacement by a Spanish adjutant who owned the beautiful name of Teopisto Perich Salat (and was beautiful in his person, as well as being a writer of plays for children) was a victory for the native sons, but Aaron still commanded the company, Pavlos Fortis Section One, Jack Hoshooley Section Two and Tabb, Wentworth and Hercules commanded three of the company's six *pelotons;* there were several American squad-leaders. (Yet we were in the vast minority.) And by and large the quality of the American rank-and-file seemed none too good. We had a

couple drunks, a couple known deserters, some guys who
had served time in labor battalions, some weaklings, some
inutiles. The Spanish never got tight, and when the Americans did they were conspicuous. All sorts of artificial respira-
tion was applied by the Brigade and the Battalion commissariats, to pump up morale and international friendship,
but circumstances were against them. We were without
doubt the tail-end of the International Brigades; thousands
of the best, the strongest comrades, had been wounded or
killed off. The Spanish eagerly read of the Non-Intervention Committee's plans (the Government had accepted it
without reservation, but Franco maintained significant silence) and the day did not pass when they did not say
to some one, "You're going home soon." It was a question
that was colored by desire. This was a real and growing
situation, and when we talked of it—Leonard Lamb, Ed
Rolfe, Dick Rusciano, Morrie Goldstein (Lamb's commissar) and Harold Smith—we shook our heads. The future
was none too bright to us.

We marched at midnight and the night was cold. There
was, as usual, confusion in the night, men lost from their
units and calling, "Company One?" "*Segundia Compania?*"
"*Qué Battalon?*" All plates or equipment that might rattle
had been ordered into packsacks or under blankets and we
moved with relative silence on the road. Trucks passed
through us, their lights casting the men's shadows against
the trees beside the road, and then they dimmed their lights.
I thought of Aaron in Barcelona, and remembering a recent
day spent at Tarragona and its beach, I was hoping that he
was having a better time than I had. Tarragona had been a

dead city on an empty sea. It was peopled with civilians; there were signs of recent bombings, but the civilians seemed sort of tentative; you expected them to disappear at a moment's notice; and the ruins left by the air-bombs might have been left by the Romans, like the Roman ruins near the shore. We had swum in the warm blue Mediterranean and eaten a fair meal in a little restaurant down by the beach, where the local children begged for our left-overs, and Yale Stuart, the life-of-the-party chief of the Battalion staff, even had some *Camels,* and some of the men had gone to the local cat-house. But I wandered through the streets, looking into stores that had nothing to sell, noting the tobacco shops with signs NO HAY TABACO and the restaurants and hotels with signs NO HAY COMIDA, and there was nothing to do. Girls walked in the streets with the usual bare legs and high heels, the light tight-fitting summer dresses, their naturally beautiful black hair bleached a strident blond. They had high, firm and separated breasts and lovely buttocks that moved with the beauty of precision instruments, but I could not talk to them; I had never been able to pick up any girl, drunk or sober. Like the deserted multi-colored *cabañas* fading on the shore, relics of a better day when Tarragona beach had seen gaiety and laughing people and their children, the town was faded and seemed fly-specked. I was glad to leave it for the Brigade again. But perhaps Barcelona was different; I had never seen it.

We marched all night and before dawn Aaron was suddenly there; he had come up in a truck, and I felt better. We marched in silence, our feet sore with the many kilometers, and at dawn we camped in an olive field about three kilometers from the Ebro, northwest of Falset. "What is this anyhow?" the men were saying. "Are we going to cross the river, or is this a maneuver?" There was no way of knowing; it might have been a tactical maneuver; part of a large-scale troop-movement, possibly an offensive on a bigger scale than ever; perhaps an important Fascist victory had been won in the south (the fall of Sagunto was rumored imminent) and we were going to initiate a diversion to relieve that pressure.

All day we rested under the trees, handling our sore and filthy feet with tender fingers, careful to watch for *avion.* Aaron looked clean and had clean clothes (he went to Barcelona with 5000 pesetas he had partly borrowed); he was close-shaved and therefore looked cleaner than usual, for his beard was very black and heavy.

"Well," I said, "did you do it?"

"Yes."

"What was it like?"

"She was very young; very pretty. We had a good supper and we went to the movies. Somehow I *had* to take her to the movies. She was very kind, but not much interested."

That night we marched again till dawn, down long and winding hills and up through sleeping villages, and when the sun rose we disappeared into a deep *baranco,* a ravine north of Mora la Nueva, about halfway between the river-towns of Garcia and Flix, three kilometers away. The day-time heat was fierce, and we could get little shelter from the sun; we were exhausted and our muscles ached, and the slight stream that ran through the *baranco* was soon filthy and scummed with soap. In this natural cleft, that rather terrified us, for we could not have climbed out of it very

fast, we stayed for two more days, and here we learned at a
Battalion meeting that the rumors were correct.

"At any moment now," said Captain Wolff, smiling at the
men sitting around him and below the terrace where he was
standing, "we are going to cross the Ebro. In this action the
entire Army of the East will participate, so we will not
be alone. That means that all up and down the Ebro, from
Tortosa to a point a hundred and fifty kilometers above it,
over eighty thousand men will be crossing simultaneously.
We do not know yet in which *echelon* our Brigade will
cross, but the objective of this entire operation is simple—
and daring. We are going to relieve the pressure on Valencia.
We are going to cross the Ebro, travel fast and light, penetrate deep into Fascist territory and hold positions while
other troops come over on bridges that will be constructed
while we're marching inland. Behind us will come trucks
and ambulances, with munitions, food and supplies; naturally, it may take some time for them to get across, and
ammo will come first.

"This action has been planned long in advance, and we
have plenty of information from our sources behind the
Fascist lines. The forces facing us across the river are the
Fifteenth Battalion of Burgos, of the Regimiento de Merida.
They are largely new recruits, youngsters who have seen no
action; they are few and they are untrained. There are only
three battalions holding the river-front from Mora de Ebro
to a point twenty kilometers to the north. We know the
names of the Fascist company-commanders. We know where
their troops are located and exactly how many there are. We
know where to find their ammunition dumps. We know
that in Corbera and Gandesa there are *intendencias,* and

we know what's in them. At both places there is chocolate, food and tobacco, and at Corbera there is supposed to be some beer! There are only fourteen machine-guns facing us at this point, some of them light guns, but this small force can withstand a frontal attack, because its fortifications are excellent. Therefore, the first *echelon* to cross will have to maneuver through, instead of attacking them. The main line of fortifications we will meet when we come to it—thirty kilometers inland, at Gandesa, which our American comrades may remember. We are going to avenge our comrades who fell there last April.

"If this operation is successful, and it *will* be successful, it will deliver a major blow to Franco. He will have to abandon his attack on Valencia and divert some of the three hundred thousand troops he has in that sector, to counter-attack us on the other side. We will have nothing to worry about on that score for at least a couple days. Gandesa is the Italian base and it will be defended. Fortification will be the order of the day. Every man is to stand by, prepared to move at a moment's notice. *Viva la República!*"

"*Viva!*"

"*Viva La Quince Brigada!*" Wolff shouted.

"*Viva!*"

"*Viva El Lobo!*" the men shouted, and Wolff joined his voice with ours. . . .

. . . Ed Rolfe, who had been transferred from Lamb's company to the Brigade staff as front-line correspondent for the *Volunteer for Liberty*, had a list. On it there were named about a hundred Americans who were imprisoned behind the Fascist lines. There were few whose names I knew—

most had been taken before the Aragon retreat. But Moish Taubman was there, and Howard Earl who had been 'cut to pieces by machine-gun fire' at Belchite was there too, as well as 'Lopez' the Brooklyn Jewish Spaniard. So we were tickled stiff . . . "What am I supposed to do in this business?" I asked Aaron, who was busy neatly folding non-essentials into his pack-sack, to be delivered to the kitchen truck. "You're carried on the company *plantilla* as an observer, you dope," he said. He was taking nothing with him, except a pair of socks and a couple handkerchiefs; he refused to take a blanket, but he had a pistol. "I'll use you as I see fit, and Christ knows what good you are." "Look," I said, "I want to give you a couple addresses." He looked at me, but handed me his note-book. I wanted to say something but it was hard to say. I opened my mouth, shut it again, and then the words came in a rush: "Do you want to give me an address?" "No," he said . . . The canteen came up on the supper truck and we both bought a pair of brand new overalls; it was good to have something that had enough pockets in it, big ones. They cost only sixty pesetas and we threw away all non-essential clothing, wearing nothing but a shirt and overalls . . . Teopisto, the new adjutant, smiled at everything; nothing seemed to worry him, nothing seemed to feaze him, and while we prepared for action he slept, his mouth open, snoring, his beautiful white teeth glinting in the sun . . . Curtis the clerk was going frantic checking on hand grenades, cartridges, rifles and sling-straps, canteens (which had to be covered to prevent them from shining in the sun), dry rations that were issued to each man. There were other reasons for his nervousness, as well . . . Harold Smith was everywhere, supervising everything . . . "Damn it," said Garfield, "I haven't heard from Gloria. I'm going to write to her and tell her she's a bitch." He bit his nails . . . Aaron wrote some letters and I wrote some letters; every Spanish boy in that battalion of almost seven hundred men wrote at least one letter. . . .

At midnight of the 24th of July we climbed and threaded our way out of the ravine, stumbling over our feet and the slippery rocks that lay in the tiny stream, falling on the slopes, touching the man in front to maintain contact. It was pitch black; conversation, smoking were forbidden. The roads were jammed with trucks, moving in complete darkness, loaded with small pieces of artillery, ammunition, tandem machine-guns, sections of pontoon bridges all ready to be put together. We began to have some understanding of the scope of this operation and it cheered us; we saw more bridge sections, huge barrels lying beside the road under the trees, boats; we saw mule-trains carrying smaller cases, machine-guns; dispatch-riders on motorcycles weaved in and out among the marching men and the *camions,* miraculously avoiding collision. The Big Dipper, which we had seen the nights before, was hidden, but the world was alive with movement on that night, and I thought suddenly of Times Square, brilliant with lights and people going to the theater and the movies; the neon signs, the barkers, the pencil venders and the newsboys; the subdued roar of cars and the smell of gasoline. Lovely girls walked arm in arm with their boy friends, smiling into their faces with bright painted eyes. The theaters were letting out somewhere in the world, people were going home to bed with each other, the kids were sound asleep in Brooklyn . . . and we left the road and cut into a wide dried stream bed that flowed down the Ebro. Two hours before dawn we camped on this stream bed, dropping to sleep with complete exhaustion on the sharpened pebbles. The smell of water was strong in the damp night; a night bird sang.

With dawn we woke to see the coffee truck bumping up the river bed, but before we had time to form up the order came to march, and there was no breakfast. Ed Fliegel, the mailman, ran up and down the lines of men, yelling out names, handing out the few letters that he had. There was no word from the kids, from any one. "I'm sorry, Al," he said. "I wish I had a letter for you." That was all right. We moved cautiously along the 'shore' of the dried stream, in single file, and the kids looked around them with the bright, sudden movements of birds. We heard the shell coming (like tearing silk) and we ducked, but it burst at least half a kilometer behind us, against the hillside. The line started and stopped; men laughed and joked, shoved each other and sat down till the line should move again. We heard the next shell, and only the Spanish boys dropped flat on the ground; it was way over. Angel, the little four-foot barber, looked at me from the ground and said, *"Malo,* Bessee, *malo." "Es nada, hombre,"* I said. *"Tengo miedo,"* he said, and we looked back at the harmless puff of white and brown smoke against the hill, and the gun did not fire many times.

Nearer the shore we entered the woods; there were thick growths of cane and marsh-weeds and we halted in the shelter of the foliage. Many men opened a can of sardines and began to cram the small fish into their mouths. Many drank half the water in their canteens; for although the sun was not yet high, we were burning up with thirst. The river was in sight; you could feel it, even if you could not see it. We knew now that we were not the first to cross; the Slavs, Czechs and Poles had crossed long before dawn, so everything must have been all right.

Aaron appeared from around a stand of cane. "Bess!" he said, "come look at this!" His face was bright like the face of a happy child, and we went around the cane and stood looking at the water. Broad and placid in the sun, it was filled with little boats, little rowboats full of men, moving sedately back and forth across the river, drifting somewhat with the swift current.

"It's Prospect Park in the summer time!" he said. "It's wonderful!"

III

THE OFFENSIVE

8

WE EMERGED from the wooded banks and were sliding down onto the beach when the plane appeared—a bi-motored Italian bomber that was being used as an observation-plane, it was painted a lovely pale blue and was almost invisible against the sky, *"Abajo!"* the men shouted, and we flattened against the bank, onto the sand below. There was a mule standing at my head when we heard the hideous whistling of the bombs and covered the back of our necks with our hands. There was a blind uproar and a deafening crash and the bank caved in onto us; the mule balked and reared and the men yelled. The plane zoomed and headed down the river, and Aaron shouted, "Let's go!" and we ran for the boats.

It was a lousy feeling getting into the little rowboats, being rowed slowly and deliberately across the wide, swift current, open and unprotected. We watched for the plane and it reappeared, roared down the opposite shore with its four machine-guns going and climbed off the bank into the sky. We touched shore, jumped out and ran for the shelter of a few trees, but now the plane was on our side again, and it combed the shore with its guns. No one said a word, no one gave a word of command, and the plane came on, not a hundred feet above the ground, kicking up the sand with

its machine-gun bullets, sewing four seams along the shore
and through the few trees, its propeller screaming like a
panther. With one voice, 1400 rifles spoke; we were suddenly filled with an unutterable exaltation, and we watched
the plane over our heads, saw the glint of its rivets, and
fired deliberately. From all over the two shores of the river,
two battalions of men with rifles and light machine-guns
were firing at the plane, and our hearts were in our throats.
It rose above us, hung on its prop, almost stood on its tail,
its motors groaning with the strain of its suddenly altered
position, and it took on altitude and disappeared. "That's it!"
the men shouted. "That's the way to treat those bastards!
Let him come back, the son-of-a-bitch; we'll put some lead
in his ass, the c ... s ...... !" But the plane did not come back.
We laughed and shouted; everything we saw was immensely
funny—the cable they were stringing across the river, on
which to weave the pontoon-bridge, a mule being coaxed
through the shallow water, straining against its halter, a
huge piece of jagged shrapnel one of the men found on the
sand. "Boy," we said, "that could make a hole in you;
hombre, that could do a thing or two!" The Spanish tossed
off their universal expletive, *"Me cago en Dios!"* One man
put it in his pack as a souvenir. "That pilot had his nerve
with him," some one said. "He had guts coming so low."

Through a narrow *baranco* we marched inland till we hit
a road, and then continued marching. Scouts were put out
on the flanks and at point; you could see the flankers, moving up and down the hills far over to our right and left,
watching for the possibility of ambush; for we had no way of
knowing where the enemy might be. He might have retreated kilometers, or he might be planning to stand us off

at any point on our march toward Gandesa. The sun was high now and the heat was intense; thirst was a torture. The men dropped their superfluous equipment; blankets and pack-sacks, mess-tins and extra clothing littered the sides of the road. I showed the Spanish boys in the *plana mayor* (the company staff) how to put leaves inside their caps to ward off sun-stroke, but worse than the heat was the lack of water. We stopped frequently on the dusty road and sent out details, but there was not enough water for all. The dust had choked us and our tongues were swollen. The men ran back and forth a dozen times with loads of canteens, but no one got enough. We were wet from head to foot with sweat; we were exhausted by the march and the excitement. Where was the enemy? Where would we meet him? Were there eyes, even now, watching us from the wooded hills, reporting by field-telephone; were replacements coming up to engage us?

When we rested, leaning against the embankments that enclosed the road, taking cover in the little shade from eyes that might be watching from the sky, we could look around. The countryside was wooded and hilly; Gandesa was only twenty-one kilometers inland from the river, but somewhere ahead of us, to our left or right, were the forces of the XIIIth Brigade, and possibly they had made contact with the enemy. They had. A captured ambulance came past us, toward the river, its cab and body jammed with wounded men in fresh white bandages; they lifted their fists in greeting and we cheered them. Behind us, at the river, we could hear other planes bombing the men on the shores, bombing the bridges as they were constructed; we felt somewhat trapped, but we could still advance; only there was no way of knowing how far we could advance before we would meet the first of their counter-attacks. It would not take long for motorized divisions to come up from the Levante front with artillery and tanks; it would take still less time for a few squadrons of airplanes to arrive.

Aaron looked low, and I asked what was bothering him. He looked back toward the Ebro and said, "The river."

"What's the matter with the river?"

"Did you know Blackie Maphralian?" he said. "He was in command of Company 2 last March. I was his adjutant."

"I saw him once, when I went on a patrol during Batea. He was a sailor, wasn't he?"

"Yeh," Aaron said. "We came all the way to the river together, in the retreat. He was a queer guy; a tough guy; a sweet son-of-a-bitch. He couldn't get across the river, though he started."

There was nothing for me to say, and so I didn't say it. "I got to love that guy," said Aaron.

The word came to move again, and we trudged along the road in a cloud of white dust. Every once in awhile the *avion* signal came, and we scattered for the sides of the road, the ditches, the wooded patches, and lay low till the planes were gone. In a way we were grateful for those planes, although they were looking for us; for their appearance was the signal for a rest, and we were burning up with the heat and the thirst; our bellies rumbled with hunger.

The guys were tired; they were grouchy. Arthur Madden, tall and lanky, was tireder than most. So was Lennond Lino, the young Italian-American, who had no business being at the front. He was really *inutile;* he was thin and undernourished; he was sick. He had a chronic gonorrhea; he had a gonorrheal rheumatism; he had syphilis as well, and a case of nichthyolopia—he could not see at night. But since he had accepted his lot with a twisted smile and did not complain, he was with us. He was a good soldier; a staunch anti-fascist; he was Italian. Madden complained all the time; he had been taken out of the auto-park to join the infantry and he wanted to go home. His wife sent him cigarettes every week, enclosed in an envelope, and on the bottom of her letters she invariably wrote, 'Censor: Please put these cigarettes back in the envelope after you have read the letter.' (The censor was considerably annoyed.) Ed Rolfe was tired, but fresher than usual. Talking to him now, I recalled the time when we marched from Tarrega to Fondarella, before he was attached to the Battalion staff, and I asked if I could carry his rifle. He refused. Teopisto Perich Salat, our adjutant, was everywhere, granting his *Pepsodent* smile to all with great impartiality. Sam Spiller, Aaron's personal runner, was streaked with dirt and sweat, and so was Joaquin, the lanky Alicante peasant-boy. The other runners did not work so hard.

"Adelante!" came the word, and we picked ourselves up with reluctance and kept going. The sun was at its height and its heat was a literal burden on our backs. It was dry, but we were sopping wet; when we stopped to rest we could smell ourselves; we had not washed in days; we had not bathed in weeks. But when a real rest was called—for an hour or so—I was sent out on patrol to determine the identity of some mysterious figures two kilometers away on a hill, that Wolff had noticed through his Zeiss binoculars. I cursed that man.

"What's the matter, poppa?" Aaron said. "Can't you take

it?" "Fuck *you*," I said. "Nobody asked you to come to Spain, grampa," he said, "or are you one of these Moscow minions I hear so much about?" "I'm a counter-revolutionary Trotskyite wrecker," I said, and he said, "Get going. . . ."

. . . That night we took up positions in an extended line along a low ridge that faced southwest. It was cold, and the men brought armfuls of straw from a hay-stack that stood nearby, to lie in when they were off guard. In a small stone barn near by Aaron, Harold Smith, Garfield and Curtis and a few of the runners found shelter from the cold wind that harassed the men. Smith had found some *White Rose* tea during a trip to Barcelona to have his eye-glasses repaired, and he had a box of *Domino* cube-sugar, but Aaron would not permit us to build a small fire in the barn, because the barn had no door and the open space faced the enemy. The Ebro lay behind us, and word had come that Mora de Ebro had been occupied by our troops on the left flank, that the advance was proceeding according to schedule, over the entire hundred-and-fifty-kilometer front. No food had come up yet, and we had run out of our iron rations, but when you cannot eat you can sometimes sleep; it always helps.

Early the next morning food did come, food and tobacco captured from a town that we had taken, Fatarella. There was a good brand of Italian canned fish in tomato sauce, there was a rock-hard brand of chocolate, better than any we had had in Spain, there were cookies (slightly sweet) and a multiplicity of tobacco, both loose and in Italian-made cigars that we broke up and used to roll cigarettes. "The bastards have got something in their favor," Harold said. "They've got good food, the sons-of-bitches." But we had little time to speculate on this good fortune—of course, the Fascists had everything they needed, no one was embargoing Italy or Germany or Portugal. They could bring in food as well as guns—for the order came to march, and we advanced again toward Gandesa, watching for the ever-present *avion,* expecting to meet the enemy at every turn of the road. We marched in close-order, and again Aaron put me out on the flank, where I had a hell of a time keeping up with the main body on the road. There was the sound of rifle and machine-gun fire in the distance, and some artillery ahead of us, and we quickened our pace; something was beginning to happen. From the top of a hill we saw a small body of troops huddled on the road, and they were not moving. Word came back that we had some prisoners, and we hurried down the hill onto the road.

Here we found a company of the Fascists, that had been taken after a brief skirmish with Captain Lamb's Company 1, and they were already under guard. We were startled to see that they looked so much like us, Spanish, dressed in nondescript pickup uniforms, dirty and uncombed, unshaved, exhausted and patently terrified. They kept their arms above their heads even when they were ordered to lower them. They timidly offered us cigarettes, of which they had a considerable supply. They emptied their pockets of anything that might be called a weapon, even pocket-knives—which were immediately returned to them. They expected to be shot on sight by the 'Reds' and their officers had obviously removed any insignia they might have been wearing, but instead of being shot they had to stand around on that road for about two hours, while their *avion*—observation planes and squadrons of heavy bombers—wheeled and banked and inspected the terrain. We did not like it any more than they, but either the forces did not look important from the air, or the enemy observers knew what was going on, for they left us alone. (Ambushed on his return from marching these young captured conscripts back to head-quarters, Yale Stuart, Battalion-staff commander, was hit by a dum-dum bullet which required the amputation of his arm. Afterwards I used to think of him, always smiling, always gay, and wonder if he would ever be so gay again.

We marched again, and again we camped at night; there was a bitter wind blowing and this time there was no shelter, not even straw. We lay exposed on the hard ground under olive trees, huddled against each other for the warmth the human body radiates, shivering despite that warmth. Worn out by more than the fatigue of marching, Aaron snored at my side; we lay dove-tailed into one another, but I could not sleep. I thought of home and of where I was, of the sleeping men lying all around; I sat up and rolled a bad cigarette and smoked it under cover of Aaron's back (neither of us had a blanket any more). I thought of the company of prisoners who had been caught behind our lines by the swiftness of their own retreat, just as many of us had been caught behind the Fascist lines last April—and I remembered the difference in the fate of these respective prisoners. For the peasants on this side of the Ebro had told us what happened to our prisoners during the Aragon offensive, how they had been taken out every night in batches of three to five, and shot down. They showed us their unmarked graves and told us (since many of them had been forced to witness these executions as an example) how our men lifted their fists in the Republican salute and shouted, "Death to Fascism!"

I was finally dropping off to sleep, watching the moon scudding behind the clouds, when the firing began over on our left. The rifle bullets snapped and hummed over our heads, and I saw Aaron rise from the ground beside me as though he had been yanked aloft by a wire. He ran a few steps and flattened to the ground. Men shouted; the crisp rattle of bolts sounded and individual men started firing in the direction from which the bullets came, but the officers were yelling, *"Halto fuego!* Stop firing! *Halto fuego!"* and the flurry soon died down. "Enemy patrol," the men said, "a company of Moors," they said, "an ambush," but later that morning a few of us were told of what had happened; a sentry of our Company 3 had seen a bush walking and fired at it; his company awoke from sleep and fired with him, and we replied. Three or four men were wounded; no one killed. "Dumb," said Pavlos Fortis, *"muy* dumb. *Mucho pinta."* I kidded Aaron about leaving his pistol on the ground and bounding for cover like a deer. "What the hell," he said. "I did it automatically; I heard firing and took cover." "But you *were* covered," I said. "You were lying down behind a tree." "None of your lip, grampa," he said.

Every step we took brought us farther from the Ebro, and there were, as yet, no signs of communication with the rear. A bit of food came up, however, dried *bacalao* (codfish, very salty) and a petrified sort of blood-sausage that was more gristle than meat. We moved on, and the sound of firing came again from ahead of us; we met patrols of our own men, of other outfits, acting as rearguards, and we learned that the 24th had contacted the enemy and was in

action a short distance ahead. We took positions on a
wooded hill facing Gandesa and Villalba (where we had
run through the Fascist camp during the retreat). Our
machine-gun company was with us, and the men rested in
the growing heat, in the dubious shelter of two-foot trenches
scratched behind the pine woods on the crest. We waited.
Most of the time we were waiting—waiting for orders, for
communications to be established, wires strung, ammunition
to come up, for food, for water, for the first-aid unit under
Doctor Simon to be established. Now we lay on our faces in
the wood, propping stones up in front of us, for a few stray
bullets were coming over the hill, and beyond the valley
there was a machine-gun talking. It began to look like action
now, and at such times the tension is intolerable. Your
mouth dries up and you spit cotton; your stomach clenches
and unclenches, your bowels writhe and there is a deep ache
in your chest. You look around and you see other men sitting, talking calmly, showing no fear in their faces, acting
as though they were on a picnic in the woods; and you
realize with astonishment that if you could see yourself, that
is exactly what you would see. For men do not like to show
fear in the presence of other men, and they put on a good
act.

As always, there was confusion. Small units ran back and
forth, looking for their proper places, men were unrolling
stretchers, bringing up wooden boxes of rifle and machine-
gun ammunition, opening the boxes and the tin cans inside
with their bayonets. Men hastily cleaned rifles; they stuffed
the bullets in their pockets; they hung the hand-grenades on
their belts; they buttoned those pockets that had buttons and
threw away any surplus equipment that might hamper

movement. It was business-like, it was efficient, it was completely undramatic. There was thorough concentration on the job in hand. Lopoff was away at a meeting of company commanders behind our hill, and we lay flat and waited. I gathered the company *plana mayor* in one section of the woods, and told them to stay covered, but to listen for a shout from me, and when I moved to follow. "Bess-*ee,*" the little *barbero* Angel said, "what's going to happen?" "I don't know," I said. He had grown a little beard while we were still in camp beyond the Ebro, and he looked like a miniature man, complete and well-proportioned, but a midget. He spoke with the falsetto of a twelve-year old.

Aaron returned and said to me, "We're going to attack that machine-gun nest on the hill beyond. Pavlos will take Section 1 over and try to flank it from the left; Jack Hoshooley will flank it from the right, and Guillermo's section will go straight ahead. There'll be cover-fire from the machine-gun company. I'm sending Guillermo and Tabb with their section now; follow me with your lousy *plana mayor* when I go. O.K., baby?" (I had seen a lot of war-pictures one time.) "Right!" I said, and Aaron glanced at me, and disappeared. . . .

. . . Seeing them crouching behind bushes, lying flat behind rocks, I understood and I wanted to stay with them, be with them myself, but Aaron was ahead now, saying, "Let's go!" so I shouted, *"Plana mayor de la Segunda, adelante! Vamos!"* and waved my arm the way they do in the movies, and followed hot on his heels, stumbling down the hill, hopping over rocks and around bushes, seeing the pistol in his hand (like in the movies), hearing the machine-gun across the little valley accelerate its rhythm, become insistent. I did not look back to see if they were following, Joaquin and Sam and Antonio and Curtis and Garfield and the other Spanish runners and the barber; it was tough going down that hill, hopping down the terraces and around the low fig trees, keeping up with Aaron, who could run like a deer and was doing exactly that, automatically zigzagging so as to avoid a fine alignment of enemy rifle-sights. I had to keep up with him; it was lonely only ten feet behind. "Be careful," I was yelling, "watch yourself, boy," but he did not answer.

They had spotted us moving down the hill and into the olive field that lay below, and now we had to move faster than before, using the tree trunks for momentary shelter, dodging from one to the other, groaning for breath. "Come on, Pop," Aaron yelled to me, "come on, old man," and we dashed from behind the tree, instinctively ducking when the bullets snapped close to our ears, running toward the right, up-grade. There was a momentary glimpse of Guillermo's section to our left, infiltrating rapidly toward the rise on top of which the enemy machine-gun was established, and we ran, scrambled, slid uphill into a sheltered place between two stone walls that bordered a sort of lane. We leaned against the wall, pleased with the natural shelter of the place; no bullets could get into it. We had passed two or three of Guillermo's sections lying on the hillside as we ran up it . . . Van Pataghan and Valentine Koppel . . . and they soon came in between the walls. But no one had followed us, not one of the company's staff, and when I stood up to look back at the hill we had left, Aaron grabbed me by the arm and yanked me down. "Keep your head down, you dope," he said, "or your kids will have to get another poppa." We sat there choking for breath and sweating. "I wish the hell I knew what was going on," Aaron said. "I can't sit here and wait." He got up, crouching, and started for the open space at the other end of the wall. He took Koppel and Van Pataghan along. "Want me to come?" I said, hoping he'd say No, and he said, "No, stay here," and was gone. Immediately I regretted my cowardice, and started after him, but then the power of rationalization got to work again and said, He told you to stay here, and he's your commander, so stay.

Teopisto appeared, streaming with perspiration, his smile wiped off for the moment. *"A dónde está El Comandante?"* he said, and I said, *"Fuera; buscando."* He shook his head and sat down by me. There was an explosion just outside, and one of the walls partly caved in. We had covered our faces with our arms, and when we looked again he said, *"Mortero."* They threw a couple more mortars, but they were wide, and we debated whether they had noticed us take cover behind the wall, or whether the mortars were intended for some one else. Mortars were bad; you couldn't hear them coming.

Aaron reappeared for a few moments, coming rapidly around the wall and sitting down. "Where is your Goddamned *plana mayor?*" he said. "I need some runners. Sent Van and Valentine up ahead." Tabb and Guillermo appeared from the lower end of the culvert, streaked with dirt and panting, their faces twisted with dismay and horror. Guillermo talked so rapidly I could not understand him; he kept throwing down his hands, cursing, gesticulating. "Where's the rest of your section?" I asked Tabb, and he looked at me as though he would have liked to bite my head off. Finally he said, "We were almost up to the machine-gun; there *is* no more to the section." They talked with Aaron, drew a few deep breaths and then went off again, with him.

Gradually, one at a time, the members of the *plana mayor* began to appear. Garfield, in his shorts, his eyes wide with terror, his heavy first-aid *bolsa* strapped around him. Then came Sam and Joaquin and Antonio Anton, and Curtis. The rest did not appear at all. "Why didn't you come before?" I asked, and they shrugged their shoulders. Joaquin was disposed to argue the point with me; that the fire was too hot, that it was dangerous, but I shut him up. No word came from Aaron and I was afraid for him; I sent Sam and Antonio out to look for him, and told Sam to stick by his side, Antonio to report back when there were orders. Koppel came crawling around the end of the stone wall, and we crawled to him and pulled him further down the little lane. "Where'd they get you?" we said, and he laughed. "Right through one cheek of my ass," he said. We stripped him of his pants and Garfield bandaged him, his hands shaking like aspen leaves. "It's bad out there," Val said, looking up through his eyeglasses. "We rushed the machine-gun and they withdrew it, but they've got it set up again." He paused; then we all flattened ourselves on the ground as the mortar went off over our heads and the rocks tumbled onto us.

"They've got us spotted," Curtis said. "Now we're going to get it."

"Go on," I said, and Koppel said, "We've got three dead so far that I know of."

"Who?"

"Kurculiotis; got it right between the eyes, leading his

squad—" he waved his arm to the left, indicating the general location of the body. "The tall guy, too," he said, "what's his name, Madden . . . Lino." Christ, I thought, how logical! They were throwing their trench-mortars in earnest now, in front of the wall, behind it, to the left and right; it would only be a matter of time before one would drop straight in. "Let's get out of here," Curtis said, and I said, "There's no place else to go; besides, Aaron said to stay here." "Any place would be better than this."

It was hot; outside, re-echoing in the valley was the sound of rapid machine-gun fire, ours and theirs, and far off to the left of the sector, some artillery. Their planes were overhead at all times, but they witheld their stuff; the skirmish was too diffuse for them to find anything to unload upon. We had no water and we had no food; we had no tobacco now, and so we just sat or lay flat, wishing they would throw their mortars some place else. The sun beat upon our heads and we lay there wondering what was going on in our particular sector, what was the significance of the intermittent firing, whether we were advancing or holding our own. For to the average soldier battle always remains a chaos and an impression of immense confusion; he has only a worm's-eye view of the affair; he has no way of knowing what it's all about. One minute he is advancing under fire; the next he is lying low; the next withdrawing. He receives definite orders and they are immediately countermanded; he rarely sees the enemy and the fire that is directed at him assumes astonishing impersonality, as though it were independent of any human agency.

Suddenly Tabb was there, his eyes glazed, his face and neck and tunic soaked in blood; he had an improvised bandage around his head, from under which the good red blood oozed in a glistening pattern, and Garfield was improving on the bandage. "Does it hurt?" he said, and Tabb shook his head. He sat on the ground, looking straight ahead of him, and it was impossible to tell whether he was merely stunned or afraid. He spoke logically, choosing his words even more slowly than usual.

"Hoshooley got hit," he said. "Nothing bad; in the other shoulder." (Jack had been wounded before.)

I told Garfield to help Tabb back to the Battalion *sanidad,* on the hill from which we had launched the attack, but Tabb said, "I know the way; I can get there all right by myself."

"No," said Garfield, "I wouldn't think of letting you go alone." His hands trembled as he adjusted the bandage, wiped Tabb's face with a piece of gauze.

"All right," I said. "Get him back to Doc Simon, and then come right back here; we'll need you." The wounded man stood up, his eyes apparently focused on far space, and he moved with deliberation as Garfield helped him, picking up his feet like a mechanical doll and putting them down again. "I'll see you later, Bess," he said.

Teopisto looked at me and said, *"Mal herido?"*

"Creo que no."

"Buen chico."

"Sí."

Bessie, the note said, *Am reforming sections, advancing flanks. Stay there till almost dark; then bring plana mayor up to new lines. Send back to E-M for ammo (rifle and m.g.) Lopoff.*

Antonio Anton Pastor was out of breath; his plump body shook, but he still retained an amusing military preci-

sion in his salute, and the step backward he invariably took
when I told him to return to Aaron with my note. I sent
Joaquin with him, and leaving Teopisto in charge of the
command post (it was his job, after all), Curtis and I went
back to Battalion headquarters, the long way around, and
asked for ammo. George Watt said it was coming up on mule-
back, and should be there any minute. Ed Rolfe was nowhere
in sight, so we hung around awhile until we were sure the
ammo was on the way, then started back.

Halfway there we met Van Pataghan, carrying Joaquin,
the runner, pig-a-back. There was a bullet through the Spanish boy's foot, and Van shook his head and said, "It's bad out
there; we tried to get across a vine field and they got him."
Joaquin kept urging Van to hurry; he was badly frightened
and his face was streaked with tears, but despite the burden
he was carrying, Van Pataghan seemed in no hurry to get
going. "You know about Kukalotis," he said, "and Madden
and Lino, don't you?" "Yes," we said. "Aaron's a great guy,"
he said.

"Por favor," said Joaquin, kicking his good leg, *"portame
al medico, camarada."* "Keep your shirt on," I said. *"Qué
dices?"* They left, and Curtis and I found our way back to
the command post in the dark, where we discovered the rest
of the company staff, including the barber and Lara, the
furiel, and rounding them all up we started searching for
the company. There was no sign of Garfield yet. . . .

Even in the dark you could make out that the Battalion
sector was in the general shape of a horseshoe. If you stood in
the middle of the shoe, facing the curve, you were standing in
a vine field that was always under fire. To your left was a

low wooded ridge, and the Fascists were dug in on a hill beyond, about six hundred meters away. Directly ahead there was a small wooded island in the vine field, where we had a couple machine-gun nests under George Cady (who took over when Jack was hit) and Nat Gross, with Scarlettos, the red-eyed Greek, as one gunner and an eighteen-year-old boy named Charlie Bartolotta as the other. They were alone in the middle of the field, with the enemy on three sides of them. On your right was another wooded hill, and somewhere farther to the right were the lines of the 3d Division (all Spanish), that faced Villalba and the church-tower from which a Fascist machine-gunner was doing effective work.

"You'll have to run back and forth all night between here and the 3d Division," Aaron told me. "You're the only guy who knows where they are. Make contact about once an hour. Meantime, sit down and take it easy." Behind the hill on which our machine-gun company was placed, there was a multitude of men of Companies 1 and 2, lying on the bare ground, trying to sleep. Equipment was littered all about; we even found some tobacco in a knapsack and divided it; we found some sardines and some canned *bonito*. It was cold; we were hungry and exhausted, but there would be no possibility of sleep. "We're going to attack at dawn," Aaron said, pointing at the hill to our left. "We've got orders to take that hill across the way."

We rummaged in the abandoned packsack as we talked, finding more tobacco and a sack that belonged to one of the other runners who'd been wounded. Aaron took his military book and put it in his pocket, and I found a small wallet that would be useful. "Poor Juan," Aaron said. "He got it bad."

We sat down and were silent, smoking the boy's tobacco; then we got up and moved over to the little wooded island where Cady and Gross were in command, and sat quietly chewing the rag with them, eating some salmon they had found. "I'll get going," I said to Aaron. "Why don't you catch some sleep?" "I think I will," he said, and they found a blanket for him.

It was lonesome crossing the open space at night (there was a moon), moving silently through the vines in the hope that the enemy gunners would not spot you, but once in awhile during the four trips I made before dawn, they must have noticed something moving in the vines, for they let fly with their gun and I had to lie still for quite a time. I thought of Aaron asleep in the machine-gun nest, and wondered what would happen in the morning when we attacked. This was only their rear-guard we had come upon; this was nothing compared to what would come. On one of the trips through the woods that topped our original position between the two stone walls, I found what was left of Harold Smith's *White Rose* tea and sugar-cubes, and put them in my pocket. He had been cursing about that; he had given his packsack to Angel, the barber, to take care of, and he had not seen Angel since. Somewhere up on the hill under which all the men were sleeping, Nick the Greek was sleeping too; I thought of him, of Madden, and of Lino who always wore a bitter smile. . . .

. . . I was still asleep when the first attack was made from the crest of our hill; Aaron did not wake me, but the sound of firing and the earth shaking with the explosion of mortars and sudden artillery came into my dream, and I rose from it to find that the Battalion had gone over. Few men were hanging around, and those who were seemed distracted. They wore an air of intense preoccupation or forced mon- chalance. I looked for Aaron but could not find him. I looked for Harold Smith, the commissar, but Curtis, who was biting his finger-nails, told me he had gone over with the rest. I ran, crouched over, to the top of the ridge and watched from behind a tree. There was nothing to be seen.

Our men would have had to cross a road on the far side of our hill, run down a slope planted to vines and stepped with terraces, charge across about three hundred meters of five- foot vines, before they reached the wooded grade that led up to the hill the Fascists occupied. The fire was hot and the mortars came over regularly, covering the back side of our hill. I retreated back down the slope and lay flat in a little depression underneath a tree. Then suddenly there was a squadron of enemy planes, low-winged monoplanes painted black, that came from our rear and dived at the hill from which we had stepped off, their four machine-guns rattling. They disappeared over the hill, pulled up and winged over and came back behind our lines, pulled up higher, went into a half-roll and a half-loop and came at us again. They were beautiful, and they kept this up for about fifteen minutes and then they went away. Our machine-gun company, on the left flank, was banging away, and then it stopped firing, and the only fire came from the other side; plenty of it, hot rifle and machine-gun, and the mortars, whose high parabola made it impossible for you to hear them coming. And since you could not hear them coming you were prepared (well not exactly) to meet them anywhere. So it was wiser to stay just where you were and hope that one would not land at your feet and smear you.

Aaron appeared with Dick Rusciano, and their faces were drawn and bitter. For once I had sense enough not to ask any questions, and Aaron and Dick sat down by my side and said nothing for a time. Then Dick said, "I knew it would happen; I knew damn well it would happen."

Aaron bit his lip. "I feel like a butcher," he said. "Kicking those kids over; I had to take a couple of them by the seat of the pants." He laughed. He noticed that he had his pistol in his hand, broke it and removed the two empty shells. He looked at me; then looked away.

"Where are they?" I said.

"Out in front. They won't advance; they can't come back." Dick got up and walked away. "Bess," said Aaron, "I had to take a couple by the back of the neck and push them over."

"I know."

Then he said, "I'm going up to see Wolff," and walked along the foot of the ridge toward Battalion headquarters, his hands hanging at his sides, his head bowed. I thought of the men out front; lying in the vines, dead or living and wounded and unable to return till dark. It occurred to me with a start that Aaron had deliberately neglected to wake me that morning, and I wanted to cry.

"Where is that c... Garfield?" Smith said. His hand was wrapped in a handkerchief.

"I don't know."

"It's your *job* to know."

"I haven't seen him since he took Tabb to the *sanidad* yesterday afternoon." I looked at his hand, but he shook his head.

"It's nothing," he said. "Clean through. The hand was useless anyhow." He found it an amusing thing that he should have been plugged through the same hand, twice in the same place, within a half an inch. The nerves had never healed where they had been severed by the first bullet, months before.

"Go to the Doc," I said.

"Later."

Aaron was back and he sat idly cleaning the pistol with a twig and a bit of rag. Garfield appeared and we bawled him out. He said he had been helping Doctor Simon at the *sanidad* and carrying stretchers all night. "Your place was here," said Aaron. "You knew we didn't have another *practicante.*"

Harold said, "There are a lot of wounded comrades on the other side of the hill, right by the road. Go up and dress their wounds." Garfield stood before us in his shorts, and somehow for the first time I noticed the great discrepancy between his hairy masculine legs and the ripe red mouth that was trembling. He moved up the hill behind us reluctantly. And in a few moments he was back.

"The fire's awful hot up there," he said. "It's dangerous to go there now."

"Jesus Christ I *know* it!" Smith said. "Our comrades are bleeding up there. Go and dress their wounds if you can't get them out!" Garfield moved away.

"The god-damn fairy," Harold said. His eyes glinted through the thick glasses; or perhaps it was the reflection of the hot midday sun. "Go to the *sanidad,* Mr. Comic-Star," Aaron said dully. "We won't need you here." "All right," said Harold. "I'll go, but I'll be back." "Don't do us any favors," Aaron said.

"Look, Bess," he said. "You'll have to go over to the 3d Division and ask for reinforcements. They may counter-attack us here." I could see the open space ahead of me, that

lay between the arms of the horseshoe, that was open to their
machine-gun, and I got sore.

"Damn it all," I said. "I'm not a runner! Since Teopisto got
hit, I'm your adjutant."

Aaron glared at me and stood up. "I *told* you to go over to
the 3d Division. Now get going."

I started away from him and heard him mumble, and
swinging on my heel I gave him the dirtiest look of which I
was capable, and said, "What'd you say?" There was a
pause.

"I said be careful," he murmured, and turned and walked
away, and I started across the open space, laughing, enjoying
the game of skill with the enemy gunners across the vine field
in the woods, falling on my face, rolling sideways a few feet
through the vines, getting up and running once again. Who
was out of the game now? Nick and Madden and Lino, dead;
Tabb and Hoshooley, Scarlettos (through the throat), Teopisto and Joaquin, Juan the runner ('bad'), Hank Wentworth and Captain Lamb (shot through the hip), Marcus
Ransom the Negro pantomimist and Morris Goldstein,
Lamb's commissar (shoulder and foot), Mike Pavlos, Garfield's adjutant (broken ankle falling off a wall), many anon-
ymous Spanish boys, many others in other companies we had
not heard of yet; many lying out in the brutal sun between
their lines and ours, who would be dead by night, or would
they be?

When I got back with word that the 3d could not spare
any men at the moment, I could still taste the ripe figs I had
picked on the way; good fruit, soft and warm to the mouth.
Aaron was not in sight, but suddenly there was a good deal
of shouting in Spanish and English, "They're coming, they're

coming, ellos vienen!" and Dick ordered every available man into the line atop the ridge, with hand-grenades. We lay behind the trees, pulling the pins with our left hand, hurling the grenades with our right in the general direction of the other side of the hill, as fast as we could throw. We could not even hear them going off, there was so much noise; the mortars were coming over, their machine-guns were giving cover-fire, artillery was landing behind us (they could not seem to range that hill), and those of us who had no grenades were firing. But gradually the noise died down a bit, and I discovered that Frank Stout, Battalion scout, was lying by my side with his fine Czech rifle, doing a little sniping. I don't know where he'd come from or what he was doing there.

"Hi," I said, and he said, "Hi."

We both did some sniping in the intervals when the mortars, that were scouring the hilltop right and left, let off. They were getting a bit too close for comfort, and he smiled at me.

"This is a bad spot," he said.

"You said it." Some one next to us got hit, and ran screaming from the hill, abandoning his rifle. The next one was close enough to throw considerable dirt over us, and the stones and earth fell for quite a time. I was suddenly acutely conscious of having legs.

"I'm hoping to get hit," said Frank, looking at me sidewise, his cheek resting against the dirt. (His glasses were misted.) "I've been wanting a nice little blighty for some time." He turned his head again.

"Looks like you'll get your wish if this keeps up."

"See that guy move then?" he said.

"No."

"Watch over there next to the poplar, the big one." I

watched; I could see nothing, but Frank was squinting down his rifle, through his glasses, and he fired. "Missed the bugger," he said; "where are your eyes, comrade; he was moving just as big as li—" We covered our heads against the falling dirt, and I heard Frank grunt, then he propped himself up and said, "Hurray, I'm *hit!*" and felt of his right side, looked at his hand, felt again and then said, "Shucks; I guess it was a stone." They must have run out of mortars for a time, for they stopped dropping them and the firing faltered and Frank and I came down the hill.

"What've *you* been up to?" Aaron said.

"In the line."

"You're supposed to be down here when I need you."

"Do you need me?"

"No."

"Well, then——"

"Did you see the guy come down off the hill?" he said. "He was dead as a doornail while he was running. He came running down the hill, absolutely stone dead; I never hope to see the like again." He smiled. "I thought for a minute it was you; he was an ugly bastard, too."

The sun was declining and the skirmish had died down; if they had actually counter-attacked, which I had no way of knowing, they had changed their minds about it, and we had a little food that the barber had brought when he was on water detail—some ripe figs and some dried ones, plums that were still hot with the sun, some canned beef and bread and thick bad marmalade. There was a small stone house near by and Aaron decided the company staff ought to move into it; there was hay on the floor and the walls were heavy. "They can drop them through the roof,"

Curtis said, biting his nails; and Aaron said, "What'ya want for a nickel?"

We had the finest rest in that little house, that night, since we had crossed the Ebro; a long sleep broken only by one night alarm, when, as usual, the Fascists were jittery and thought we might be attacking them, and started throwing grenades off their hill and generally raising hell. Lopoff was hard to wake, and I remember Dick Rusciano shaking him and shaking him, yelling (Dick was slightly deaf from too much artillery), "Lopoff, for Christ's sake, come on; something's happening!" Aaron only mumbled, "Nothing, 'snothing, sleep," but Dick kept at him till he got him up, when we all went outside, Sam Spiller and Curtis and Dick and Aaron and I, and dodged among the falling mortars till the flurry died down again.

Curtis had drawn up a preliminary report; of Company 1, Lamb's company, only thirty-six men could be accounted for; of Company 2, only sixty-six, and there was some talk of combining the two companies under Aaron's leadership. There was no authentic record of the wounded or the missing, but as each company had originally numbered over a hundred men, they must have been high. Yet our losses, because they *were* our losses, could not be discounted in the face of the success of the offensive. We had taken over three thousand prisoners; we had taken several hundred square kilometers of territory; many towns; Gandesa was practically surrounded, but Villalba would have to be taken first; we had relieved some of the pressure on the Levante, but as yet there were no signs of the Fascist motorized divisions, of their heavy artillery, their *avion*. . . .

I was hauled out of the hay early in the morning, just before dawn, to take Eli Biegelman, Brigade observer, over to the headquarters of the 3d Division, and while I was there waiting for him, there was nothing to do but sit in a little stone house with a group of Spanish comrades and listen to their conversation. Occasional mortars fell outside, and machine-gun bullets rattled off the walls. It was hard to get onto what they were saying, because they were talking Valenciano, which is a curious dialect, but after a time I gathered that the conversation, which was heated, was about spiritualism, and that half the men believed in spirits and the other half did not. Arguments were adduced; one of them had an aunt who had definitely seen a ghost; she *knew* it was a ghost because she got out of bed and tried to touch it, and it went right through her when she tried. There was also a tame magpie in the hut, that the men called Maria, and we played with it. And one man threw an epileptic fit.

Biegelman and I got back in the late afternoon, and we were sitting around the little stone house when the mortar exploded and we saw Pavlos Fortis running toward us, and we ran to him. "Are you hurt?" Aaron cried; Pavlos was holding his face, that was streaming with blood where a piece of his nose had been nicked out and his cheek laid open. "Ah, the *bos*-tards," he said, "the *bos*-tards," and we found a bandage for him. (Garfield had never come back.)

I looked at Aaron and saw him take off his beret, throw it violently on the ground and stamp on it. "God *damn* it!" he said. "God *damn* it, this *would* have to happen!" He looked at Pavlos and said, "Well, *chico,* they finally got you, so I suppose I'll be the next." "Ah," said Pavlos, "is nothing," but he couldn't speak so easily through all the bandages, and we had Curtis walk him to the *sanidad*.

Late that night the silence was dissolved into the shuffle and the many sounds of multitudes of men trying to move silently—the 24th Brigade had come up to fill in our gaps, and to make an attack through our lines at dawn. They made the attack and it was reported to have been successful, but there was no way of knowing. Orders came and went with every runner; we were ordered to follow the 24th in the attack, and the order was immediately countermanded; we were ordered to pull out and march south toward Gandesa, and we did not march; we finally were ordered to attack with the support of the 24th's machine-guns, early that afternoon, and preparations went forward to that end. The good breakfast of coffee, marmalade, sliced ham (American), corned beef and plums tasted sour in our mouths. The tension had been heightened by the 24th's early morning attack, and the enemy was nervous. They kept throwing their artillery and mortars all that day, burning the bores out of their machine-guns, and as the hours passed (for we learned soon enough that the dawn attack had been far from successful) toward the moment when our attack (our second) would have to be made, the tension became intolerable. Raw nerves mean acute agony; the sound of the shells, the bullets whining and whacking (even though when you can hear them you know they are already gone), induce a rise in temperature, hot sweat (cold sweat in some), a sickness at the stomach, and heightened faculties. Fear is real and there is nothing you can do about it except to keep functioning, keep your hands and legs and body moving, your mind focussed on the task in hand.

We made the attack with what men we had—a handful of Internationals and a larger group of demoralized and terrified youngsters, who, before they went over, were remembering the first attack and their comrades who had not returned from it, and who again could not be led or driven more than thirty meters past the crest of our hill. They lay down in the vines; they would not move ahead; they could not get up and run back. The terrain was bad; there was no cover; the fire was murderous. Sam Spiller came running to me (Aaron had ordered us to stay behind), and his eyes were full of tears. "Where's Aaron?" he said. "I gotta find Aaron; he may need me." "He told us to stay here." "No!" he said, "I gotta find him right away; he needs me to be with him; he may be hurt." He dashed up the hill and over it, with me in hot pursuit. He saw me following him, rifle in hand, and he yelled, "Be careful, Al, get down, be careful!" He was right. The few men left in the lines, our own and some of the 24th Brigade, were flattened to the earth on the edge of the little clearing that topped our hill. I dropped into a depression behind some tilted stones and kept my head down. Sam was at my side; but when I turned to look, the kid was gone. Running to position I had passed Kurculiotis; I smelled him before I saw him, and I knew him from the uniform, for it would have been impossible to identify him otherwise. Lying there in the beating sun, his smell came to me and sickened me, and I applied myself to the job of doing a little sniping with Pavlos' Czech mauser.

The heat was alive with the cries of a wounded man over to my right, and I saw him coming toward me, crawling along the top of the hill in the open, dragging his bloody broken legs, saying, "Comrade, help me; help me, comrade." I motioned him to lie flat till it died down, but he kept on coming and for a moment I debated whether or not to get up and run to him and carry him. He was heavy and the fire that was coming over the hill just then was deadly. I was filled with shame as I looked at his wide eyes, saw him lift his hand to me and then saw his white face blossom red, his body sag and fall. I turned back to the valley that faced me, and kneeling upright, started to fire conscientiously until it suddenly occurred to me that I was exposing myself to the waist. Nick smelled dreadful and I wanted to get away from there. I lay flat, seeing the grains of white dust under my eyes magnified till they looked like cobbles. I watched again and saw a man moving on the hillside opposite; drew a fine bead on him and fired. I do not know whether I had hit him or not, but he did not move again, for he had fallen from a little stone bluff into thick undergrowth. I was soaked in sweat and sweltering; perspiration dripped from my nose and eyebrows; I wanted to get away from there, from that sweet stench of broiling, festered flesh; in my mind was an image of Nick when I had passed him on the run—he was a presence there; he was a challenge and a menace. I had thought, running past him, crouching low, 'Well, there *you* are, there you *are!*' I can't describe it better; he was *there*. He would always be there; nothing could take him away from there. There is nothing to fear from a dead body; surely there is nothing to fear—except that it is always you.

From below me and to the right Aaron came running; he had lost his beret and his automatic pistol was in his hand. He was running like mad, coming over the hill as in a moving picture, and he saw me, ran for me and dropped into the depression by my side, groaning for breath. When he had caught it, he turned to look at me with utter exhaustion in his eyes, and he said, "Did *you* have to get mixed up in this mess, too?" We lay side by side in the hammering heat and he rolled a cigarette and passed it to me; we passed it back and forth. Then, without saying a word, he got up and ran for the woods and down the hill, and since I knew he wanted me to follow him and had done that so I would get up and follow, I followed.

"Where's Aaron?" I said, and Curtis told me he had started toward Battalion headquarters, and I found him on the path. He didn't speak and I didn't speak, but we walked side by side till we came to the *estado-mayor* under a spreading fig tree. Wolff was there and Watt and Ed Rolfe, and a number of other men, transmissionists and runners and observers and scouts (Luke Hinman and Frank Stout), and we sat around saying nothing. The firing had died down, but occasional artillery shells came ripping over to burst against the hill behind us. Ed Rolfe had a set smile on his finely structured face, but his eyes were following the landing of the shells, and he did not feel like talking. He had a *Chesterfield* that he had received in a letter from his wife back home, and which he shared with me. I'm sure he knew what I was going through, and I was grateful to him for knowing it.

"The hill across the way," said Captain Wolff, "is the only point that is holding up the advance upon Gandesa. Brigade says it must be taken." We looked at our commander, this twenty-two-year-old Brooklyn student who so much resembled the young Lincoln. His face was serious; his cheeks were covered with a week-old beard. "What do you guys say?" he asked.

It was the opinion of the few men in command of the companies that we could not take the hill. "The kids won't go over," Aaron said. "They're scared stiff; they're lying out there now; they can't advance or get back to the lines."

"What'ya mean they *won't* go over?" Wolff said, and it was possible to hate him for a moment. But he did not believe, himself, in what he was saying. "We've *got* to take that hill; Brigade's orders. We'll have the 24th Brigade in support, and between the two of us we'll take the hill." He talked for a long time on the telephone, but nothing conclusive came across. He sat looking at his maps, his young face preternaturally old; older than his years. You could not help respect the man, for at twenty-two he *was* a man who could handle more than many men would even attempt at twice his age. He was a natural-born military leader, if such exists, for there is no way to understand how a man comes by such a talent. He did not like what he was doing, but he did it with the grace that comes to those who know they can.

Aaron and I walked back in the failing light, and just beyond Battalion headquarters we passed a comrade, dead upon the grass beside the path. I don't know who he was, but he was lying on his face and, absurdly enough, his trousers were pulled down exposing his bare buttocks, which were blue. We did not pause, but we looked at him, and Aaron looked down at the path that we were following. "Why don't they bury that guy?" he said; there was some resentment in his voice, and I think that at that moment we were closer to each other than we had ever been before, or were later to become. There is no way of saying why; there are no words for certain human feelings.

Just after dark I organized a patrol to go out into the space that lay between our lines, to check on the dead and bring back the wounded. Garfield had not been seen since Smith sent him up the hill the day before, and we were using the Spanish *practicante* of Lamb's old company, Victor Seriñana (he pronounced it Bictor). Victor was a curious-looking bird with the face of a hawk, who wore a poncho with a deep fur collar, no matter how hot the sun. With four stretcher-bearers (without stretchers) and with Hercules Arnaoutis, Greek *peloton* leader who came in just at dusk, to lead the way, we went over the top and down the hill. Hercules knew where the wounded lay; he had lain out in the sun all day himself, waiting to return. We split our forces, and I went on solitary patrol, scouting among the vines between our lines and theirs, looking for the patch of darkness, just a little darker than the night, that would mean a body. The newly dead, those who had been killed by their wounds and the sun that afternoon, had begun to smell, and the sweet stench lay over the vine field like an evening mist. It was absolutely silent, except that at moments the Fascist gunners, on watch upon the hill across the way, suspected what we were up to and opened fire. At such times you flattened to the ground and waited. It was a weird feeling lying there, halfway between the lines, knowing there were many silent men on either side, feeling the silence that could, at any moment, erupt into hideous sound. You began to learn the meaning of the word, alone. I could not locate the patrol, although I scouted

back and forth, tripping over the tangled vines, easing myself up and down the terraces. And so I started back.

There was a bad moment when I recalled that I had not
warned the men in the lines that a patrol was working out
in front, but some one apparently had had more sense, for
they did not challenge me when I returned. I climbed over
the parapet and a Spaniard touched my leg. "Comrade," he
said, "there is a dead comrade over there"—he pointed in
the direction where Nick was lying, close at hand—"and
he smells bad. Why don't you bury him?" "I know," I said.
"We didn't have the time." I worked back down the hill,
moving toward the stone house, and I called. "Aaron," I
said, in a low voice, "Aaron," and suddenly his voice was
at my feet.

"Where have you been?" he said.

"On patrol."

"Hercules came back long ago."

"I know."

"I thought I'd got rid of you," he said. "But no such luck."

"Why, what did you *think* had happened to me?"

"I heard the firing," he said.

We sat side by side in the darkness, and I thought of the
wounded we had found—Emiliano Marin, the Puerto Rican
with the Pekingese eyes, whom every one had thought was
worthless. He was a squad-leader now, and yesterday his
steel helmet had been deeply creased by a bullet in the attack. Today he had received the bullet in his leg, but he was
smiling when we brought him in. There had been no trace
of Garfield, and it was the common opinion that he had
fucked off, but we never did find out. (Garfield was not
his name.) We searched the terrain from the point he was

supposed to have entered it to the other side, just below the Fascist trenches, and there was no trace of him. "The bastard," the men said. "He had a bar of chocolate in his *bolsa,* and some sugar."

"Bess," Aaron said. "Orders have come to attack tonight at eleven, and take that hill, quotes, at all costs, end quotes."

"That's bad."

"It's suicide," he said. "It's murder." The Brigade and the Battalion commands did not seem to acknowledge the low morale or condition of the men, their youth, their political innocence. But perhaps they were in as tight a spot as we; this was a war. The title of a story by Richard Aldington came to mind, *At All Costs,* and I suddenly said, aloud, "Fiction come to life."

"What?"

"Nothing. I was talking in my sleep."

We were silent, then Aaron said, "I want you and Sam to stay behind when we attack."

"Why?"

"I'll need some responsible guys back here to give cover-fire and help the wounded, if possible. Curtis too; there's no one else but you guys I can trust."

"I want to come with you," I said, but I'm sure he must have known the request was half-hearted; just as I knew why he was ordering me to stay behind.

"You'll stay here," he said.

"Is that an order?"

"It's an order. Come over with ammo when we take the hill." We sat and were silent for some time, and I heard him open his mouth once or twice and close it. Then he cleared his throat and said, "You remember I've told you about a girl I know; the one I write to. She's a swell dame; you'll have to meet her when we go home."

"Yes," I said.

He put a piece of paper in my hand. "This is her address," he said. "In case." I looked at him, but it was too dark to see his face; I wanted to.

"What about your Pop?" I said. "What's *his* address?"

"She'll tell my Pop," he said.

We did not attack; instead we received orders to stand by to move, and at dawn, just after sixteen Fascist bombers had dropped a load at the entrance to the valley, we moved off in Indian file, having been replaced in that position by the 24th Brigade and another outfit that came up during the night. We marched to a *baranco* a few kilometers to the south of this sector, where we camped on the side of a steep hill that did not permit us to lie flat. And here they held us in reserve—the question was, how long and for what purpose, which is two questions after all. But it was possible to take off our shoes for the first time since we had crossed the Ebro, and I used the water in my canteen to wash my hands and feet and face (at which several comrades exclaimed in horror), and the time to have the little Angel-barber shave my face, a sensual pleasure under these conditions, that defies description. Angel was a good barber, but we Americans could never get accustomed to his horrifying Spanish habit of stropping the razor on the palm of his hand; it was easier to get used to cold water.

Curtis drew up an itemized report of the losses our company had sustained in the nine days of action: originally effective were one hundred and twenty-six men, of whom forty-odd were Internationals. There were seven known dead (of whom four were Internationals), twelve known sick and evacuated, forty-five known wounded and evacuated, and ten unaccounted for—dead, wounded, captured or fucked off—which left an effective list of fifty-two. Our company fared better than the others, but no figures were available and the count was difficult because new replacements began to arrive almost immediately.

All that day on the side of the hill the men slept while the sound of heavy fighting went on to our right—artillery and mortars, rifle and machine-gun—and their planes (and a very few of ours, the first we'd seen) moved over the landscape among heavy clouds. "Christ," said Curtis, "here they come!" and disappeared into a hole. But no one else paid much attention to them, for they had other work in hand. The company was reorganized, and consisted of two sections of three large squads each, under George Cady and Julian Andrés, the only two remaining *peloton* leaders. For one day Aaron had had an adjutant and second in command (old style) named Julius Deutsch, but he was wounded in the last attack we made; so I was adjutant again. Then we were suddenly merged with the remnants of Company 1; Dick Rusciano became the second in command, Archie Brown (West Coast longshoreman leader, of the machine-gun company) became political commissar, and I was chief of the *plana mayor*. Word came that the Brigade was 'proud' of us, for our 'spirited attacks'; for it seems we had been opposed for two days by the Mohammedan Moors Franco had brought to restore Christianity to Spain, and then by his infamous Foreign Legion—two of the toughest fighting units in his army. So spirited were our attacks, said Brigade, that the enemy had concentrated a great quantity of materiel opposite, believing that we commanded a key position in the Government's offensive. Did we laugh?

Late that night we moved again, from the reserve position to a hill somewhat to the south, and learned that there was to be a mass attack on Gandesa. (The two outfits who had relieved us, we were told, had taken the hill we tried so hard to take, and the way was clear.) We were told that we would have artillery and aviation to support us, and as the hot dawn came up we had a magnificent breakfast; there was really too much to eat for once, and the sliced ham was left lying in the sun, where it spoiled inside of fifteen minutes.

When the order came we moved down off that hill in single file, the taste of breakfast still in our mouths—coffee, chocolate, ham and sardines, bread, marmalade and plums. There was a comfortable weight inside us, and there was, too, the inevitable nervousness, the pre-action tension that sharpens the senses and makes you take notice of things you never saw before—a lizard sticking his head out of a crack in the dry, volcanic rock; a broken shoe-lace; a streak of dirt on another man's face. Two divisions were moving through parallel *barancos* toward the town.

The ravine was narrow at the top, wide at the bottom, a perfect bottleneck. Ahead of us, our 24th Battalion had engaged the enemy; they were out of sight ahead of us, among the foliage, but the machine-guns were singing their crisp metallic song, the rifle bullets snapped over our heads as we waited, flattened onto the dry earth, seeking cover below terraces, behind the olive trees. You could look around and see men flattening visibly into the ground, disappearing, their rifles canted against the natural parapets ahead. (Curtis disappeared completely.) A runner would appear from below, dash from tree to tree, to re-appear later, sweating. The sun rose straight above us, hanging over our heads, beating on our backs and necks. There was no water as we waited for the word to go ahead, wondering how long it would be before the word came, what would happen when it did come, how much opposition we would meet at the mouth of the *baranco,* as we emerged to the attack. You could hear our Hotchkiss talking from the hill on our left; a heavy Maxim on the right. (You could always tell when an American was on the gun, for he could not resist playing Shave-and-a-haircut, two-bits.) There was *avion* overhead, seeking—finding? We waited for it to find us; we watched its impersonal evolutions, bank and turn, soar and glide, looking for something it would find in the course of time. We watched the stretchers coming back from the line the 24th was holding.

It is possible to watch the stretchers coming back in an entirely impersonal fashion. You note the severity of the wound (a man's intestines piled neatly on his belly); you try to catch a glimpse of the face; you think, 'There I go, back to the hospital,' and you think, 'Does it hurt much?' One by one the stretchers came back from the line, weaving between the twisted olive trunks, the *camilleros'* backs exposed to the enemy fire. You could not envy them their jobs, their lives dependent on and weighted with the weight and the lives of the comrades they were carrying. You watched them, thinking, 'There I go,' or 'How soon will it be?' and 'Will it be bad?' You wondered how things were going ahead, and how soon the word would come, and you wondered where our artillery was, and how soon it would be before it opened up, and where was the promised *avion?* You listened for it.

You woke with astonishment to find that you had been dozing in the sun; the heat and the dust and the thirst, the tension—all had combined to undo your senses and relax your vigilance, and the body snatched at the rest it needed, the rest it had foregone during the hard days of action that had gone before. You woke with a start, wondering how you could possibly have gone to sleep in the face of the fire—you felt a sickening sensation at what you had done, like a man who has come safely through an accident and suddenly recalls how close he had been to death and feels his guts turn over in his body. Vigilance returns, and with it the heightened sensibility, the tension. Some one is eating a tin of sardines near by; you can smell the warm olive oil. (He will use the oil to clean his rifle.)

All day, in the stifling furnace heat and the searing thirst we waited, the sun pounding our backs, the hammering song of the Hotchkiss loud from the left slope of the *baranco.* 'The damn fool!' we thought, 'Can't he shut up for awhile? He'll ruin the bore. He'll give his position away!' Dusk brought the order to advance—and it brought other things as well. The unbearable tension snapped; the parched lips were wet by the still moist tongue. Over the right slope of the ravine there came sailing, precisely spaced and beautifully colored in the failing light, tracer-bullets like small slow balls of pink fire. They soared across the valley into the Hotchkiss' position, but the gun kept firing.

From somewhere the enemy artillery awoke and the

shells came over—you could count them as they came. And
then you couldn't count them; they fell in no regular order,
one-two-three, but with a conscious knowledge of where
we were—to left, to right, ahead, behind, crashing like enormous garbage cans heaved by gigantic men. The broken
earth fell on us, the cracked rock spattered against the unbroken stone of the hillsides. The growing night was loud
in our ears, and the men, ordered up the right slope of the
ravine, were huddled in a long line against the hillside,
crouching, sitting, lying flat. My rifle was smashed to pieces
in my hand. A comrade, wounded and lying in a stretcher,
had to be moved out of the line of fire, and nobody wanted
to leave the dubious shelter of the hillside, where the
angle was comparatively safe, to help. Archie Brown helped
carry him to safety. The screaming of the many wounded
was an impersonal sound amid the other sounds; it was
getting darker all the time and we prayed for it to get
darker suddenly, but it didn't. Faces were fading rapidly.
"Plana mayor de la Segunda, no—Primera, aqui!" I shouted,
but I could only find the barber and the *furiel,* Matias Lara.
We shouted for stretcher-bearers, could not find them in
the dark, and no one came. I shouted for Aaron, could not
find him; could not have heard if he had answered. We
were deafened by the sound, terrified by the barrage that
moved closer to us all the time, coming from over the hill
on whose slope we were standing, sitting, lying. As though
on cue, as though trained by a stage director, the men
moved slowly back and forth depending on where the shells
were falling, in huddled droves like sheep, crouching, their
faces frightened in the growing darkness. No one spoke;
no one said a word.

9

[*August 4th–19th*]

THE NIGHT was full of confusion and shouting. Soon after it became dark the artillery lifted, for artillery cannot see to fire at night; it must have its eyes posted on distant hills or in the air, for each powder charge varies by perhaps a few milligrams, and the gun creeps upon the ground each time it fires. Everywhere men were shouting for their companies, calling names, stumbling over each other and the rocks and foliage in the dark. "Company One, back up the hill!" Archie and I shouted, and we grasped individual shadows by the arm, asked, "First Company?" and if they were ours sent them to the top of the ridge among the trees. Many could not be found, but after about an hour a sizable number had been rounded up on the steep hillside, and Aaron had reappeared again. It was pitch black on the hill, and in the distance we could see buildings burning on the mountain side, fired by that day's bombing and the shells. All night there was the intermittent sound of heavy firing, artillery and mortars, and no sleep was possible.

Food came up at three in the morning; coffee, ham, sardines and tomatoes, and squabbling broke out among the men. "*I'm* first in line," they'd say. "Get the hell back there!" "When does this section eat, anyhow?" "Christ, we didn't get any *comida* today; hey, Lopoff, how about getting a little system in this mess?" Their nerves were unstrung; their tempers at the humming point; they shoved and pushed and cursed each other, and Matias Lara, the quartermaster, protested vainly to all and each in turn. *"Hay que formar una cola, camaradas,"* and *"Cola! cola!"* the men cried. "Pipe down there; you're in the lines now!" Aaron said. "Get your grub and take it back into your places." We lay huddled, Aaron, Dick, Archie, Curtis and the rest, trying to get some sleep; being stepped on by straggling men, wondering what the dawn would bring. Dawn brought the order to return to the last hill we had occupied, in the reserve position, and it brought some mail. . . .

Dearest Guys (I wrote)

Don't know whether this will reach you, and I'll write again as soon as possible, but we've been in action now for 9 (?) days and communications were naturally haphazard. As of today I'm well and all in one piece. Day before yesterday we were retired from the lines to a reserve position. Yesterday we went back in again and took an awful load of their stuff, trench-mortars, machine-gun and rifle fire, artillery. Today we're out again, in a reserve position. Things are moving fast; I continually lose track of the days or add ones that don't exist; I try to make notes in non-existent spare time.

This morning the first mail in 5–6 weeks; none from you, but Jerry and Simon give me my first word (indirect) of you and the kids in over a month, and under the circumstances was happy as hell to know you are all well, and managed to get to the beach. But where are your letters?

Yesterday's action was the worst I've met so far. We were in a deep gulley between 2 hills, expecting to advance. The advance was postponed by heavy fighting ahead of us, and we suffered all day from the terrific heat and thirst. Then just at dusk they got our range with their artillery, and filled the valley with a heavy barrage from end to end—horrible and terrific. The men were amazing, considering that most were in their first action—but there is little you can do except to hug the earth and hope for the best. It was hell on wheels; there were and are no words for it.

What can I say except that I'm thinking of you guys all day and night; that I love you all with a love that will end only with my life; that your images in my heart and mind go far, far, toward sustaining life at its worst and (paradoxically enough) greatest moments. I feel confident that my determination to live will in some way overcome the hazards of the present, and bring you all back into my life again—for it is for all of you that I hope to live when it is time to live again (and not just merely cling to life). . . .

What would it be—rest (a real one), reserve or action? We spent the day on the side of the hill, jittery with constant *avion* alarms and speculating on the immediate future. Rumor said we would move again during the coming night; that the entire Division was being gathered together, that there might be a rest for us. And food came up again that night at one in the morning; coffee with the Spanish cognac to warm our bellies, tinned corned beef and sardines. And at two-thirty we did move to a hill about three kilometers from Corbera, and to a dawn loud with the sound of airplanes, droning, humming, against which we lay, dug slightly into the hard baked earth, clinging to the dubious shelter of rocks, shrubs and trees, expecting the planes to find us and unload. (Curtis found a good spot underneath a ledge, and would not stick his nose out.)

It appeared that neither Gandesa nor Villalba had been

taken, though the hill that had absorbed three unsuccessful attacks had finally fallen. That had been the first serious engagement for the Spanish *quintos,* and with notable exceptions, it had showed them up. The Internationals, soldiers and leaders, did their best; they went over (not only) as an example to the younger men, but the youngsters would not follow; they could not be urged, threatened, kicked or shot (two of them were) into advancing in the face of that fire. And there could be no doubt that the nature of our set-up accounted for our position as 'reserves,' though as reserves we had done a passable amount of fighting. The prospect seemed discouraging, for each day we were held from the Italian base of Gandesa and its important communications-network, gave them that much more time to bring their men and their stuff from wherever they were bringing it. And it was their equipment, not their men we had to fear; their infantry was worthless, for it did not want to fight.

(Ed Rolfe had said, before we crossed the Ebro, 'This will be your last action.' He was quite mysterious, but he hinted that he had been solicited for a man to do a writing job, and that on the basis of my 'experience and ability,' I had been elected. 'After this action,' he had said, 'you and I will go some place.' He did not say where we'd go or what we'd do; he just said, 'Wait and see.' But I put little faith in his predictions, for months before I had played the prophet too. 'You'll be out of Spain by the first of July,' I'd said. 'I have a hunch.' I was only trying to cheer him up.)

At one in the morning we did move (You are afraid of your life, I thought), marching through the moonlight—avoiding shadows by marching in single file on either side of the road, under the trees—to the outskirts of Corbera, destroyed by air-bombs, and along the main road for a time. Then we turned off left into a long, winding *baranco,* and followed it for about five kilometers to a point three miles from Gandesa, where we relieved two battalions of the XIth Brigade that were entrenched there. (Of course you are afraid for your life, but really you have learned all you can learn from this; but really you are no good as a soldier; you have no qualities of leadership; your weight in the sum-total is negligible and you should get out, but really you are afraid for your life.) The balance of the night was spent getting the lay of the land, placing the sections and squads in the trenches, establishing the company *puesto de mando* a short distance behind the lines, in a dugout.

"Christ!" said Aaron, "but this stinks. The trenches are two feet deep. There's no way of getting in or out of them without being spotted; there are no picks and shovels to improve them. That means the men will have to come out one by one, after dark, for their grub and water. God damn this lousy outfit!" he said. "Have they no respect for the lives of their men!"

The dugout was sunk into a four-foot bank, and looked like half a doughnut in shape. There were two entrances, and immediately Curtis established himself in one, with Harold Lee, our new (and cockeyed) *practicante.* "Get the hell out of there," Aaron said. "We have no room for you." "There's no place else," the secretary said. "Find a shovel and dig yourself a hole." "There *are* no shovels." "Fuck off," Aaron said; and we lay in that semicircular hole waiting for dawn. "No cover," he said, "no decent trenches, no tools." When we brought the telephone box inside with the telephonist, there was no room to bend en elbow. But we went to sleep.

Dawn was lovely, rosy-fingered, spectacular with pearl-gray clouds and rare tints of rose. Dawn was beautiful with airplanes, a twelve-plane flight that came over, high and moving toward the river, that they regularly bombed every day and all the day, destroying our bridges, preventing the mobilization of reserves. There were mortar-pits and parts of exploded mortars everywhere, but theoretically we were not to be there long; only until we could be relieved. Our instructions were to stay on the defensive, fire only if we were attacked, lie low. We did. The Division was still being gathered—to be withdrawn for rest, or for attack? We lay low; the men lay flat in the baking sun in the shallow trenches in the vine fields, and we stayed inside the dugout, for they were throwing mortars. (Curtis was still there.) Our offensive on the Ebro front had obviously been stopped; it was said we had not relieved much pressure on the Levante, for the forces Franco withdrew to bolster his Gandesa fortifications came from the Balaguer-Lerida sector instead. (Sure, you think, you ought to get out now and try to help by being a writer; that's your job. Writing is a weapon too. Is it a more valuable job, or just a different one? He who fights and runs away lives to fight another day. Or, he fights who also turns and runs away. But Ed, who was planning to go to Barcelona any minute, and was stationed with the Battalion *estado-mayor* half a kilometer behind us in the woods, had nothing to say. He did not know when he would go to Barcelona; he did not know when he'd be back. He did not say what he was going to do there.)

A few shells came over, feeling for the Battalion's headquarters in the small stone house; a few mortars fell—one was a dud and a Spanish boy came running with it in his arms, till

Aaron told him to take it far away and let it lie; and we found an earthen jar sticky with honey and crawling with flies. We ate the honey; it was sweet, and sugar was so lacking in our diet we craved it night and day. The men came singly from the lines to get their food, and then returned. The Fascist planes came and went all day, but they paid no attention to us at all. Word came that we would be replaced that night and go back for rest and reorganization. That was a shit-house rumor, for we were still there that night when a hundred *zapadores* (engineers) came up to deepen the trenches for us, and we were there the next morning, making out lists for citations and promotions. I walked back down through the fields to Battalion headquarters in the stone house, and heard them laughing in the upper story. A few shells came over now and then, but they had not found the house. Upstairs there was a poker-game in progress; Wolff and Watt and Rolfe and others, and their flunkies had brought some good wine from Corbera. Ed was winning all the money, which proves that intellectuals are in some way superior to other human beings; even in an army, and everybody was a trifle tight.

"*Vino bueno!*" Wolff shouted to his orderly. "*Mas, chico, mas y mas!*" I hung around (Ed had no news) and talked to Luke Hinman for a time, who told me of his experience organizing factory workers back in California, in the canning industry. He was thin and drawn, but his fine lips were as firm as ever; his blue eyes as steady. Then I went back to the dugout, where Aaron was perpetually sleeping, and where the sand got into your hair, your teeth, your eyes, your socks, your food and drink. We heard yelling outside and came running out; all the company staffmen were shouting and pointing and running around like chickens without their heads, and we looked. A plane was falling in flames, and the men danced with excitement. *"Fascista!"* they yelled. *"Criminales!"* *"Una trimotore, una negra!"* I don't know how they knew it was a Fascist plane or a trimotor. It might have been a friend, but the sight was beautiful, a lovely pear-shaped flame, slowly falling through the pale blue air. But Fascist or not I was with the pilot in that plane; I burned with him as he fought with his safety-belt, struggled to bail out—but perhaps he was dead by then, for no parachute blossomed white beside the falling ship, and it disappeared behind the hills.

At midnight the 27th Division came up to relieve us, and we were so glad to get out of that hole—where nothing had actually happened—that we ran through most of the five kilometers of the *baranco,* back onto the Gandesa-Corbera highway. There we reformed our lines and started to march toward Mora de Ebro to a place where we would rest about fifteen kilometers from the lines. In the moonlight we passed through Corbera, and as we approached the outskirts of the town the sudden stench of the dead nauseated us. There was nothing left of the place, for half an hour after our first forces occupied it and continued to march toward Gandesa, the Fascist aviation had come and bombed it. It had returned hourly for the balance of the day, systematically pounding and grinding the town to pieces, for although we had neither troops nor munitions in the place, it was an important town on the highway, and its broken buildings cluttered up the road. There was not a sound as we marched through, except the shuffling of our feet on the broken pavement; the smell of the dead still buried beneath the refuse—women, children, old men—was rotten-sweet in the deserted moonlit streets;

the shell-like houses cast wide fantastic shadows on the road. No one spoke as we passed through; there were no words to say.

We lay in an extended olive field that covered many broad terraces and was bounded on the sides by low hills on which there were posted guards to warn us of approaching *avion*. But they did not need to warn us, for the planes came and went all day long in ever-increasing numbers. There were flights of five bombers, fifteen bombers, twenty-one bombers, Savoias and Junkers, with their accompanying chasers, higher up. They came and went to and from the river, and from where we lay we could feel the deep reverberation of the earth and see the black smoke rising like columns on the shore. They must have known that we were there, after the first few days, for the paths used by the food-trucks and the water-tanks were plain in the white dust of the earth, and the men did not exercise too much caution about remaining under cover. They were coming and going all the time, after they had caught up on their sleep, visiting men in other companies, other battalions of the XVth Brigade, running to and from the narrow trench-like latrines dug on the hillsides, for every one was suffering from diarrhea.

Replacements came up, about a hundred fifty, including twenty-five Americans. Joe North, the *Daily Worker* correspondent, came in a fine *Matford* sedan, with Louis Fischer, the *Nation's* correspondent, and both had cigarettes. "Here's one for you," said Fischer, standing before a group of seated men, "and here's one for you and one for you." And with Joe's appearance, the rumor Rolfe had mentioned became somewhat clarified. The writing job might be one of two—

either Ed would soon take over Joe's job and I would take
on his as *Volunteer for Liberty* reporter at the front; or there
might be a job for both of us with the Ministry of Propaganda
in Barcelona. It all depended on a trip that Ed would shortly
make, but at the moment he did not seem to be leaving. So
the possibilities of the job's materializing assumed the nature
of a race against time; for we would be in action soon enough!

North and Fischer left and the airplanes were still there.
"This is a hell of a place to rest," the men said as they lay in
the shadows of the trees, pretending not to see the planes
droning slowly overhead, V after V of them. You could tell
whether they were going to drop their stuff; as they came
toward you there was a point, at about sixty-five or seventy
degrees off horizontal, when they would have to lay their
eggs if they expected to make a hit. You watched as they approached, and when each V passed that point you could sigh
with relief and wait for the next. But all day long they came
and circled overhead, and white clouds in long streaks issued
from them. "A signal," the men said the first time, "you can
expect the shit any minute." But these were leaflets they were
dropping, and as they finally reached the ground, some minutes later, the men could not resist running for them:

Come over to us [the leaflets read], *with your officers or alone.
Nothing will happen to you if you surrender; if not, you will
all die, for you have no more bridges.*

The men laughed and said, "Humph! ain't got no union
label; scab printing."

*Do not let yourselves be killed in a war already lost. Hoist the
white flag and come over to our lines. Do not be afraid that any-*

*thing will happen to you. You will be well received in our camp
and will enjoy peace and a commodious life; abundance, tran-
quility, justice and liberty.*

"Poor quality stock," said Dick, who was a printer. "Good
ass-paper," said the men; "we've run out of *The Daily*."

In Franco's Spain [the leaflet said], *justice reigns; there is
abundance, peace and liberty. No one is hungry. No one is
persecuted. No one is received with hatred. Come over to your
brothers. Come over to our lines.*

All this was very touching, quite naïve and somewhat pa-
thetic, but it had a slight effect. In the course of the long Ebro
campaign there were a few deserters. "Get me a job with
Franco, Ed," I said. "He needs a good publicity man; this one
stinks." "What's wrong with Carney?" said Ed. "He's not
doing such a bad job for the bugger." . . .

. . . We were filthy and alive with lice; a bath and clean
clothes had been promised. The clothes arrived, but the bath
was impossible, for the bath-machine gave off black smoke.
So one night we rode in trucks down the main highway to
the Ebro, and into Mora. But it looked somewhat different
than it had last April. There were a few inhabitants remaining despite the daily bombings that had reduced the once
thriving industrial town to a wreckage; they were people who
did not want to leave their homes, and preferred death to removal; which is hard to understand, but not too hard. (They
were mostly old.) Gaping ruins bordered the streets; whole
walls had been sheared away by the explosives, leaving completely furnished rooms exposed to view in the moonlight,

and we rode through and down to the shore. It was like a stage-set; it was indecent too.

It was warm in the water, but the current was swift. We began to feel familiar with the Ebro; we'd crossed it twice and now we were bathing in its stream. The men laughed and shouted, splashed each other like little children at the beach, played and stood on their hands in the shallow water. They dived to the bottom, retrieved pebbles, swam under-water, pinched each other's buttocks or rose between each other's legs like porpoises. On the far shore we could see the occasional lights of trucks moving toward the river, munitions and supplies of all sorts, that came over only at night, and we were reluctant to come out of the water and dress in the clean clothes waiting for us. We were clean, but cold water will not kill your lice. Yet with lice and a week's growth of beard, it was possible to feel like a king, clean and renewed and rested by the bath, refreshed by the old clean clothes. We slept well that night, when we got back.

But now our anxiety that our rest would be terminated by a sudden call to action changed to a different—but only slightly different—form of discomfort. We knew that every day that passed brought us nearer to the front again; the rest-period was shortening every hour, and the men compensated for the nervousness they felt by expressing a desire to get back to the lines. We could hear the artillery all day and night. "Anything is better than this waiting," they would say. So with few exceptions we did not work too hard on the circular trenches we were digging around the base of the trees, for refuge against possible bombing. We were careless about leaving white objects lying around, tin-cans and water-bottles, light-colored blankets and torn newspapers. We walked calmly across the open spaces when the planes were overhead, and paid no attention to frantic comrades calling to us to get down for Christ's sake if your life doesn't mean anything to you mine does to me.

Joe North returned again, this time with Ernst Toller, the exiled German dramatist, and a young man whose name was Daniel Roosevelt, who told me he was a correspondent for my old paper, *The Brooklyn Daily Eagle*. That is to say, he had agreed to send them articles from Spain that they might publish if they cared to, but he had not written any and was going back to Paris any day. Toller was a quiet, heavy-set man, who wandered about talking to the soldiers, asking questions; how much did we get to eat, and did we get enough to smoke, and watching the Fascist airplanes through a pair of opera-glasses, when everybody else was under cover. "Who's that dope standing out there in the open?" some one shouted; but Toller stood and watched, changing his position to get a better view, and saying quietly, "We did not have so many planes during the World War."

It was quite definite now that Joe North was going to go home; that Ed would take over his job as correspondent, and that I would take Ed's job. It was only a question of how long, and Ed said, "When I get back from Barcelona." Somehow I expected confirmation of this fact almost any day, but nothing was said to me; it was a deadly secret. I wandered around from company to company, made a half-hearted attempt to clean up my persistent scabies (which I had undoubtedly caught from Aaron), by reporting to Doc Simon's *sanidad,* where he gave me two solutions, one that stung and one that stank, and neither of which did any good. "Bessie," said the absent-minded little medico, "it won't make any difference if you cure 'em; you're gonna get bumped off anyhow, and no one will look at you and say, Why how disgusting, he's got a skin disease." He was a curious bird, this medical student acting as a doctor; he was so absent-minded and distracted most of the time that he gained a reputation for outrageous courage. There was no place he would not go; nothing he would not do with calmness and deliberation during the hottest fire, and there was a perpetual debate among the men whether his courage sprang from strength of will or was a by-product of the fact that he 'didn't know enough to come in out of the rain.'

"Still up to your old tricks, I see," said Aaron, when I handed him the cigarette I'd bummed from North.

"What would you do without me?"

"Manage to struggle along, I guess," he said. "But what does your pal North have to say?"

I told him that our offensive appeared, after all, to have relieved some pressure on the Levante; that it had given courage to our partisans behind the Fascist lines; that it had demoralized the Franco rear-guard; that it had effected still another swing in international relations, for there was a strong movement in Great Britain to force Chamberlain to revise his Spanish policy; the Daladier Government was said to be fed up with Britain's perpetual concessions to Hitler and Mussolini, and the French border was unofficially open again. Sympathetic elements everywhere had been heartened by our resistance and our offensive, and were bringing pressure on their respective governments to give aid to Spain. You could not fool the decent people anywhere.

"Yeh," said Aaron, "but have you seen the Spanish papers? The Japs are raiding Soviet territory; Lord Runciman is in

Prague, and Mr. Chamberlain is going to sell the Czechs down the river, mark my words. Hitler has mobilized almost a million and a half men. . . ."

Dear Pop [the letter said],
   David says 'a hunk o' hugs, Poppy.'
   We went to Riis Park Beach. Mom bought two pairs of sneakers, one for Dave and one for me.
   When you come home, buy a bag of ice-pops for us all to eat, down around at Eddie's.
   Big hug and a kiss. You're a bum! You bum you bum you bum!

DAN

"My older son says I'm a bum."

"He shows more sense than his old man," said Aaron. "I hope to Christ you get that job of Rolfe's soon; then you can bother Wolff instead of me."

"You know what I'd like?" I said.

"What?"

"A T-bone steak smothered in mushrooms."

"With cauliflower on the side," said Aaron.

"A bottle of Chateauneuf du Pâpe."

"Crêpes Suzette."

"And afterwards, a slug of Courvoisier's V.O. cognac, in a big bubble-glass blown by Steuben."

"A hot bath."

"Smoking in the bath; bath-salts."

"A piece of tail."

"Two of them."

"Two of them with salt on 'em. Where's that sonofabitch Curtis?" he said.

"Are you going to send out for 'em now? Order me one with red hair on it."

"No, I want him to translate this for me; it looks like an order." Curtis was in his hole, the deepest on the battalion-grounds, and he did not come out until the two flights of airplanes overhead, that were mixed up in a dogfight, went away. They had started at twenty thousand feet, mixed it up till you couldn't tell what they were doing, and the scream of their propellors as they dived sounded in our ears as though they were directly overhead. Three went down in flames, one after the other, with two parachutes blooming suddenly like spring flowers in the air, and floating slowly down. You could see the men hauling on the shrouds to guide the chutes, swinging wildly from side to side like pendulums as their own planes, Fascists, dived at them and tried to machine-gun them. "The bastards!" Aaron said. "Look at them, the sons-of-bitches!" Two of our planes spiralled slowly around the descending pilots to protect them. "This is one hell of a war," Aaron said.

"What is it?" said Dick, who was reading a newspaper. "I can't hear anything."

"You're deaf."

"What?" said Dick, "what did you say; don't mumble your words."

"It says to turn in all picks and shovels," Curtis said.

"I see where a guy started to fly for California and landed in Ireland," Dick said.

"He's wacky," Aaron said to me. "Don't mind him; he's shell-shocked."

"My Toots don't think so," Rusciano said.

"What is she?" Aaron said, "Black or white?"

"Now comrade," said Dick, "no chauvinism."

"Take care of this," said Aaron, handing me the note.

"You don't *know* my Toots."

We organized some reluctant men to carry all the picks and shovels to Battalion headquarters near by, and then word came via the grapevine that an uprising of Franco partisans —the Fifth Column—was expected that night all over Spain; Franco had boasted of it, and even named the date; so it was thought best to put half of each company on guard against possible ambush, and detail a large squad to guard all commanders and commissars.

"What nonsense!" Aaron said. "I don't need a guard, except from Rusciano; he gropes me in his sleep."

"Sleep with your pistol, Loppy," Dick said, and Aaron laughed. But nothing happened during the night, and in the morning Aaron said, "I told you so." Captain Leonard Lamb, with a newly-healed bullet-hole through his side, had escaped from hospital, the damned fool, and was now attached to the Battalion staff. North and Toller and Roosevelt and Ed Rolfe had returned together to Barcelona. At three that afternoon word came to stand by to march that night; that we were going to relieve the Lister Division before Gandesa, and I had a premonition that there would be no writing job for some time to come.

There was still some light in the sky as we moved out of the rest-camp under the olive trees, along the narrow trail leading over the low hills toward Gandesa. We followed this trail for quite a time, then emerged onto a well-travelled highway. Ahead, muffled by distance, was the sound of artillery in the night—always more terrifying than it is by day, though less effective. We marched, in all, for twelve kilometers, reaching and passing through the small town of Pinell, and then the road wound steeply uphill, bounded on one side by a precipitous gorge out of which came the sudden sickly smell of the dead, and on the other by towering peaks and crags that would have been fantastic even in the daytime. There was one rock-peak shaped like the prow of a great ocean liner, steep and sheared to a point, that menaced the road with its bulk and its shadow, and the men toiling up the grade. Then we turned off the main road onto a goatpath that led into the hills.

For two and a half hours we bent to the forty-degree angle, twisting and turning, slipping and stumbling up the almost impassable way. There was one thought in our minds: it's going to be hell getting food, water and munitions up this hill; it's going to be tough for the wounded; it would all have to be done by mules, and mules were only flesh and blood. There was a moon, and the smell of burnt wood; halfway up the mountain, the sudden, incongruous sight of a soldier sitting on a rock by the path (it was past three A.M.), reading a letter as though it were the last chance he would have in the world to read that letter. It was unreal. And as we progressed up the slippery broken stone the unreality augmented until it all seemed part of a bad dream. For God never made a more desolate stretch of territory, and man never contributed more to its further desolation. We sweated and groaned under the weight of our equipment, our guns. Rock walls bordered the goat-trail that led to the wind-torn summits, and near the crest we came upon terrain that had been fought over, lost and recaptured by the famous XIth Division, Lister's men. Here they had withstood heavy shelling; here the Fascist planes had rained incendiary bombs and, temporarily, driven our men off. It looked like a landscape on the moon—tumbled, crumbling rock, black and slippery; burnt-off shrubbery that caught our trouser-legs and tripped us up. We slipped and fell, stumbled and cursed; there was a bitter wind and the smell of wood-smoke.

Even before dawn it was possible to see that there was no cover here; there were no trees; there were no bushes; there were no natural cavities in the rock; the earth itself was stone—you could not dig in it. And there were no fortifications facing the enemy. Lister's men had done the best they could; they had scraped shallow trenches into the crest of the hill, and they had erected stone parapets topped with a few sandbags. These were the lines we had to hold, and they were important; for if the enemy could retake this hill (number 666 on our military maps), and hold it, he could dominate our main bridge-head at Mora and the entire sector would become untenable. There is no way to understand why the Lincoln Battalion, in fighting strength the weakest in the XVth Brigade, had been detailed to hold this position, but these things sometimes happen.

Before dawn Aaron established the men in the lines; moved the *plana mayor* back down the central crest about a hundred meters, against a relatively low stone bluff. Here the company staff was to be in the direct line of fire, and here it was to stay, for there was no other place to put it. The position was heartbreaking; there was no food, no water on the hill, and if we could escape the fire, there would be the sun. Sam Spiller, Antonio Anton, Rafael the youngster whose clipped head looked like a cocoanut, the other runners and the observers, Virgili and Albareda, the barber Angel, the *furiel,* Lara, the

American secretary Curtis and the Spanish secretary, Sans, the stretcher-bearers and the *practicante,* Lee got to work constructing what looked like modern bathtubs, cradles of loose stone against the wall of the low cliff. And when the dawn came we climbed into them with the field-telephone and the Battalion telephonist detailed to us. Aaron went up into the lines, where the men were already cursing the impossible fortifications and the lack of cover against anything the Fascists cared to throw at us.

With the dawn we could really see what we had to work with; a bare mountainside thrust into the empty sky, facing a concealed enemy slightly below. Gandesa was a kilometer or so below us. Corbera was to the right of the Battalion sector, on the road below; Pinell was behind us and to the left. On our left flank was the Canadian Battalion, the Mac-Paps; behind us somewhere were the British, in reserve. On our right flank there was nothing but the steep slope of the hills, falling away to the valley through which the road ran to Gandesa. The mountain-side was pitted with shell-holes, strewn with splinters and casings. (We used some of the larger pieces of shrapnel to construct our parapets.) The back side of our hill was folded; our company staff was on one grade; no men were stationed on the other but stretcher-bearers were to pass across the opposite slope on their way toward the *sanidad* behind the right-hand hill.

All day we waited in the heat; there was no water. Then some water came up—water disinfected with iodine and mixed with Spanish cognac; it was warm to drink and rotten to the taste. A squadron of Fascist planes came over and unloaded upon the Mac-Paps, on our left. We waited patiently for our turn, but they ignored us.

They came and they ignored us, but Curtis would say, "Christ, here they come! Christ, we're gonna get it now!" To which we said nothing.

"This is a hell of a place to be," he said.

"You're right." He was lying low in the 'bathtub' next to mine, with the telephonist.

"What?"

"I said, You're right."

"This is a hell of a spot—*look* at 'em!" he said. "Thirty-two of 'em. Jesus, are we gonna get it now!"

"Shut up!"

"Why?" he said. "I didn't say anything. I was just saying look how many there are——"

"We can count."

"Well, I didn't mean anything; I was just saying—Holy Christ!" he said.

There was a meeting of company commanders going on, back of the hill at the *estado-mayor,* and we lay baking in the unbroken sun, our mouths dry with the heat, the thirst, the tension. Aaron finally came back, near dusk, with Archie the new commissar and Dick Rusciano, and he told us an attack would be made that night to capture an isolated peak of our hill that was held by the enemy. "It'll be a cinch," he said. "A handful of men could do it." He stayed up in the line that night, sending occasional messages to me, telling me to stay near the telephone and send one of the runners when an order came. I lay in the little niche we had constructed for him, hard as only rock can be hard, waiting. Late that night there was a flurry of hand grenades and machine-gun fire, which lasted ten or fifteen minutes, but no order came down from the line, and I was nailed there anyhow. In the morning we were told that our Company 4 had captured the isolated point without firing a shot, without a casualty; there had been nobody there when they arrived, but the Fascists on other hills, thinking we were attacking, had cut loose with hundreds of grenades, mortars and even artillery, and then later sang in triumph at having repulsed our attack! Word therefore came that that day or the next our Battalion, Brigade and Division was attacking in force, our particular objective the capture of a series of hills to the south of Gandesa. There was fog early that morning, but before noon the sun began to burn it up and the sound of airplanes filled the air. All the night before food had been coming up at intervals of an hour, and we woke the men each time it arrived; there was coffee (fairly warm), a sort of vegetable imitation hamburger cooked in olive oil, sardines, bread, fruit, cookies and wine. Some mail came too, with cigarettes from Carnovsky and Brand of the Group Theater, and my flying club. We looked at ourselves in the morning; we were black from head to foot, from scrambling among the burnt rocks and the shrubbery.

"Christ!" said Curtis. "Here they come!"

At three we moved up, by order, to the back side of the main crest, where we were to wait till the attack began. Artillery support and aviation had been promised, and now there were about three hundred men sitting and lying on that slope, in plain sight of the sky, waiting. We sat, our backs to the hill, looking down the long *baranco* that led, eventually, to the road, and waiting. We streamed with sweat and lay snuggled among the hot broken rocks, flattening ourselves to the earth as much as possible. We did not talk much; some men ate their sardines and bread, others merely stared at their toes. Promptly at three-thirty our artillery awoke, and we enjoyed the sound of it coming over our heads tearing through the air like ripping silk. The sound tapered off and then, from the distance, came the report of the explosions, one-two-three. Shell after shell came over; no heavy barrage, but enough to keep them busy and uncomfortable. Then the shelling stopped and all of five of our *Chattos* appeared over the lines, diving across us and opening their machine-guns at the Fascist entrenchments across the way. It was good to see them, though they were so few, but they stayed for only about five minutes, and then they too were gone. No order came, and so we merely sat. I looked at Nat Gross, who was lying next to me, his Czech machine-gun wrapped in a piece of blanket. The lines in his young hard face seemed deeper, harder than usual, but he smiled. "This is a hell of a way from Wall Street," he said.

Then he said, "I knew it," for the Fascist artillery, stung and annoyed by us, had opened up in its turn, and was throwing its stuff over our lines. At first it was far over, and we watched the shells with a speculative interest, bursting far below us down the mountain side. "That's where the British are, in reserve," said Nat, and we both laughed. We flattened, perhaps unconsciously, a little closer to the broken rock on which we were lying, and we found a tin of sardines and began to eat it. But even as we concentrated on the food, we were aware of the fact that the Fascists had lifted their guns (there was an observation plane far above us) and we watched, since we had not been told to move, as the shell bursts came closer to us, crawling slowly up the slopes. We looked around for a runner, who should have come up about that time and told us to scatter, but no runner was in sight. We looked around at the hundreds of other men, calmly lying there as the fire crept slowly back up the mountain side toward us; they did not move, they were cleaning their guns or eating or lying on their sides talking, or trying to catch a few winks of sleep. It was getting too close for comfort, and now we were as flat as we could be. They were falling a few hundred meters below us; I was watching two men carrying a stretcher (it was empty); I just happened to be watching them, and then they were not there. The shrapnel whined viciously over our heads, slapping against the stone of the hillside, whirring away into the middle distance. I heard a brief conversation between two men I knew belonged to the Mac-Paps (I don't know what they were doing in our lines).

"Jim's gone," one said.

"How?"

"Bumped himself off; I tried to take his gun away."

"Why?"

"His leg was off; he said, 'Kill me,' but I couldn't, so he reached for his pistol."

"That's shit," the other said.

All the time we expected their planes; we listened for them, but they did not come. We could not understand why they did not come, for the enemy must have known by our barrage, by our planes, that we were planning an attack; they must have known we were lying there naked on the hillside, exposed to anything that came along. But no planes came, and it was getting dark, and no word came from the lines, from the Battalion headquarters. And so we stayed there.

Then Aaron sent Antonio for me, and I crawled up onto the crest of the hill. "Get in here, Poppa," Aaron said from behind the parapets, and I crawled over and dropped in, where the men were crowded against each other, arm to arm, waiting. "Listen," he said. "We're going over when it gets dark. We didn't take that point last night; we're going to take it tonight."

"What do you want me to do?"

"Stay here with Curtis and Sans, and when we take the point, come over with ammo."

"How will we know when you've taken it?"

"Well, it will be quiet for awhile, then you'll hear a lot of hand grenades and rifles going off, and a lot of yelling, and when it quiets down, come over."

"I'd better go with you, hadn't I?"

"You'd better stay here; I won't need you. I'll take Sam and Rafael. There won't be anything to the job." He was smiling, standing in the trench, his head about level with the stone parapets. Rafael, the young runner, was sitting up on the parapet, firing a rifle, grinning like a Cheshire cat. "Get down from there, you dope," said Aaron, and pulled his leg. The shelling had died down with the growing dark, and only a few rifle bullets were coming over now and then.

Aaron took the rifle from Rafael, and climbing halfway up the parapet, began to fire. He looked back at me, and said, grinning, "It's so long since I've had a rifle in my hands, I've forgotten what it feels like." He smiled, taking careful aim with his Mauser, and fired conscientiously for a time. He was a good shot; I remembered from the practice maneuvers, when he had always taken his place in the line, either with a rifle or a light machine-gun. He looked younger than ever, younger than his twenty-four years, standing there, firing over the parapet. The men near by stood or crouched in the shallow trench, watching him, smiling. . . .

. . . The dark forms moved silently over the parapets into the darkness, moving off to the right into the greater darkness that lay in the pocket between our hill and the little point that was to be taken; and for a long time Curtis and Sans and I kept our heads raised above the stones and watched and listened. The silence was absolute; it was suspicious. We felt that either they did not know what we were doing, or they knew too well. It was difficult to breathe, to swallow. It was difficult to watch, for there was nothing to see, and we strained our ears with listening. We crouched in the trench; then we climbed out and began to assemble ammo boxes, carrying them by their rope handles to a central point, from which it would be easy to bring them to the men.

For fifteen minutes it was absolutely silent, and we wondered how our men could move so quietly; then it began. Curtis ducked behind the stones, but Ramon Sans and I watched (I could see his scholarly face with the horn-rimmed spectacles, occasionally lit by the flashing lights)— in the distance, toward the point, there was noise; the spectacular pink roman-candles of the hand grenades going off; the hysterical chatter of the machine-guns going full blast, taken by surprise, confused shouting and yelling. Then it

stopped. "Do you think we have the hill?" I asked, and
Ramon said, "I don't know." Then it started again, and the
echoes multiplied and reverberated among the peaks; it
seemed miles away, though it was only a few hundred
meters at best. There would be a sudden, heavy explosion
and a bright flower-pot of bursting flame as a mortar exploded; silence, the shouting and the subdued murmur; a
few bullets cracked near by and it was quiet. Alternately,
every few minutes, this went on, then silence. Then it
was silent for a long time and suddenly we were aware that
there were men near us, coming by us silently, not very
many men at first, but soon more and more of them, filling
the emptiness around us with heavy breathing. Some one
was sobbing. Some one said, "Help me, I'm wounded."
Antonio was in front of me, he saluted and said, *"La pistola
del Comandante,"* and thrust the automatic into my hand. I
grasped it; it was sticky, and I held it up and could see
it was wet with something. *"El Comandante?"* I said, but
Antonio was gone, and Sam was in front of me, breathing
rapidly.

"Aaron's hurt," he said. "In the head. It's nothing. Don't
get excited; take it easy; he'll be all right."

"Are you sure. Where is he?"

"They took him out; they got him out. Did you get his
pistol? He said to give it to you to keep."

"Yes."

"Christ it was shit up there," the kid said. "They had
machine-guns; they had barbed wire; why didn't they tell
us they had barbed wire? How were we to know they had
barbed wire?—" He was out of breath.

"Where's Dick? Where's Archie?"

"I don't know. They wouldn't go ahead; they lay down in the woods——"

"Who?"

"Who do you think? The same guys; the bastards, the cowards."

I could see in the pale light that filtered from behind the streaming clouds that he was crying. I remembered that Aaron had told me about that day on the first hill, when Sam had finally found him, after thinking him lost in the attack, and had become hysterical.

"Take it easy," I said.

"Aaron's all right," he said. "I helped him walk a little way back. Did we take the hill? he said; I told him Yes; How's the company? he said; I told him Fine. He'll be all right," he said. "*He'll be all right!*"

"Go lie down," I said. "Get some rest."

"Oh, Jesus," he said. "The bastards."

Dick appeared, and Archie, and we rounded up what men we could find and posted them in the line and behind the parapets. We distributed the hand grenades and the munitions as far as they would go, and sent back for more, in the event of a counter-attack. It was bitter cold, and we lay on the bare rocks, waiting, waiting for what we did not know. They were singing over on their hills, a weird Moorish song that curdled your blood and made your spine run cold. We listened to them singing, and we watched the sudden moon come from behind the wet clouds, and then disappear again. The wind came up and blew the clouds away, and we lay strewn all over the hilltop like the dead, waiting. Seeing the men in these grotesque positions I remembered a play that I had seen, "Johnny Johnson," and it occurred to me that this was life imitating art again, or was it that the play had been so accurate a mirror of this life? I couldn't make up my mind.

Wolff was up on the hill with us, and Lamb and some of the Brigade staff, consulting in a sandbag dugout, lit with a candle, over maps and possibilities. He asked for a report, and we did the best we could; one known dead, fifteen known wounded, many missing, a rout and a retreat without orders; that was all we could determine. You couldn't find any one in the dark anyhow. Stretcher-bearers had disappeared; the men were all mixed up by squads and *pelotons* and companies; the wrong companies had gone first, misunderstood the orders; the wrong information, or worse, no information at all as to the extent of the enemy fortifications. So we hung around, and the British were brought up from reserve, and with all our men in position in the lines, the British went through just before dawn and attacked in turn, and the same thing happened to them. The Mac-Paps, who had come up to hold our positions when we jumped off, returned to their original position on the left flank; we returned to ours; the *plana mayor* of the company which was now commanded by Rusciano, retreated to its stone *refugios* alongside the cliff face, and dawn came up through the heavy fog.

Fog meant no airplanes, so we could relax. Yesterday they had been active all day, bombing Pinell behind us, Corbera and the road to Gandesa on our right, Mora and our lines of communication. We could see them from the hilltop, cruising slowly in formidable array and with damnable slowness over the terrain, sowing their seed up and down, back and forth over large square areas, and for hours the air was full of smoke and dust and trembling with the constant drumming of the explosive. Our 'pom-pom' guns sniped at them pitiably. This is a long, light anti-aircraft gun that was fairly effective, but we had so few that they paid no attention to them. Seventy-five planes merely sailed with exasperating ease through their sparse fire; then when ten of ours appeared they had to run a gauntlet of fire that blackened the sky for hundreds of acres. It was heart-breaking, and you could thank France for that; you could thank England and its Non-Intervention Committee; you could thank Italy and Germany, and last but not least you could thank the good old U. S. A. and its 'Neutrality' Act, that permitted the sale of American-made munitions to Italy and Germany for transhipment to Franco.

By ten in the morning we could hear them, however, above the fog, and Curtis, flat in the next hole, said, "Here they come!" "Don't worry," I said. "There's no ceiling; they can't see through the fog," and so we remained silent and listened to them droning and droning overhead. Then I thought, Hurray, the bastards are lost and trying to find their way downstairs, and I began to hope passionately that they would misjudge their altitude and crash into one of the jagged peaks, but they kept on droning overhead, invisible to us through the heavy blanket of the fog, moving back and forth across the range, fading into the distance and returning. And then, suddenly, there was the familiar whistling and a load fell directly into the *baranco* behind the hill, across the way from us, and the earth rose under us and threw us off and we fell back again, our hands clasped over our heads, hearing the falling rocks and dirt, waiting to be hit, our ears ringing.

Later that day the ceiling was unlimited but there were no further planes; the afternoon grew deathly quiet and the heat grew intense, but nothing happened. No rifle fired; there was no shelling; no mortars came sailing in their high parabola over the hill. *"Qué pasa?"* I said to Ramon Sans, the intellectual secretary, and he said, correctly, *"Nada."* That was the end of our third day in that hole. Earlier there had been mail with cigarettes, and I had sent two of them in an envelope to Ed Rolfe, who I thought must be back from Barcelona now, with the Battalion *estado-mayor. Still here and in one piece,* I wrote. *Enclosed please find. Hope you are the same.* I could not say, For Christ's sake hurry up and get me out of this hole; for Christ's sake *do* something; Lister's men were here for twenty days and this is only the end of our third. . . .

. . . For a change there were plenty of cigarettes, that had come from my kids, from Carnovsky and Brand in London, from others, and I had them stuffed into the pockets of my leather jacket, my shirt (where they got soaked with sweat, but tasted just as good), everywhere. We were crouched in the shallow *refugios* alongside the cliff; I was lying on my back and Dick was catching a little sleep at my feet, with Archie behind him with Sans. It had just passed noon when they opened up, and from the start they had our range. We could count about seven batteries at work, all of them concentrated on our sector, that was no more than five hundred yards wide. They began coming over, and we stayed down; they came, you heard them from the start to the end, the three low harmless thumps of the faraway guns, then a brief silence, then a low hissing growing crescendo into a riffling whistle (a scream if they were coming close) and then a deafening crash that reverberated between the two slopes that enclosed the *baranco* behind the hill. We stuck our heads up to see where they had landed, saw the brown and white smoke drifting away, the rocks falling as though in slow motion, possibly a couple men running. Then they were coming again and we ducked again.

"That was close," Curtis said. "They've got us spotted."

He was in the next hole with the telephonist, Felix. I turned onto my back, saw Aaron's automatic pistol tucked between the two rocks where I had put it, still streaked with his dried blood. (Doc Simon had sent word that he would be all right.) I heard them coming again, and closed my eyes, put my arms over my face and waited. You felt nothing at such moments except a tightening of the belly, and you drew up your legs instinctively and then it was all over. There were occasional duds; occasionally a shell whistling close overhead would suddenly lose its twirling motion and, turning end over end, go scuffling through the air making a noise like a small boy blowing air between his lips. You wanted to laugh when you heard those.

"Oh, Christ," said Curtis, "this is awful!"

"Shut up!"

"Why, what's the matter?"

"Nobody likes it any more than you do."

From where I was lying, if I lifted my head, I could see the built-up parapets of the other men in the *plana mayor,* the stretcher-bearers, the barber, the quartermaster Lara. When the shells were coming they were nowhere to be seen; after they had landed and the shrapnel had stopped screeching and smacking at the stone, they all sat up, sticking their heads over the parapet as though they were puppets in a Punch and Judy show. It was funny. Dick was crouched in front of me, with Archie behind him and Sans lying on his face the other way. "What about it?" Archie yelled, and Dick shouted, "What about what?" "We ought to be up in the line," the commissar said; then they both ducked and the thing went off and deafened us and the stones fell in on us from where the shrapnel and concussion had chipped away the cliff.

There was a terrific tearing smash and everything was black and a voice was screaming, screaming. I went out for a moment and came to, and put my hand on top of my head and looked at my hand, but there was no blood on it. It was difficult to see, the air was clogged with rock dust and smoke and the ringing was continuous and the voice kept screaming on a high note. Far away, I heard Dick say, "Who got it? You, Bess?" and I said, "I don't think so," and sat up. The screaming came from behind me, so I got up and looked, and there was Curtis, lying on his belly, his buttocks torn away, holding them with his hands, his face turned to me, dead white and powdered with rock dust, and his mouth open, his eyes looking at me, his mouth open screaming. I could not take my eyes away from his.

"Come on!" Archie shouted, and he and Dick ducked out and up the hill.

Felix lay behind Curtis, his legs bloody and his face still, and I climbed over the few stones that remained standing between us, and Felix said, "Take him first, he's worse." Curtis kept screaming although his mouth did not move, looking at me with his eyes wide and staring, and I was saying, "Take it easy take it easy take it easy," and suddenly it was *good* to be moving, good to be doing something instead of just lying there waiting for something to happen. I yelled for the *practicante,* but he was in the lines; I yelled for a bandage and was handed a small one-inch roll that was worthless. I called the stretcher-bearers, who came and we lifted Curtis out under the arms and knees (he was not screaming now), and they went away with him through the fire that was falling before us, behind us (Rafael was looking up over a near-by parapet, his mouth open), the noise terrific and the shrapnel whining and slapping around.

Felix's legs were badly torn and his foot was broken to bits, the bones stuck through the torn leather of his shoes. I gave him a cigarette (like in the movies) and tried with my wet red hands to light it for him, succeeding after a time. Rafael threw over a canteen of wine, and he took a slug or two. There was a pool of rapidly congealing blood, like half-stiffened *Jello* on the floor of the *refugio,* and I threw a blanket over it, spread the other over Felix and climbed back into my own hole. Dick and Archie had gone, but Sans looked at me and asked for a cigarette, and we both lit them and laid low.

They were pounding the shallow lines on the hill-crest; with artillery and anti-tank shells they were hammering away from left to right and back again, and it hurt to watch; it hurt in much the same way that a sore knee hurts when you clumsily bang it again and again. "God damn the bastards," I said to myself. "God damn the lousy c . . . s . . . sons-of-bitches," but that didn't do much good. They hammered at the lines and the men ran out from behind the parapets, seeking shelter on the bare back of the hill; then they came back to the lines again. They pounded at the same place time and time again, and you would see forms that looked like moving-picture dummies rise slowly in the air and fall back again. You knew that they were men.

The telephone was dead; the telephonist had become unconscious, the cigarette dead between his thin white lips, and he moaned in his stupor, over and over and over. The blood on the earth stank in the heat, turning your stomach, and I moved to look at Sans. He was calmly smoking the butt I had given him, lying on his belly, facing me. He did not smile when I smiled at him. They were coming over all the time, on top of the little cliff, in front of us, behind, and I thought, It's only a question of time before another lands right in this place. I had sent a runner to headquarters for another telephonist; the *camilleros* had not yet returned, for they had to run the gauntlet of that fire with Curtis's dead weight (dead ?), down the slope and up the opposite, around the hill to the *sanidad,* where the men must have been arriving every minute. I saw the little barber's head and little beard, and he saw me and said, "Bess-ee, this is a bad place."

"I know," I said.

"We ought to go some place else," he said. Then he ducked, and when he reappeared I said, "*Chico,* this is the company command-post; *El Teniente* Rusciano needs us here."

"It's a bad place," he said, and then the shells came again, and I saw Lara, the middle-aged quartermaster, run out of his hole and down the hill. I grasped Aaron's pistol, expecting that his example would provoke a panic among the others in the hole, but they obeyed my order to get down and that was a relief, for I knew I could not have shot one of them for running away. I could not even have fired after one.

All day, hour after hour they kept it up. They covered our parapets and every inch of the back side of the hill. They wanted, by the sheer weight of their steel, to blow us off that hill. Hour in and out they kept it up, and the body was utterly exhausted and indifferent to conscious fear, but straining to the snapping point. There was sweat, and there was internal pain; the word 'waiting' came to mean something more than it had meant before, for you were definitely waiting for them to find you and to finish you. It was impersonal; it had nothing to do with men or with machines; the steel and the noise that filled the air—they came from nowhere, but you knew they were directed at you by some agency with more than human guile. The boys in the trenches were hammered, their rock parapets smashed down; there were many wounded, many killed, many missing. There was no connection with the Battalion, and you twisted the handle of the field-set just the same, knowing that you would not get an answer. Planes came over, but they withheld their bombs, possibly because our lines were so close to theirs; you did not care. Time stood still—but absolutely. What do you think? What do you feel? Everything and nothing . . . saying over and over, "Dan and Dave stick with me now, and all the days to come, stick with me now." And it was astonishing, how you could not hold their image in your mind. Talking in a rational tone of voice to Ramon Sans, to Joe Riehl, the new telephonist who arrived a couple hours after it started, but who could not go out to repair the line. Listening to him say, "Boy, I never knew before today what a good Catholic I was," you laughed, and he laughed with you. (He had been to Spain earlier, gone home and then returned.) Talking rationally, remaining where you were, when everything in you said, Run for your life and scream out loud!

The pauses were worse than the shelling, before and after, waiting for them to cool their guns. When they are dropping the mind is impersonal even if the body is not, but waiting for them to begin again. . . . A fly is attracted to your bloody hands and clothes; you shake it off. A louse is crawling in your groin and you think, At least you're safe, you louse, and laugh. Dry lips, rising gorge, sweat and shaking limbs. You look at your hands, filthy and covered with the blood of two men who have finally been taken where? you lie and insanely cover your face with your leather jacket when you hear them coming, as though it offered any protection. You throw it angrily from you, knowing yourself a fool, but grasp it again instinctively when the whistling is growing louder and your mind tells you *this* one will be close. Hour after hour, waiting for them to find you and finish you, waiting like a rat in a trap, chained to the command post by the commander's simple words, 'I'll need you here.' And chained by more—for you cannot run away from this struggle; it is everywhere; you could not look yourself in the face again. For six hours, no word from the Battalion, no connection, and then, coming through the fire there are two men, one of them bent with the weight of a spool of wire on his back, reeling it out across the bare *baranco*. Orders. You speak calmly, trying to keep your voice even and level. "What's happening up there?" "They're throwing the shit all around." "Keep a few men in the lines and let the others seek what cover they can find; the Mac-Paps are extending their lines toward your left flank; the British are coming up with reinforcements. In the event of an attack, put all the men back in the line; get up munitions now." That is Wolff's voice speaking, a young man who is not here.

It all seems very far away and meaningless although you know the meaning or you would not be there; there is no immediate reality in this. You can think of Times Square with all its cars and all its pople, and the focus narrows down and you can see their faces, ordinary commonplace faces like the faces you have known all your life, like the faces of the Spanish men and women and children you have seen in the cities and the small towns and the country, who are waiting back of the lines now, maybe reading a newspaper: Our forces in the Sector of X . . . repulsed, with heavy casualties, a violent enemy attack and withdrew to predetermined positions on Hill Z. . . . And what does that mean, tell me, and do you know? Faces. Do they care about us over there? and do they even think of us with love? The women and the children and the men; do they know we are so far away from them and dying for them? Do they know this is *their* struggle too? There is no connection between the fact of war and people; not when you are in it. It seems to be something taking place upon another, insulated plane of existence that does not, while you live it, touch the people whom it really touches. You think of love.

Yes, you can think of love. The love you have never had and could not give; the love that does not need words to create itself, but exists as a bond between the man and the woman who can look at each other and say inside their minds, I love and I am loved. The body is precious to you; the body wants to live. It wants to live to touch again— ('Hell,' he said, 'this may be the last chance I ever get to sleep with a woman.')—those tender parts of a woman's body that are so much of woman (her symbol and her essence), those parts you only need to touch so lightly with your hand to know again that you are a man and she is a woman and that there *is* a meaning to the world and to the life we try to live, but which they are trying to steal from us. For it is love alone that can, for even a moment of our time, give you the illusion that you are not alone, penetrate your loneliness and separate it from you for that moment. And you are afraid that you will die without that love; you are not just afraid to *die*. And this is the meaning of it all (the people's war); these men behind these fragile rocks, these men whose tender flesh is torn to pieces by the hot and ragged steel; they could not accept their death with such good grace if they did not love so deeply and so well— were not determined that love must come alive into the world. What other reason could there be for dying? What other reason for this blood upon your hands?

10

[August 20th–September 24th]

IN THE early darkness, after the artillery stopped firing, there was a brief flurry; our men stood in the shallow trenches and hurled grenades; there was a little rifle-fire and then silence. Apparently they had decided not to attack; that their sheer steel had not blown us off the hill. And after all these hours, eight in all, when you tried to walk, rising from the narrow niche in which you had been lying all that day, it was almost impossible. Your legs refused to obey your mind, and you had to look at them to assure yourself that they were there, and *will* them to move. It was like the children's game in which you cross your arms and then clasp your hands and fingers, and you have to touch a finger before you can localize it and make it move. Now you had to look at your feet to make them walk, and when you walked it was like a cat in paper boots; you lifted each foot an exaggerated distance off the ground, and placed it down with care, testing it to see if it would hold. Your body was weak and light as a feather; your hands shook uncontrollably, your intestines quivered. Trying to relieve yourself some distance from the shelter—ready to jump and run at the sound of a distant gun—you tottered on your feet and fell back into your excrement. You wondered how much of this it would be possible to bear.

But sleep was possible; a deep, exhausted sleep that did not rest the body; a sleep broken by endless phone-calls from Battalion. In the morning there was a light rain that soon cleared; a few shells and mortars came over, feeling for the range they had had the day before. Tobacco helped to keep you sane, and you smoked endlessly until your tongue was raw as a barked knee and your lips cracked. It was fortunate that there *was* something to smoke; cigarettes from home, others from Nat Gross who received four cartons on the mail that came up during the night. It was possible to talk with the others—Sans and Dick and Archie (cut above the eye by flying stone)—to talk rationally about Joe Bianca, who had been killed by a shell the day before (no one believed that Joe would ever get it; no one believed it now, but there it was); about Paul Wendorf, transferred from the machine-gun company to a 'safe' job as liaison-man between Brigade and the Battalions, who had been hit by shrapnel way behind the line, and killed—it was even possible to joke. The British Battalion had withdrawn to its reserve position, and ours, the weakest in the Brigade, still held its weakened lines. Our Company 1, merger of two companies, could account for fifty-two men; each original company had had over a hundred when we crossed the Ebro less than a month before.

And then it began all over again about ten in the morning; not quite as intense, but much more accurate. Their electric batteries pounded our parapets viciously with shell after shell and mortar after mortar, smashing them to pieces. The men ran out, sought shelter and returned; the Fascists advanced under cover of the barrage, and received hand-grenades for a reception. They withdrew and our morale rose visibly—and audibly. Archie had the men singing *The Star-Spangled Banner* in the lines, and the barrage began again. The pocket behind the hill howled and re-echoed with the shrapnel, the howling amplified by the peculiar acoustics of the place. A shell that fell a hundred meters away sounded in your very ears; ricocheting steel twanged and whined in all directions until four o'clock, and then there was a sudden silence; a silence that grew on us and enervated us till we said, "Christ, I wish they'd start again; anything is better than this silence!" But they did not start; there was no sound over the hills, not a rifle-shot, a grenade or a mortar, nothing. I thought of the burned-off hills in

Pike County, Pennsylvania, burned years before and desolate as badlands always are. This was the same; or much the same. Death lay over both; the silence and the desolation of the grave. . . .

. . . Near dawn of the next day we were relieved in that position by the British, and moved back down the mountain-side to the places they had occupied, shallow gravelike holes dug into the hard soil of the hills. Here we lay and slept, filthy, unshaved, crawling with lice, with no water in which to wash, no change of clothes possible. What would it be? the men asked, how long would we be there? They were unnerved; they had the jitters; I remember George Cady's hands shaking uncontrollably for days; I remember the short stick that Sergeant Leo Markowitz carried between his teeth, to prevent them from chattering. All day we lay in these lightly camouflaged grave-holes, waiting, sleeping, talking of the action, of the men who had gone defending that position, of the possibility of more.

I remembered particularly Albareda, the youngster who had been one of our observers. Plump, always finding it diffi-cult to keep up with the rest, we had had to use him in the Pandols as a runner. There was something about the kid that, from the time he first appeared late in May, made me feel that he was doomed. He was young—nineteen—preternaturally grave. He was homesick, and shortly before we crossed the Ebro, he had received a letter that his father in Barcelona was gravely ill. We arranged for him to have forty-eight hours leave, and he returned and told us that his father had died. Then the day of the great barrage—the nineteenth— he had run his legs off in that sector, carrying messages from unit to unit, and on one occasion when I had to send him out again, he said,

"*Sargento, no puedo andar mas.*"

"I know," I said. "But some one's got to go. If I could leave this post I'd go myself; all the other runners are away."

"*Muy bien,*" he said, and went. An hour later he returned, saluted to indicate that he had carried out his mission, and collapsed, sobbing on my shoulder. He had been slightly wounded on his way to the Mac-Paps, and they had bandaged his side; he was done in. "Get some rest," I said, and he lay down and cried quietly onto his sleeve. Then yesterday, carrying a message to the lines, he had really connected with their steel; and lost a leg. The sequence was logical. Somehow I had expected that to happen, but I could not easily forget his frightened face. Sam Spiller had been wounded, too, some shrapnel splinters in the buttocks, nothing much.

Now Joe North appeared again, puffing up the long exhausting hills, and we met at Battalion headquarters below a cliff that hung above the road. On the road below, through a pair of opera-glasses Ernst Toller sent to me, we could see a burnt-up truck, our food-truck that had been hit days before by a shell that killed the driver. (There had been no food that night and the men had been pretty sore.) The noise of fighting was loud and constant over near Gandesa. Messerschmidts and Junkers, Bredas and Savoias were bombing and strafing all the day. An occasional stray shell came over us and landed farther down the valley. Joe said that Rolfe had been disaffected from the International Brigades, would soon take over his *Daily Worker* job as correspondent.

He said that I would be given Ed's job; he did not know when. This was hard news to take, for the indications were that we would go back up the hill at any time; we could hear the British taking all their stuff; the echoes reverberated down the valley. And looking at the men, you wondered what would happen if the going got too tough up on the hill, and we were called again; they seemed hopelessly demoralized. Our company strength was rated at fifty-eight; the Battalion strength, that had been seven hundred and sixty-eight when we crossed the Ebro, now stood at a little more than three hundred eighty, including all the services—transmissions, *sanidad* and kitchen, as well as fighting men.

North's news of Europe was disheartening. Hitler had mobilized a million and a half men on the Czech and French borders, presumably for 'maneuvers'; probably for aggression against Czechoslovakia if the democracies, as they are euphemistically described, remained supine. Roosevelt and Hull had, it is true, made strong speeches against Fascist aggression within the week, and called for united democratic opposition, but when would the talking end and what good did it do? Franco, unlike the Spanish Loyalist Government, had given a categorical refusal to the Non-Intervention Committee's alleged plan for evacuation of foreign volunteers; he did worse, he said he would accept it in exchange for belligerent rights, immediately granted. The British Trades' Union Congress (soon to open) offered a ray of hope, *if* it could be united and if, by the crystallization of opposition it could overthrow the Chamberlain Government; which seemed unlikely. The Soviet Union, Joe said, would not act unless France came to the aid of Czechoslovakia, and France still seemed to be tied to the tail of England's kite.

In the bargain, there seemed to be a small but influential group in Spain that favored compromise with Fascism. There had been a crisis in the Negrin cabinet, when two ministers voted against new decrees that had centralized the war industries and militarized the ports. The people of Barcelona awoke one day to find twenty-five armored cars lined up in front of the Presidential Palace, troops in the streets and aviation overhead. But the next day, as a gesture of confidence in his authority, the magnificent Doctor Negrin had gone to Zürich to attend an international conference of physiologists! It was true that one of the new ministers favored compromise, but with the exception of the Basque and Catalonian Nationalists, every major party and workers' organization had given its endorsement to the new regime. As always, the Anarchists and President Azaña's personal coterie remained an unknown quantity.

Still exhausted, still unnerved, the men went back up the hills at night, their rifles slung over their shoulders, to fortify the positions the British were holding. They spent the night rebuilding the parapets that were smashed during the day. "Stay here," Archie said, "and keep an ear cocked. The men don't know it, but we're expecting a large-scale attack at three in the morning. The Fascists have brought up five or six divisions." "Oughtn't they to know it?" I said, and he said, "They will if it comes off; if it doesn't, it's better that they don't."

I lay in my grave, wrapped in what blankets I could find, listening, but the night was silent and before the dawn came I was asleep. Every night the men returned to fortify, and during the daytime we improved the shelters that we had, for occasional shells came over and fell close by, and the black wings of the Fascist *avion* were overhead all day. All day the constant drumming of their bombs sounded from near Corbera or Pinell, and the sky was dark with constant smoke and dirt. No word came from Brigade about the job; there was a violent wind and bitter cold; diarrhea was epidemic. But despite the sickness, we could enjoy a jar of jam and a tin of Belgian butter that Harold Smith had brought from Barcelona. His wound just barely healed, he had returned; had been sent back again.

Sam Spiller came back from the hospital at La Sabinosa. "I saw Aaron," he said. "He lost an eye; he may lose the other, and he says to tell you to write to his girl and say he's wounded but he'll be all right; and to tell Wolff and Gates to see what they can do. He wants to get out of Spain, to some place where they can save his other eye. He's scared." So we saw Wolff and Gates, and we told them what we knew, and they got in touch with Gallo at the *Comisariado* of the International Brigades in Barcelona, to see what could be done about getting him to an eye-specialist. They got hold of a copy of *The Book of the XVth Brigade,* and they asked all his friends to autograph it for him, and write something that would make him smile. Wolff wrote, 'For Aaron, a good guy to have in a tough spot.' I wrote, 'From the worst adjutant you'll ever have.' Others wrote Cheerio or Happy Landings, and we sent the book to him in hospital; we knew he would be pleased to have it.

It was blazing hot during the day and freezing cold at night, and it was true that Rusciano must have dreamed he was sleeping with his Toots. The food came up, laboriously,

after dark, and was distributed in the dark and eaten. Day
followed day until we had been nine days in the Pandols,
five days in action on the peak and four days in reserve.
Would we go back to relieve the British, or was it true that
a fresh division was coming up behind us? If we rested,
would we go back across the Ebro, really rest; or would
they drop us in some hole that was naked to artillery and
avion? The Battalion had been cited during the early part
of the offensive; now Brigade itself was cited by Division,
for its 'magnificent resistance' on Hill 666. Somehow we
could not relish the citation in view of the persistent rumors
of imminent attack, to which we might be called. First *they*
were going to attack; then *we* were going to attack. For it
seemed they were determined to smash through at this
point in our lines, and their strategy was quite correct.
They had concentrated enormous quantities of men and
materials (Italian men, Italian and German machines), and
we laughed at their leaflets that said: *How many foreign
prisoners have you taken in this sector? Not one! And yet
your press keeps yelping about a foreign invasion. All is lies
in your propaganda.* True, we had taken no foreign prisoners; for they had used no foreign troops.

It was quiet, and then it was loud with noise; the famous
43d Division, that had once been surrounded in the Pyrenees
and forced over the border into France, was below us in the
folded gulleys and pockets of the mountains. Word came
that we might all attack, in force, to finally pinch off and
close the pocket that had been thrown around Gandesa.
Orders came up advising us to return all surplus equipment,
picks and shovels, to the armory, to clean camp and remember that 'the Battalion is still in reserve and the men are

to be prepared to go into action at a moment's notice.' The old stomach quivered in anticipation of the next twenty-four hours; the hands shook and the smile was forced. . . .

But we came down off the Sierra Pandols at dusk, eleven days after we had climbed into them, and we came down a whole lot faster than we had gone in. Passing us on the narrow goat-paths, going the other way, were the men of the 43d Division, mostly more mature than we, heavy, solidly built men wearing overalls and caps in many cases; hard, determined fighters who with many like them formed the backbone of the Spanish Republican Army—working-men. They cheered us, in the dark, and we cheered them; and then we were on the road that wound down beside the gulch from out of which the stench of the dead rose strong as ever, laughing and shouting, and we went back through Pinell (that was no longer standing), and cut off the main road and marched eight kilometers toward the Ebro, where we camped for the night. Rumor said we would move again the next night, possibly across the Ebro; men who had been slightly wounded in the early part of the offensive joined us in the night, and the next day, stretched under olive trees on piles of straw that happened to be there from the glean-ing, I was told to report to the Brigade Commissariat as front-line correspondent for our sheet, *The Volunteer for Liberty*. It occurred to me that it was the 28th of August, my older son's sixth birthday. And since I'm sentimental, I felt that it was a good present for him.

It was a job that would have taxed the ingenuity of a man with more newspaper experience than I possessed. Front-line correspondent for a publication that was printed over a hundred kilometers away; there were no dead-lines, no dummy was possible, no proofs were shown, Brigade had no control over the sheet and there was no contact with John Tisa, who made up the job in Barcelona, except to send the stuff by mail and hope it got there, or wait till some one was going into town. You had to be a leg-man, reporter, rewrite man and editor all at once. The men were fed up with the *Volunteer;* it published too much 'horse-shit' about how-to-win-the-war and we-must-keep-our-mo-rale-up, and our-glorious-aviation and our-glorious-XVth-Brigade and our traditions and the machinations of the Fascist powers. The men knew all about that stuff. They wanted to read about themselves, their exploits, human-interest stories about 'Gabby' Klein, the clown of the Battalion (who had cast-iron guts in the bargain), about the time Captain Goddard talked a Fascist company into surrender, about Captain Wolff, who had been cited for promotion to Major for his work in the offensive, about the humorous incidents and the queer things that were said, the gripes and gags, the jokes and the guys who really did the stuff. They were the men who should have written the paper; but either they were in action, fighting; or they were in reserve, resting, and they had neither the time, the inclination nor the talent.

I tried to establish reliable correspondents in each Battalion of the Brigade—the Lincolns, MacPaps, British, 24th —and it is true that four men promised to round up stuff for me, but no one did except Ralph Bates's brother, Ronald, who turned in an article on the British that could not be used. If you went around and 'interviewed' the outstanding leaders of the various units, they would either say, 'Here comes that man again,' and laugh it off, or else shut up like clams and refuse to coöperate. So you ferretted out information about the interesting men, and your dope was generally inaccurate and the men in question pounced on you for that. Or, considering the lapse that occurred between the time you sent the stuff to Barcelona and the time it would appear, the news would all be stale and have to be killed, only to be supplanted by an inspirational article by Commissar Gallo. You got a headache, and the men found that the *Volunteer* stock was much too stiff for comfort.

The Commissariat of the Brigade was a weird place anyhow. Presided over by Sandor Voros, Hungarian-American who had an accent you could cut with a knife and an opinion of himself you could not puncture with a sabre, there was a job-lot assortment of Spanish and International comrades. Dave Gordon, who had a small mustache and fingered it continuously, got out a daily bulletin, largely inspirational, called *Our Fight*. Bill Griffith, whose Welsh accent was almost as thick as Sandor's, was a sort of personnel men between the various battalions; Ernst Lesser (British for all his name) supplied 'information' of a secret, military nature, handling reports on the daily actions, the internal workings of the units, their number of effectives, the state of their morale. There was a jolly young Spanish sports delegate, who did nothing, although he *had* imported an assortment of bright orange *futbol* shorts from Barcelona; there was a fat Spanish secretary who wore a broken pistol, a Spanish cultural and statistical expert (who was the most lugubrious human being I have ever met—and one of the finest), a person named Sanchez who was in charge of press and propaganda, and was a coward from the word go.

None of these boys got along very well with the others, and it was a matter of considerable shock to me (at first), to find that in the one spot where the political development of the Brigade should have been the highest, it was actually the lowest. The Spanish argued continually among themselves, and stuck to each other; the Internationals felt somewhat contemptuous and fraternized with each other, when at all. No one listened to anything that Voros had to say, except Voros. Gordon maintained a discreet silence that seemed intended to convey a profound knowledge of the higher information. Griffith wore an air of polite bewilderment; Lesser barked at everybody, but was as sweet a guy as you will ever meet; Sanchez was deaf, greedy, egotistical and argumentative, and the fat secretary giggled all the time. It was a madhouse; so I went my own way, walking kilometers from one battalion to another, where they were resting off the road from Ascot to Corbera, having lunch with the Lincolns, tea with the British and supper with the Mac-Paps, and gathering no news at all. There was none.

The only news came from outside, and some of it was startling. It was rumored that the Government was wondering what to do about the International Brigades. Men were no longer coming in from other countries; the Brigades themselves were shot to hell, and it was being considered whether they should be allowed to peter out, or be sent home in a blaze of glory. Some substance was given to this rumor in a speech by Harry Pollitt, British working-class leader, who hinted vaguely at a 'satisfactory answer' to 'the problem that is bothering you all.' Within an hour, the battalions were ablaze with rumors and conjecture. Hitler had demanded non-aggression pacts of Jugoslavia, Hungary

and Rumania, guaranteeing their neutrality in the event
that he invaded Czechoslovakia. They were refused. France
was apparently itching to open its Spanish frontier formally;
had announced it would stand by the Czechs if Hitler
marched. The Chamberlain gang was still powerful, but it
might be forced by the Trades' Union Congress to make some
concessions in regard to Spain. The Loyalists had made
advances in Extramadura, and had initiated a 'mosquito-
bite' campaign that kept the Fascists busy everywhere at
once, repulsing short but vicious jabs at their lines, and thus
stalling their counter-offensive at Gandesa.

But still the pressure on our lines around Gandesa became
stronger all the time, and the air was thick with heavy
bombers unloading on the crossroads about five kilometers
away, and it shook with the reverberation of artillery that
lasted day and night. We heard that they had succeeded in
advancing their lines in the sector, and were trying hard
to push a V down toward Mora de Ebro, our main bridge-
head. And in the event of action, our respective tasks were
outlined by Voros, with much verbiage and many significant
pauses; I was expected to stay with the headquarters of the
Brigade, wherever it would be located, and make trips out
to the battalions in the lines, gathering material for stories.
There was also the matter of helping with the daily bulletin,
but there was nothing certain, except that if our lines gave
at any time, we would go in. Hence, the trip I had been
promised to Barcelona, to contact Tisa and gather material
for a pamphlet the Brigade was interested in seeing published, was stalled off. The possibility, voiced by Voros, that
I would be sent to Barcelona to work there vanished when
he was sent instead, did not come back. So the time while we

were waiting was occupied with walking to and fro, and making vain efforts to combat lice, fleas, scabies and diarrhea. The days and nights were cooler now; it felt definitely like fall....

It was necessary, however, to do something about the rumors that were floating around the camp, and the feeling that had been inflamed by another factor. During our first rest period on this side of the Ebro word had come that the Government was going to grant foreign leave to men with fourteen months' service, who had seen six months at the front. Now the first batch of International veterans was leaving for furlough in Paris, and the men did not hesitate to predict that they never would come back. This was felt to be a form of repatriation that foreshadowed the beginning of the end, but combined with the other information—that conversations were actually going on in the Government about the disposition of the Internationals—it called for concrete action, for the men might have to enter the lines again at any time. Therefore a meeting of all commissars was held at the Brigade, and the law was laid down.

Are we needed? it was asked. Yes, or we wouldn't still be here. The Fascists had announced by bulletin and radio that their efforts to push us back to the river were being impeded by 'the Government's best troops—the Internationals.' This proved that our propaganda value still persisted. The Ebro victory was important for its national and international repercussions. It had definitely strengthened the Government's position both in Spain and abroad; it had won the admiration of the democratic world, and it definitely helped to check Hitler-Mussolini aggression elsewhere. Hence the importance, said Brigade, of our maintaining, at all costs, the gains that we had made. The

Government, said Brigade, is the only source qualified to say when we shall go, or when our rôle in Spain is ended. "The men must be kept prepared for action; those on foreign leave are returning, and no lowering of morale, which would be occasioned by International or Spanish conviction that the I. B.'s are leaving imminently, can be permitted." That was that. And fierce fighting was going on near by.

The same afternoon at one o'clock, waiting at Brigade to talk to Gates, I saw Captain Malcolm Dunbar, Chief of Staff, pick up the field-telephone and call each battalion commander. "Have the men stand by," he said in his well-modulated British voice, "to move when the next order is received. . . . Have the men stand by to move. . . ."

There was a song the men used to sing at that time, in a comic, wailing voice, laughing while they sang. It went like this:

> I, want to go ho-ome,
> I, want to go ho-ome,
> Machine-guns they rattle,
> The cannons they roar,
> I—don't—want—to—go—to—the—front any more.
> Send me over the sea
> Where the Fascists can't get at me-ee,
> Oh my, I'm too young to die,
> I, *want to go ho*-OME!

It was an old song. . . .

The sun was brilliant, hot and white, and one by one the auto-park *camions* were ordered out of the scant shadow of the trees. The men came down to the road from their rest-places in single file, and piled into the trucks. They were nervous; they could hear the bombing at the crossroads, see the high columns of smoke rising on the horizon, hear the artillery going in the sector to which they were being rushed. It was rumored that the lines had broken; that we were badly needed. The road was under fire part of the way to the front, and the trucks would have to run through that fire; there was no time to wait for us to march the five kilometers. One by one the trucks came out from under the trees, loaded with men crouched in their bodies, and moved off into the direction of the sound. We sat under the trees, waiting to see if they would come back, and they did. Then, when all the men had been transported to the front, the comrades of the Commissariat were loaded on. "Don't worry," Easey Goldstein said (he was in charge of the auto-park), "only one *camion's* been hit so far." The truck picked up speed and we reached the crossroads, where there was barely room to pass because the road was torn to pieces, and turning right roared on toward the front. Watching from the truck, you could see the shells landing to the right and left of the road, on the road itself far ahead, behind. You crouched and waited. We piled out at a point beyond which it was inadvisable to go, and sat alongside the road, waiting.

Our artillery was firing over our heads; the batteries were quite close, close enough for us to see the dust rise from the ground when they fired from the woods near by. We didn't know where Brigade headquarters was located, so we waited several hours as the sun declined, and when a runner came to us we followed him down the highway, stepping carefully over the fallen telephone-wires, noting the shell craters in the road. We came off the road to our left, down into a *baranco* where a small stream flowed, and up a long grade between two hills. At the top of this little valley there was a natural cave, and in this the Brigade head-quarters was located. Gordon, who had become acting chief of the Commissariat when Voros went to Barcelona, told me I would not be needed that night, so I came back down and picked up a truck back to the little house where we had been quartered before.

Here, the next morning, I wrote and had mimeographed the English bulletin, *Our Fight.* "In the zone of the Ebro heavy fighting continues without interruption. Our forces continue to resist heroically the strongest enemy attacks, and have made him pay dearly for a slight rectification of his lines. . . ." (It was suddenly more unreal than ever!) Or, from Paris: "In view of the international situation, all officers and soldiers on leave have received orders to return immediately to their garrisons. All the reservists of the cele-brated Maginot Line have been recalled to the ranks. . . ." (Mussolini had ordered all Italian Jews who had entered Italy since 1919, to get out. Hitler's Czech stooge, Henlein, was conferring with him.) I had orders to remain on tap to see if I was needed; but the chances of going to Barcelona seemed slim indeed. At noon that day I went down to head-quarters again on the kitchen-truck, crossed the road and climbed the valley into the cave that topped the hill. Here it was possible to learn what had happened: one brigade of the famous Lister Division had broken in the sector of Corbera, and we had been called in to hold the line. We held. Something else had happened, but I did not learn just then what it was. Night was coming on and the cave at the crest of the hill was alive. . . .

Here, at one time, peasants had utilized the natural shel-

ter, filled its mouth with masonry and constructed a home.
(Spain was still full of cave-dwellers who had no place else
to live.) The cavern was partitioned into many large rooms,
and each room was now crowded with men. From each
room there rose a hum of conversation in a low tone, the
rattle of typewriters, the buzzing of the central, the separate
voice of one or another of the *jefes* on the telephone. For
this cavern in the rocks was the central, the nerve-center
of our Brigade; from it there ran a network, a spider-web
of wires, down the mountainside, over the *barancos,* to the
separate command-posts of our four Battalions, deployed in
front of the enemy lines. Over the wires, strung precariously
from hill to hill, went the information that coördinated our
activities, that bound us together and permitted us to function as an integral corps. And at the center of this web of
wire was the man who held all the wires in his hands, whose
will and intelligence was felt at the extremities of the lines.
He was a small man, as stature goes; he did not afford the
stereotyped picture of the military man. But you would not
have needed to read a record of his achievements as a commander since this war began, to feel that he knew what he
was doing and that his adjutants had confidence in him.
This small, unimpressive man was Major José Antonio
Valledor, Commander of the XVth International Brigade.

Midnight:

Candlelight has a way of distorting shadows; they wave
and flutter over the stone ceiling, augmenting the atmos-
phere of unreality. You cannot overcome this sense of unreality, of walking and climbing through the quiet Spanish
countryside, mounting the terraces, skirting the olive trees,

and then, entering a cave to find activity that should only rightly have its place (or so it seems) in some large meeting hall in some large city.

"Pongame con la Cincuenta y Ocho," says the voice. Then, "Wolff . . . four hundred *zapadores* are coming up there; use them as you see fit. Hello. *Oiga, oiga! Central, yo estaba hablando con la Cincuenta y Ocho. . . ."*

In the distance there is a machine-gun speaking; it has a sharp, authoritative voice in the silence of the night. There is a moon behind mottled clouds, moving in and out of them, and the night is alternately bright and then, suddenly, the light fades out of the sky. The huge black hill that the enemy is holding is afire, a creeping line of flame, like a glow-worm, crawls across its face. . . . Inside again, Valledor is standing near the doorway; he wears a short leather jacket that hangs open; his hands are in its pockets; he wears no hat. In the course of the night, that seems interminable, that is filled with mechanical and human voices, you notice that he is never alone—he is always talking to the soldiers, to his officers; he always has time to talk to his men, and there is no difference in his demeanor, whether he is talking to the Divisional Commander or to a soldier posted as a guard at the door. He is always cheerful; he gives the appearance of possessing a boundless fund of good humor; he laughs frequently, talking in a manner that is entirely characteristic of the man—short, staccato sentences.

"Digame," says the voice. *"Quien? El capitán Dunbar? Un momento."*

The enemy is putting pressure on our lines in the Corbera sector; Corbera is a no-man's land they say. In the past few days we have seen their black vultures in droves; we have

heard the *avion* signal from the observers on the hill, and
we have lain quiet in the shadow of the olives, the olives that
will remain forever in our memories of Spain, and watched
them soar overhead, bank and turn. Then we have heard
the whistling, seen the 'eggs' falling, swelling, felt the earth
tremble under us with indignation as the roar rose, rolled
and died away. 'Where are our planes?' we think. And
then they come. And then, one day, after many days in
rest, the word came. It came at one o'clock that afternoon,
'Prepare to move when the order is given.'

   "Where's Valledor?" says a voice, but he is not there.
The Lincolns are effecting a shift of their lines, and he has
gone off to be on the spot, to aid and criticize, to see that
the new positions utilize the best aspects of the broken
terrain. The soldier has a worm's-eye view; he rarely gets
to see his Brigade Commander. But the Commander is
there; this particular commander is as likely as not to turn
up, unobtrusively, beside a sentry at night, in the *puesto de
mando* of a battalion, within the sector of a company under
fire. That, too, is characteristic of the man, just as it is a fact
that this is a different sort of army. Our commanders are
not likely to be found kilometers behind the lines, drinking
champagne, strutting in polished cavalry boots. Do you
remember Merriman? Do you remember Doran?

Two A.M.

   There are men stretched in their blankets against the rock
walls of the cavern, transmissions men, guards, runners resting temporarily from their endless rounds of the battalions;
they lie in grotesque postures like the dead, the heavy sleep
of exhaustion upon them for the moment; although they

can rise from sleep with their senses wide-awake. But the hum of the central never ceases; the 59th is reporting on fortification work, the British, in reserve, are getting ready to move into the lines. *"Digame,"* says the voice. *"Aqui La Quince. De parte de quien?"* "Damn it all!" says another voice, "Goddard was here to show them where to place that anti-tank. Get busy on it!" *"Pongame,"* says the voice, *"con La Batallon Sesenta . . . Oiga . . . oiga!"* The candles flicker in the draft through the open doorway, where the guard stands wrapped in a blanket; there is a hum of conversation from a point on the dirt floor where Valledor and Brigade Commissar Gates are talking. They are huddled close together; Gates's voice low, indistinct, Valledor's sharp, accented. These two, years apart, continents distant in culture and training, are here together in a cave in the hills of Spain, talking together in a manner characteristic of old friends who have never parted since they met, years before. Gates gets up to go; he is visiting the lines before he turns in for an hour's sleep.

There is something in the night air; there is tension to be felt both in the silence and the still persistent hum of conversation; in the sound of feet coming and going. It had been felt during the day just passed when the enemy artillery was active, when the shells dropped in the dooryard of the command-post, when the walls of the cavern trembled under the load of air-bombs, when the Fascist observation plane was wheeling overhead like a broad-winged vulture. Now it is felt again in the silence of this night, a silence broken only occasionally by a heavy gun in the near distance, by the rattle of our tanks moving on the main road below, the authoritative voice of the distant machine-gun.

Valledor and Dunbar, chief of staff, examine maps on which the hills are numbered. Goddard speaks in his slow, precise voice. Brigade scouts and observers are listening. "That point is under observation in the daytime," some one says. The heads draw closer together over the maps, the voices are lower, the tension seems to mount. The central buzzes continually and Valledor bends over the phone at his side; he consults the map. Outside the moon is uncovered and there are mules moving up the *baranco;* the patient, tireless beasts are bringing up endless cases of munitions. They pass over the crest of the hill on their way to the battalions.

You think of the men, sleeping now under the moon, men who will be in battle when the sun stands in the moon's place again; men who will suffer the agony of combat, and the beauty. For there is strength and beauty in our fight. Otherwise war would be a limitless horror, a ceaseless waste of life and energy. And this is a different sort of war; just as ours is a different sort of army . . . a people's war; a people's army. . . .

The moon was still high at three A.M. when I left the *estado-mayor* and walked over the crest of the hill onto the well-defined path that sloped down the mountainside into the gulley where the stream ran silver. The moon cast my elongated shadow on the white path, and I felt like a duck in a shooting-gallery ('That point is under observation in the daytime'—it was light as day). But no one saw me or no one cared, and I reached the bottom of the hill, followed the *baranco* to my left and met a sentry who directed me to the headquarters of the Lincolns. Many hundreds of meters farther on I found Wolff and Watt and the rest, squatting in a low cave under the lee of a small hill, eating a box of chocolate candy George had received from home. They were busy and could not talk to me, and I could not say, "Got any news? Anybody perform any heroic deeds today? We must have news for the *Volunteer*." I met Jim Lardner, Ring's young son, back from the hospital and attached to the Battalion once again, as squad-leader. I hunted out Luke Hinman, Battalion scout, and gave him a cigarette I had.

"I want all the news that's fit to print," I said.

"I can give you some that's not." And then he told me.

"We came into the lines day before yesterday," he said. "And that night the scouts were sent out to look over a little ridge ahead of us, and report what was on the big black bitch beyond. We told them it was held by the Fascists, and they sent word back that it couldn't be."

I couldn't see his face when he was talking; we were sitting in the shadow of a fig tree, but I could imagine what it looked like.

"Well, we told them that they sure enough held that hill, and they said, 'It's impossible; Brigade says *we* have that hill,' so they sent Bill Wheeler's company up that night, together with the scouts and observers, and we camped there and went to sleep. We woke up this morning to fire from three sides; they were marching on us with banners flying—can you imagine it, flags! Some guys tried to run up a white rag and Tom Page shot a couple of them; a lot got wounded and the rest of us ran. Gabby Klein saved a machine-gun. Fifteen of the company got back."

On the way back through the moonlight I reflected on how curious a thing it was that this story had not touched me too deeply; possibly because I had not seen it happen.

Working in this way, a little bit back of the lines, although within sound of what was happening, a new detachment had come into existence, and these second-hand reports acted upon me the way a newspaper account acts upon most readers. They cannot hold the image in their minds—'Bloody fighting is going on in the Sector of X?' What does that mean to you? For although I now occupied a relatively safe job, fear of death swelled in my mind to proportions it had never assumed before, even during the heavy barrage of August the 19th. Just as I was about to climb the hill back to the *estado-mayor,* machine-gun fire sounded from behind me, from the Lincolns' sector, and bullets began to crackle overhead. I flattened myself onto the path, beside a bank, and I waited an unconscionable amount of time after all firing had stopped, before I dared expose myself in the moonlight on the climbing path. Out of the actual fight itself, death assumed a more immediate reality, because it was less likely!

Dawn came to the sleeping and the waking men in the cavern atop the hill and the front awoke. Squadrons of planes battled directly over our heads, not two hundred feet above the mountain-top, and we watched them eagerly through the open space above the blocked up entrance to the cave. One Fascist plane fell, and word came by telephone that the pilot, who had bailed out, had been captured and would be brought to headquarters. The enemy artillery, that had had our command-post spotted from the beginning of the engagement, filled the long climbing *baranco* and landed regular shells in the very dooryard. You did not dare go outdoors for a leak, and so you held your water all day long. The acoustics of the cave amplified the sound; dust fell from the rock ceiling, it was an echoing void of noise, and we sat calmly enough on the floor, waiting for the inevitable shell that would come right in the doorway.

"What are those bastards trying to do?" said Cookson, the transmissions adjutant, "If they keep this up, they're going to hurt somebody." He spoke in a high nasal voice that was pretty enervating, but worse than that, he insisted on reading the Spanish newspaper aloud to every one within earshot. The linemen were continually going out on the lines; the Lincolns' line was broken, the Mac-Pap, the British, the 24th. One man lost a leg.

Dave Gordon handed me two letters that had come up on the breakfast truck; I was sitting with a lousy typewriter on a rock between my legs, trying desperately to think up a couple articles for the *Volunteer*. I recognized the handwriting; I had had some correspondence with this person before.

Comrade, the first one said,

I've written you before about this, but once more and then I will take action. Don't draw pictures (even for your children) of panoramic vistas (?) or views 'from where you are.' Explanation for this is superfluous, you should realize.
Censor,

MRR, responsable

The other one, from the same gentleman, said:

Dear Comrade

We would be grateful to you, if you would write in a more legible hand. It is often with great difficulty that we are able to decipher your correspondence. This slows down

our work. We would also like to inform you that the
censors do not steal cigarettes. Salud y Republica!

MRR
Censura Militar

Johnny Gates came from the other room of the cave,
where Valledor and Dunbar had their map-table. He was
looking at me; he was smiling. I showed him the two letters
and he laughed and handed them back to me. He turned to
walk away, and then he said,

"You know about Aaron, don't you?"

"No, what?" I said.

"He died."

They brought the Fascist pilot in, and he was a Spanish
youngster in a beautiful Italian flying suit, with a bullet
wound in his arm and a broken face. The Spanish company
commander in the sector where he landed had smashed him
in the jaw in a fit of rage (and we all agreed that while
this may have been humanly understandable, it was politically incorrect). He was obviously terrified; he shook
like a leaf from head to foot and expected to be shot out-
of-hand. Valledor questioned him and Smyrka, our Czech
chief of intelligence, questioned him, and he was most polite.
He was a native of Majorca and had been a pilot before the
war. When the Fascists took Majorca, they had asked him
to fly for them and since there is nothing a pilot would
rather do than fly, he had accepted. He had raided Barcelona
many times. Like most pilots everywhere, he had no political
convictions whatsoever, and it is relatively easy to drop high
explosives on people you cannot see. (I had often thought of

it while flying over Flatbush Avenue in Brooklyn.) He was utterly astonished and tearful when we took his picture, and even more so when Smyrka gave him his name and address and said, "Write to me in a month or so and let me know how you are." The artillery that was landing outside horrified him.

The artillery was venomous that day; there was heavy rifle and machine-gun fire and the *avion* (ever more numerous) was bombing and strafing all the time. For hours on end they bombarded our positions and then late that afternoon they attacked. Their attack was repulsed with heavy losses—our Cuban-Spanish battalion caught them in the open with its machine-guns and mowed them down in heaps. Then we attacked, as had been previously planned; the Mac-Paps took a hill (which was valuable for their morale, since they had had fifteen International desertions since the order came to march), and we advanced our lines throughout the sector. For a time, at Valledor's request, I lay on top of the hill and watched the battle through binoculars. It would have taken a trained observer to know what was going on, and I was not a trained observer. I could see the flash of their artillery, in broad daylight, from behind Corbera, and I could see where ours was landing in their lines. It was a panoramic vista (as the censor suspected), in which, occasionally, you would catch a glimpse of tiny men moving slowly forward or back; but largely it was a lovely, empty landscape. Then, early the next morning, before dawn, I returned to the former headquarters to write the English bulletin, and have Sanchez translate it into Spanish.

. . . *the men of the XVth,* I wrote, knowing that what

I wrote was true but scarcely believing it, *have demon-strated that they understand the slogan, RESISTIR ES VENCER. The slogan came to life! They resisted; they at-tacked; they will know how to achieve the final victory.*

The faith the Brigade places in our men, that our men place in themselves, is an ample demonstration of the depth of their anti-fascist understanding. They understand that our resistance is not only preventing a Fascist victory in Spain, but that it is also holding off Nazi Germany's planned aggression against Czechoslovakia, and is curbing the march of Fascism throughout the world. Our victory will restore Spain to a free and democratic people; it will deliver a death-blow to the plans of the Fascist International.

Well, the paper was at least soft enough for use, and at dusk I caught the food truck back to the Brigade. When-ever I met it, Jim Fowler, the driver, smiled at me. He had a humorous face, an American face, and he was a mag-nificent driver. I sat with him in the cab and he said. "Wait till you see the road. This is a new truck I got; the other was blown to hell yesterday. I wasn't in it." When we got near the lines we had to park the truck against the bank and wait till dark; they were filling the gulley where the stream ran, with everything they had.

That night I went out to the Lincolns again, but the box of chocolate candy was all gone. "Hell," said Wolff, "if we'd known we were going to have company, we'd have sent out for another one. Come along," he said, "I've got to go out to the companies." We walked a long way across the fields and low hills, and came to the lines where a good many Spanish *zapadores* were deepening and lengthening the shal-low trenches, and the men were helping or trying hard to sleep. Dick Rusciano emerged from a dugout they had made, and we sat around a time, chewing the rag. Harold Smith, back again and now attached to the Battalion as chief-of-staff in place of Yale Stuart, guided me back to headquarters, and I started back to the Brigade. The men said it had been hell on wheels and worse was expected with the dawn. "We just lie low and wait for them to stop," they said, "but they don't stop." "Gah," said Herman 'Gabby' Klein, who had miraculously stopped talking long enough to allow the other comrade to get his sentence in edgewise, "It's nothing. I got buried twice yesterday by air-bombs. They sent over two hundred planes at once, can you imagine! I got bounced all around like a cork. I ran through their fire lots of times. They can't get *me;* they're lousy shots; I'm just beginning to enjoy this war." I think he did.

The men's predictions were correct, for with dawn they opened up again. "Christ," said Cookson, who stopped reading the paper long enough to listen, "if they don't stop that, somebody's going to get hurt." But he had little time to read, for runners came in a dozen times before noon with word that the lines were down, and since all the other transmissionists were out (three had been wounded), he had to go out on the lines himself. The cave was as noisy as a boiler-factory, dust was filtering from the ceiling, rising from the floor. First-aid men were being called out continuously to take care of comrades in the near vicinity, and the runners ran their legs off. (Wolff had put the little Angel-barber to work as a runner too; he appeared once at the Brigade, worried as the devil, shaking his head, saying, *"Muy malo,* Bess-ee, *muy malo la guerra."*) I banged on a typewriter, making a few notes for the next day's bulletin; how Jim

Lardner, who was back, had lost a front tooth in the hospital ("It was a false tooth anyhow," he said); I quoted Gabby Klein; I made a note of the fact that Juan Periz, former adjutant-commissar of the Mac-Paps, was now commissar of Mac-Pap Company 4, and Antonio Perez, former adjutant-commissar of the Lincolns, was now commissar of Lincoln Company 4. (They were not related; this was news.) I was told that a Fascist prisoner had said, 'I know that I will die; but please shoot me; don't feed me to the lions in the Barcelona zoo.' (Franco told them that these 'Reds' were capable of anything; and at that the Barcelona lions were pretty hungry.) I was told that Voros was replacing Tisa on the *Volunteer* in Barcelona, and that it might be possible for me to get Jim Lardner to help me with the bulletin, since Gordon was now *jefe* of the Commissariat.

A couple transmissionists came in the door, panting and filthy, covered with dirt from head to foot. They asked for Jim Ruskin, British transmissions-chief, and one of them said, "Cookson—" and threw out his hands. Jim bit his lip and turned back to the central; Cookson was his closest friend. I thought of Aaron then, or tried to, and could only remember Johnny Gates' smile when he had told me. ('From the worst adjutant you'll ever have.') Then there came a hideous whistling scream and the ear-splitting crash that always comes with that scream, and the animal howling of men that always seems to come with that crash, and the cave was opaque with brown rock-dust and dirt and the sound of the wounded crying and moaning and men coughing and spitting with the dust. It took half an hour to clear up, and no more shells came, and they took out the eight wounded, including Captain Dunbar and the fat Spanish secretary who wore the broken pistol. Then the planes came over and unloaded directly over our heads and we hugged the earth floor as the cave rocked and trembled with the weight and the concussion, but no stone fell in. The planes went away and returned and strafed the men, their machine-guns going full blast for minutes at a time, like sewing-machines. And two hours later they directed their artillery at the *estado-mayor* again, but they were not lucky enough to make another direct hit, and at five-thirty the next morning, in the bitter cold of early September in that part of Spain, I returned to the old headquarters to get out the bulletin. . . .

. . . The Commissariat truck carried me back through Mora de Ebro the night of the 13th of September, across the solid steel bridge over the river and into the town of Marsa, near which we had spent the summer in training. The train for Barcelona did not leave till two A.M., so there was plenty of time to wait—too much time—and I never enjoyed waiting for anything. The station, even at that hour of the night, was crowded with the poorest of country folk dressed in the simplest of clothes, going to the city with covered baskets out of which stuck the neck of the inevitable bottle of wine. Soldiers were going on leave; there were girls who had come to see them off; solid peasant girls who wore light dresses even on this cold night, no stockings, no hats.

The compartments were crowded, and the dim, blue-painted bulbs were too feeble to permit a glimpse of your travelling companions. So I sat near the window and tried to go to sleep. There was no pane in the window and the air was cold. But the combination of still persistent nervousness,

upset stomach and excitement (train-rides always excite me
for a time), made sleep impossible. So the mind went back
over the past few days. The Brigade had been pulled out of
the lines 'for a few days,' and installed in a long winding
valley that seemed to be half-way between their lines and
ours. It wasn't; but the impression derived from the fact that
our batteries were on one side, firing all day, and their batteries on the other side were trying to find ours. So the air
above the men was loud with whistling shells, criss-crossing
overhead. They lay exhausted in the slight cover of scrub-
pine, their clothes off, hunting for lice. I combed the battalions for news, but there was none fit to print, for the XVth
Brigade did not retreat, it never was surrounded, etc. The
men were hoping for withdrawal across the river and a real
rest, but it seemed unlikely, although I could not tell them so.

Largest in your mind bulked the discrepancy between the
morale of the men and the fight they had put up in this
sector, the Sierra Cabals. Always, before action, they seemed
demoralized enough to desert in droves, or at least to keep
their heads down and retreat without orders. Always, when
they went in, they put up a terrific resistance, and they
attacked like devils. It had been the same on Hill 666 of the
Sierra Pandols. But give them a few days' rest out of the lines
and they would be talking about Paris leaves again, about
repatriation, and griping and swearing never to go into
action again. This was a phenomenon of a rather curious
nature, but it proved the essential solidity of the men's anti-
fascist convictions. The Spanish kids, too, though largely
conscript troops, had done a good job despite the presence in
their ranks of many weak and unreliable elements. They
were beginning to learn what the fight was all about. They

did not yet know, as surely as the international soldiers, that this was a fight from which you could never run away, but they were learning. (And perhaps they know it even better now; those that live.)

I asked George Watt, Lincoln commissar, for Jim Lardner, but George said they could not spare him; that he was a fine squad-leader, one of their best men, one of the men around whom the Battalion would have to be rebuilt again.

"He'll be more useful as a writer," I suggested.

"I don't think he's a very good writer yet," said George. "He's learning things now that will mature him, make him a good writer——"

"If he lives," I said, and George laughed and said, "Of course." Wolff seconded Watt's opinion, but laid more emphasis upon Jim's value to the Battalion as a 'cadre,' now that the outfit consisted of only 280 men. I was considerably annoyed, but I got Luke Hinman instead. "Luke's pretty tired," Wolff said. "It would be a good job for him; he's seen a lot of action; but has he ever done this sort of work?"

"He's a good writer," I said. "He's been a newspaper man before." (Neither was true.) So Luke took my place when I went to Barcelona, and would assist me thereafter; and I was glad to have him, for he was a good companion and a solid guy, and in some curious fashion he took the place of Aaron in my mind.

With the dim light of dawn in the slow, dilapidated train, I could see that the compartment was filled with peasants. Across from me there was a young girl who was rather pretty; her knees touched mine. Her clothes were shabby; her bare arms and legs were not too clean, but she had a pleasant face. She smiled at me and offered me some *ave-*

llanos from a paper bag she was carrying. I thanked her.
"You were tired, *camarada,*" she said. "You were asleep."
"Yes."
"Do you come from the front?"
"Yes."
"Inglés?"
"No. *Norteamericano; de los Estados Unidos."*
"My sweetheart is an International," she said. "Perhaps you know him. He's a cook for the Eleventh Brigade."
"No," I said.

I was sorry when she got off at the first stop in Barcelona; I got off at the second, Paseo de Gracia, but I have not forgotten her, and I wonder where her sweetheart could be now.

Ed Rolfe's hotel, the Majestic, was only a few blocks from the station, and I got him out of bed; it was only eight in the morning. The transition was too sudden; it bewildered me and overcame me with emotion. Here was a quiet, clean and well-furnished hotel room. In the room there was no sign of the war, except the criss-cross paper strips on the window-panes. Ed ordered coffee, which was brought by a liveried bellhop; he had sugar and condensed milk. He had French chocolate, *Chesterfields,* butter for the toast and marmalade. (The foreign correspondents used to send a car to France and buy their food.) He let me take a bath in his tub; the water was copious and scalding hot, and the Turkish towel was as broad as a blanket. I knew while I was taking it that a bath would mean more to me from that day on than it ever had before. Also, a deep upholstered armchair, a bed, a room with a carpet on the floor and a mirror in the closet-door. He wore civilian clothes of a good quality; he looked well. Outside, on the roof gardens below, children were playing in the sun and their happy voices made my eyes wet. There were graceful palm trees in the court, the sky was blue and peaceful. Then I remembered that I had left all my manuscripts on the rack in the train compartment, and I had to leave immediately.

At the station they told me that the train made still another stop, Estación de Francia, at the port. It meant a walk of three-quarters of an hour, for there was not a taxicab in Barcelona in those days and you had to wait, literally, for hours to get onto a street car. The streets were crowded with people going about their business; there were hundreds of young girls with filmy dresses that revealed their excellent contours, high heels, too much make-up and the peroxide hair that seems to be a passion with these women who have the most magnificent black hair in the world. Hundreds of small shops were open, to sell—nothing. Imitation tobacco was hawked on every corner. There were innumerable lines of tired women waiting for milk rations for their children. The cafés had signs, NO HAY CAFÉ, and the restaurants and hotels, NO HAY COMIDA, and the city wore that same air of tentativeness that I had noticed months before in Tarragona . . . as though it might disappear from sight at a moment's notice. I did not see these things so much as I felt them; I was in a dreadful hurry and was terribly worried about the manuscripts for *The Volunteer;* it would mean a hell of a mess if they were lost. And the station-master at Francia shrugged his shoulders when I asked about a blue portfolio. I offered him a cigarette that Ed had given me, and he went into his office and emerged with the folder; asked for another. I almost ran back to the hotel, arriving exhausted from the unaccustomed asphalt, remembering the thousands of poorly dressed but cheerful people, the sight of buildings demolished in the hundreds of unjustifiable air-raids to which the city had been subjected for over two years, the hundreds of children in bare feet and ragged clothing, begging for bread.

I made contact with Voros at the *Volunteer;* he was going up to the Brigade for a day or so on business, and he had received one of his innumerable packages. It was enormous; there were cigarettes and chocolate and cookies—anything you could want. Cautiously, he gave Tisa and me one small piece of chocolate candy each. He gave a cigarette too, after I had annoyed him for ten minutes. So I hung around and looked over back files of our paper, turning over possible material for an anthology of 'literary' work Gordon said the Brigade wanted to print; material for a pamphlet on the Ebro. The sirens went before we heard the planes, and we ran into the dooryard of the building, where there was a deep *refugio.* The anti-aircraft guns on the hills behind the city were speaking in their sudden, staccato voices, and we heard the motors droning beyond the broken clouds. We heard the whistling and the detonation of the bombs; it seemed far away, but late that afternoon when I had dinner with Ed at the Majestic, he said he had gone to the scene— a fish-market in Barcelonetta, where thirty were killed and a hundred and twenty-four were wounded, women almost all of them, waiting in line to buy a bit of fish. "They carted them away in trucks," he said. "They were piled into the trucks, their heads hanging back, gray in their faces, the heads joggling."

The food at the Majestic was not bad—good soup (a few

spoonfuls), herring (a square inch), a peach and wine, excellently prepared and served by a waiter in tuxedo who did not see anything wrong in the ragged clothing I was wearing. It was just enough to whet your appetite, however, and this was the second-best hotel in Barcelona. After we had eaten, Ed said, "Let's run down to Child's and get a meal," but I thought Keene's Chop House would be better. The dining room was crowded, and then the sirens wailed again and the lights went out, and we were suddenly acutely conscious of the huge glass dome over our heads. It was silent for a time in the dining room; we were listening to the anti-aircraft guns batting away, and we could dimly see the great beams of the searchlights, crossing and inter-crossing through the glass. The motors hummed and droned, up and down on a single note, and Joe Taylor, Negro section-leader who was with us, on leave from the hospital where he had convalesced from a bullet wound, said, "Boy, I sure wish I was some place else." And it was silent, and then, quietly at first, and then with more and more confidence, there was a voice singing, a girl's voice, a single voice in the dining room full of silent people. She had a deep and rich soprano, and she was singing *flamenco,* that variety of song most accurately described as *canto hondo* (deep song); a song rich in Moorish overtones, sung on a scale we do not know, its material and execution largely improvised. In it there was the hope and the sorrow and the aspiration of a nation, and it seemed exactly right in this darkened dining room full of invisible people, waiting patiently for possible death. It was, although its origins were deeper and far older, the quiet and perfect expression of this war; it was the voice of an entire people crying for freedom and for human dignity, a people who had endured a living death for centuries, and then, after momentary surcease and the light of promise (given them by the young Republic), saw themselves about to be thrust back into the darkness they had so long endured, and went out with their bare hands and with no training, to fight a clever, well-armed enemy. They were still bare-handed; they still fought. And I thought again, These people can never be defeated, even though they *are* defeated; but I was trying to imagine the face of the singer, and when the lights came on again I saw her, and as I had suspected in the dark, she was completely beautiful.

We walked in the darkened streets; the automobiles were permitted to show lights, but no window light could show and the street lamps had been blinded two years before. Hundreds of people passed you in the dark, people you could not see and barely touched—they were habituated to seeing in the dark—people going about their business, young lovers taking advantage of a humanly intolerable situation to seek each other. People rarely touched each other, and the streets were black as pitch. You were aware of the broad avenue of the Paseo, and the enormous square of the Plaza de Catalunya, crowded with strolling thousands, as in the daytime. But this nightly, ghostly existence of a crowded population moving in almost total darkness, held both monstrosity and enormous beauty. Just as the crowded Ramblas in the daytime, with their jostling throngs, their innumerable flowerstands and their lounging prostitutes, offered a spectacle of human life and courage you would see under no other circumstances—evanescent and yet heightened to the pitch of human fever.

The city was full of International soldiers, on leave from

the hospital at Matero, or Las Planas, the concentration-point for recovered wounded, ready to go back to the front. Ed told me, confidentially, that the decision had been taken to withdraw the Internationals from Loyalist Spain, but the act was waiting on a more propitious moment. There was hideous irony in this—in the fact that hundreds more would die or be wounded before the decision was announced; would die in the very minutes before they were to be sent home or into further exile—for many had no homes, Germany? Italy? Why is death at such a time ironical? It should be no more ironical or undesirable then than at any other time. Joe Taylor said that no Internationals were being sent back to their Brigades; that many had been sent to Olot, near the French border, and we met many other comrades who told us the same story; Morris Goldstein; former commissar of Lamb's original Company 1, now recovered; Louis Gayle, formerly Battalion first-aid man; Jack Boxer, a curious character who could invariably win thousands of pesetas at poker, and who was now luxuriating in a radiant display of expensive and ill-assorted haberdashery; Carroll and Thompson, Battalion armorers, whom I met in a café on the Rambla de los Flores, drinking the barley-water that passed for coffee. They were 'fucking the dog,' spending what money they had, and gracefully suffering under-nourishment, for they could not find enough to eat. And it was felt in Barcelona that Franco's counter-offensive on the Ebro had spent its force—that he would not attack there again, although he had brought up thousands of fresh Italian troops he dared not use. But they were wrong. . . .

The city was so crowded with people, refugees from all parts of Spain who had fled the coming of General Franco's liberating forces, that food was scarce. Food was so scarce that every train that left the city carried jam-packed hundreds going into the countryside to try to barter goods for food. (Money would not buy it.) And the trains were so crowded that it was imposible to get onto one without rising hours before dawn to be first in line at the ticket-window. So I caught the press-truck that carried newspapers and other printed material to the front, and rode through Valls, where we had an airfield, Montblanch, a concentration point for new troops coming up and men who were returning from the hospitals, and Reus, almost destroyed by air-bombs, to the XVth Brigade postoffice in the mountains at a town fantastically called Gratallops. (There was also a Cantallops, but that's irrelevant.)

And after this six-hour ride, which brought me to the small town on this side of the river (there was a letter from Tabb, recuperating from a machine-gun bullet in the head, and enclosing cigarettes and a stick of chewing gum), I had to wait all afternoon and evening till nine o'clock, when the mail-truck, which crossed the river and stopped at every battalion-kitchen, was ready to leave. So I arrived, my clean clothes pucrhased in Barcelona, somewhat dirty, at Brigade headquarters at half-past three in the morning, to find that we were still in reserve. (And to stay awake another half-hour while Dave Gordon told me how much Gates thought of him.) And I found the first and only package that ever reached me in Spain, a box from Dave Zablodowsky and other friends at the Viking Press, which contained—four cartons of cigarettes and eight large bars of chocolate.

Our lines were being held by the 45th Division, and the next morning the enemy pulled a couple small-scale attacks that were easily repulsed. The artillery was still duelling across the *baranco* in which the men were lying, but they were in a somewhat better frame of mind, for a good number of packages had arrived through the Friends of the Lincoln Brigade, and almost everybody who was liked by anybody had something to smoke (for a day) and perhaps even a piece of chocolate. Wolff was elated over a huge bundle that some guy who expected to arrive in Spain had sent himself. He never did arrive, so Wolff was enjoying the prospect of wearing a magnificent leather jacket (fleece-lined), and every sort of change of underwear, socks and other accessories. The guy had been considerate; he was big. George Watt had a glass jar of sour-balls. And life was made somewhat bearable by being sent, that night, to the auto-park behind the lines, where Luke Hinman, who was installed with the Commissariat personnel and its equipment (and was struggling with a total lack of Spanish), had managed to find a real mattress, which we stretched under a tree.

"I'm glad I gave you those cigarettes this summer," he said. "I always felt I'd get them back." We laughed, and I told him about Barcelona; about the six baths I had taken in three days (which made a start at cleaning up my scabies); about the real scotch-and-soda Herbert Matthews had set up in his room at the Majestic; about the food Ed Rolfe had produced and the wonderment I'd felt at the fact that I still knew what to do with a knife, a fork, a spoon, and felt quite natural sitting at a table laid with a white cloth and glasses, plates and cups. "Stop it," he said. "You're breaking my heart."

So we set to work on the bulletin, attacking the Franco

propaganda, greeting the new 'comrades' who had arrived to reinforce us—they were a scurvy lot, ex-prisoners, ex-deserters, weak and unreliable elements that were being rounded up, for by that time the Government was experiencing some difficulty in finding men. We quoted the proclamation of President Benes of the Czechoslovak Republic: 'Certain elements are attempting to bring about a civil war. . . .' With Henlein's flight to Hitler, the Nazi party in Czechia had been outlawed, martial law declared in eighteen districts. We were, momentarily, satisfied that the right course was being pursued to crush Hitler terrorism. But it was a distracting day. The sky was loud with constant dog-fights, and an artillery-duel that was going on, with our guns trying to find theirs and theirs trying to find ours, resulted in both batteries finding the auto-park. We were forced to leave our typewriter and mimeograph-machine every ten minutes, when the shells started coming over, and seek refuge in incompleted dugouts. (The mimeographist got the pages mixed as a result.) Luke had been sitting on the running-board of the Commissariat truck; I had been stretched out on the mattress. We heard them coming and we left the place, to crouch behind a terrace further down, and returned to find that the mattress had been ripped to shreds by shrapnel, that there were three holes in the truck-door, its tires punctured and its gas-tank leaking. "Must be, we're being spared for a higher destiny," Luke said, and we talked about how much more jittery we felt out of the lines than we had when we were in them.

"I wanted to kiss you when you got me out," said Luke, "but now I'm not so sure I don't want to be back. It's safer there." But the food at the auto-park was remarkable; they had the same materials to work with, but they had only thirty men to feed and they had a man who could be called a cook, without fear of any one contradicting you.

I returned to the Brigade after supper, and found the battalions still blazing with rumors about our imminent withdrawal. Spanish comrades invariably greeted you with the remark, "Well, you're going home soon, eh?" and we had to deny the allegation with all the conviction we could muster. Gordon said he knew that the decsiion to withdraw us had been reached, but in his most judicial manner, he said, "I feel that this tendency toward liquidation of the I. B.'s would be a serious international mistake."

"Why?" I said. "We're not a fighting force any more."

"You talk like a *derrotista,* comrade," he said. "I know we're not a fighting force; but we could, if the repatriation business were properly handled, and if there were a decent system of leaves, recruiting and the rest, be rehabilitated and resume our former importance, both in Spain and internationally."

"Why not leave it to the Government?" I said.

"Of course," he said. "If the Government's taking these steps toward liquidation, it apparently feels it could gain more by retiring us than it could by rehabilitating us. Our rôle has been consistently played down by the Spanish papers for many months, even though the Government recognizes our importance. In this campaign particularly, both in its offensive and defensive phases, you can't deny that we held the lines when other units couldn't."

"I wouldn't deny it for a minute."

"Well?" he said, as though he'd proved something or other. That was on the 19th of September; the next morning

I returned to auto-park, which had been moved a couple kilometers back toward Mora, to avoid artillery. I stayed there that night, and returned again to the Brigade at lunch-time the next day. We drove under their planes all the way, with the Spanish comrades on the truck yelling and jumping up and down, pointing to the sky and demanding that Jim Fowler stop the truck. Sanchez, when he saw the planes, jumped out and ran away. (He had a good long walk ahead of him.) The road was being shelled, in the bargain, and we reached the mouth of the reserve *baranco* with a sense of considerable relief, but the battle had been joined again; the firing over our heads never stopped for a moment, and we had to shout to make ourselves heard. Although, since I had been transferred into the Brigade, I knew less about what was going on than I had before, I did learn that they had decided to attack again; that they had taken two hills in the vicinity of Corbera; that the hills we lost were very important to the maintenance of our positions on this side of the Ebro, and would have to be retaken. Two companies of our 24th Battalion had already taken up second-line positions, which seemed to indicate that the entire Brigade would be in action again within the day. (It was the end of our ninth day in reserve, and we rarely stayed more than ten; that was the system, when it could be worked.)

The news from Europe was worse than ever, with England and France agreeing to the dismemberment of Czecho-slovakia and presenting a 'plan' of compromise to her. This plan was cynical in the extreme: it involved outright cession of the Sudeten areas; the autonomy of other regions containing a large German population; the 'neutralization' of Czechoslovakia in the event of a major conflict between other powers, and the usual 'guarantees' of her frontiers by England, France, Germany and Italy. The murderers were guaranteeing to respect the corpse! These terms, we believed, the present Czech Government would never accept. It had an army second to none. Its people had tasted years of true democracy. It had a munitions industry that any one could well have envied (many did). And so we expected that France would respect her previous commitments, that popular indignation in both France and England would bring about the fall of their respective cabinets. And we were wrong.

The Fascists were attacking strongly on the entire sector; the British and the 24th, in position on the other side of the main road to Mora, reported casualties as a result of artillery and air-attacks. And the night of the 21st the Lincolns moved into the *baranco* below the previous position of the Brigade *estado-mayor,* to be ready. The guns spoke in lower tones these days; they were bigger guns; they were farther off. They spoke all day and all the night and they told us that Hitler and Mussolini were anxious to bring an end to their invasion of the Spanish land, before they moved farther afield in Europe. Valledor and Gates had left to establish a new headquarters, and by noon of that day there was heavy machine-gun fire to be heard, hand-grenades crackling like pop-corn in the pan, artillery. Word came late that afternoon that the Lincolns, waiting in position to move into the lines, were bombed and suffered thirteen casualties; four dead and nine wounded; no names. The Canadians, last to move, were on the march in single file over the hills leading to the front and a few of us—Gordon, Lesser, Sanchez and Comrade *Cultura,* were sitting about under the trees when the

planes came over. They came in single file, a line of heavy
Junkers, and as the whistling sounded we dived for a shallow
dugout we had never completed. I could see, over my
shoulder, the landing of those heavy bombs; I could see it
before I heard the sound, and the hill just behind us was a
sudden deep crimson flame and it rose slowly into the air (I
thought, How beautiful!); then the sound came and the
concussion knocked me flat into the shallow hole with the
others and our heads split with the sound and we lay on top
of one another.

Gordon left that afternoon, returned late that night. The
whole Brigade staff had moved, and I had attempted to get
to auto-park on foot, but had been stopped by a guard on
the road, so I was back. Gordon lay down next to me and
said, "Can you keep something under your hat?" "You
know I'm the soul of discretion."

"I've been to Division," he said. "To stop the mail and
press. Yesterday Negrin made a speech before the League of
Nations, in which he said that the Government was going
to retire all its foreign volunteers."

"My God!" I said.

"What's the matter?"

"Nothing," I said. "I was just thinking of the guys who're
going to be killed tonight and tomorrow; we're counter-
attacking tonight."

"You can't think of that," he said.

"Why not?"

"It's all part of the game."

"Oh, nuts!"

"What'ya mean, nuts?"

"It must be wonderful to be so objective," I said. He was right, of course.

"Anyhow," he said. "That's the way it is."

"Will they be in long?"

"I don't know. Go to auto-park tomorrow morning; a truck will come before then; wait for orders. I'm going back to Brigade now." I lay there in the night, hearing the fighting going on, desolate and torn by the information he had given me. Nothing could be done about it. Negrin had done a wonderful job; the announcement was timed to perfection and it caused a sensation in the League Assembly. It showed up the farce of Non-Intervention once and for all; it made magnificent propaganda for the Government; it concealed the practical non-existence of the International Brigades; it would salve a certain amount of international discontent over the fact that foreigners were still fighting on our side; it would appeal to the Spanish on the Franco side. They would feel, Now Franco, you can shit or you can get off the pot.

Before dawn we got to the auto-park and I woke Luke and told him. He looked at me and said, "I'll believe it when it happens; I've heard the like before." Certain men in the park had also had the news, and one copy of the paper *Las Noticias,* which had somehow reached the place, had been confiscated by Joe Hecht, the commissar. We got hold of it, and moving off some distance from the park, we spelled it out:

And now, Mr. President, the Doctor said, *I wish to raise the concrete point that is the motive of my declaration.*

The Spanish Government wishes to contribute not only

*in words but also in deeds to the appeasement desired by all,
and resolves to dispell all doubts as to the completely national
character of the cause for which the armies of the Republic
are fighting. To this end, the Government has decided upon
the immediate and complete withdrawal of all non-Spanish
combatants now participating in the struggle in Spain, in
the Government's ranks; and it is to be understood that this
withdrawal will apply to all foreigners, without distinction
as to nationality, including those who may have assumed
Spanish nationality since the 5th of July in 1936. . . .'*

He asked for the appointment of a commission of the
League to witness and control the withdrawal, and to testify
to the world that it had taken place. And he continued:

*We are overcome with a feeling of the deepest pain at the
idea of being separated from this body of brave and self-
sacrificing men who, with an impulse of generosity that will
never be forgotten by the Spanish people, came to our assistance during one of the most critical hours of our history. I
want, here, to proclaim the high moral value of the sacrifice
they willingly accepted, not to further any egoistic ends, but
in the service and defence of the purest ideals of liberty and
justice.*

"It sounds real," I said.

"It sounds real all right," said Luke, "but I'll believe it
when we get to Paris and you show me all those places you've
talked so much about. Particularly, the chastity belts."

"I'll believe it when we're six days off the coast of France,"
I said.

That day was loud with artillery, that did not find the
auto-park, but was continuous to the point of incredibility.
"This sounds like the World War," said one of the *chofers,*

who had been in it. News and rumors of all sorts were arriving at the park; we heard that Captain Lamb had been wounded again, this time by a piece of shrapnel through the neck; we heard that Jim Lardner, on patrol the night before, had been killed or captured when his squad met sudden and unexpected fire; we heard that the entire Brigade had broken, and was in strategic retreat. We sat on the ground, listening to the noise of near-by battle, and we agreed that we were glad we were not there. No minute passed without sight of airplanes. A flight of our *Moscas,* low-wing monoplanes, suddenly broke over our heads like a covey of flushed quail, coming from the river. They were hedge-hopping and were on us before we heard them, roared overhead not a hundred feet above the ground, moving toward the front. It was a surprise maneuver, and apparently it worked, for we heard their guns strafing the enemy, and they returned a few minutes later in the same formation. We stood and cheered them and they dipped their wings to us when they went over. "That's where *we* should be," I said to Luke, and he agreed we should. "Hell," he said, "it's ten years since I've flown a ship; I learned in an old Jenny, and took my wife-to-be and wife-that-was up on my second solo flight." "I've got eighteen hours solo," I said. "We'd be a hot pair of combat-pilots." "None better," said Luke.

They were fighting far above our heads. At ten or fifteen thousand feet, they were fighting, dozens of them. Sometimes you could not see them and sometimes you could; you could make no sense of what you did see, but the roar of their screaming propellors was amplified till it sounded almost among the trees. They snarled and howled like a pack of wolves, and we finally picked out a pair and isolated them from the others and watched. I felt my arms and legs growing tired as I watched; automatically kicking rudder and hauling the stick around, diving and pulling up into half-loops and half-rolls (the Immelmann), snap-rolling, executing chandelles and wing-overs in an effort to keep the Fascist off my tail. It was a terrific strain, and then we saw one of the ships pull up and kick over into a tail-spin. "He got him," Luke said, and we watched. We could not take our eyes away from the falling plane; he was winding it up something terrific. The throttle was wide open, the propellor was howling as he spun around his longitudinal axis toward the earth. "He's not on fire," I said. "It's a maneuver; he'll pull out."

We waited for him to pull out, and I was aware that I was saying, "Pull it out, pull it out, opposite rudder, stick forward, pull it out." It was our ship that was falling, we could see its wide red wing-tips flashing as he spun. He was going to fall close to us; I glanced at Luke and he was watching, his lips tense, his fists clenched at his sides. I looked back at the ship, spinning like a top and howling like a maniac. It looked too late now, and I was no longer saying Pull it out. It *was* too late now, and he passed behind the hill; the sound was cut off as by a knife. I glanced at Luke and I could see that he was counting too. I counted, one-two-three-four-five, and then we heard the crash, deadened but definitive. I glanced at Luke; he was looking at the ground. The boys in the auto-park started running toward the hill and scrambling over, and I said, "Do you want to go?" and Luke said, "No."

We sat there looking at the ground, and it was difficult not to see in this common incident a symbol, obvious as it might have been, of the end. It was pure coincidence; we knew we would be leaving soon, those of us who lived; we knew we were taking a terrific beating at the time; we saw our man fall from the skies, and it was a period (in the literary mind), a period put to an adventure—if you wanted to call it that—an adventure unique in human history. For never before in the history of the world had there been such a body of men—a spontaneously gathered international volunteer army, drawn from every stratum of human life and every human occupation, handworkers and professionals, intellectuals and farmers. The very existence of this army, that had played so crucial a rôle in this Spanish war, was the guarantee of international working-class brotherhood; the final proof that those who perform the work of the world possess a common interest and an identical obligation. It was the living embodiment of the unity that exists between all men of good will, whatever their nationality, their political or religious convictions, or their way of making a living on this earth. Every occupation, every color, every nationality, these men had fought and died with and for each other; their roster was the roster of mankind.

Bessie, the note that afternoon said, *You will take a car and go to Brigade post-office, where you will order the mail and press delivered again. All comrades of the Commissariat are to remain at auto-park till further order.* GORDON.

We made a fast trip in broad daylight, through Mora and across the river up the mountains into Gratallops. Then we returned; were halted in Mora la Nueva while they bombed the town across the river, and then we came across. Speeding out of Mora de Ebro, there was another dog fight, directly over our heads. Our man had spun down and out of the fight, thinking to escape (perhaps he was wounded), but contrary to their usual tactics, the Fascist pilot had followed him to earth. Now they fought not a hundred feet over the road, and it happened that they kept exactly ahead of us, moving at an identical rate of speed like a pair of bluebirds fighting in front of a speeding automobile. It was the most amazing exhibition of aerobatics I had ever seen, and the road on either side was being sprayed with their machine-gun bullets." "Shall I stop?" the driver said, and I said, "No, keep going." Men ran out onto the road and fired with rifles and light machine-guns at the Fascist, but they kept twisting and turning, rolling and looping overhead, until our pilot suddenly went out of control, crashed and burned beside the road. We kept on moving fast.

The air was full of planes; we saw as many as three hundred of their bombers and chasers in one flight, moving back and forth over the lines six kilometers away; we heard their stuff dropping and we sat in sodden silence on the ground, looking at our feet. Gates' chauffeur came walking in, covered with earth to the eyebrows, telling how he had lost the staff-car that was blown to pieces; how he and many others had been buried by the bombs, had to be dug out. The Lincolns had almost been surrounded; the new replacements had done what was expected of them—ex-deserters, some Fascist sympathizers, they attempted to go over to the enemy at the first opportunity; the lines had broken under the extreme pressure of artillery and *avion;* it was a fuck-up. There was nothing for us to do, and so we sat. We sat all the rest of the afternoon and all that night, trying to sleep, unable to sleep. There was no way of knowing what was happening, but late that night we heard the marching feet, the shuffling feet dragging on the road, moving toward the river. It was a low shuffle; there were no voices; there was no singing. And at dawn the men of the Commissariat climbed into a truck and started toward the rear. The sky was wide and blue, bluer than it usually was. For a change there were no planes, although the front was just as active as before. We were aware of enormous impatience as the *camion* rolled toward the shattered town. Many others were moving too (there were many exhausted, ragged men walking toward the town), and there was a traffic-jam in the center of Mora de Ebro that took half an hour to untangle. We were terribly impatient; we were jittery, and the truck moved slowly down the long ramp toward the bridge, and slowly across the sounding, narrow planks. To your right was the collapsed skeleton of the old bridge that we had blown up to cover our retreat last April; it lay half in and half out of the water, like a wrecked dirigible. The farther shore was pitted with enormous craters left by the bombing that had been going on every day for two months now. We moved off the bridge and up-grade into the twin town, Mora la Nueva, and I looked back at the yellow Ebro before we turned the corner. It was wide and placid in the brilliant sun; its surface shimmered with a million broken moving flecks of quiet light. I thought of Aaron.

A FOOTNOTE

The facts are known; they are recorded, and you need not look for them in the columns of the Communist *Daily Worker* (although you would find more of the unadulterated truth there, than elsewhere). You may read them in the columns of *The New York Times,* a paper that is proud to print all the news its owners feel is fit to print. In those columns you will find the facts, attested to a thousand times over by correspondents whose integrity is beyond cavil, as well as by liars who also point the way toward truth.

The people of Spain, who had lived for centuries at a level lower than that enjoyed by American livestock, in 1931 overthrew their monarchy and, in an attempt to rise from medievalism, established a Republic. They wanted to put an end to a state of affairs which countenanced the possession of 50 per cent of their land by 1 per cent of their population. (Another 40 per cent owned no land at all.) But their Republic was weak and indecisive and its enemies were everywhere—the class upon which the monarchy had rested, the owning class and those whose interests tied in with the interests of the owning class. Every mild reform that the Republic attempted was opposed and sabotaged by these people, who fell into four groups: the landlords, the industrialists, the Spanish Catholic hierarchy and the Army. The liberal government of the Republic was superseded for a time by a dictatorship under Lerroux and Gil Robles. And this dictatorship, in 1934 and 1935, proceeded to nullify every mild reform the Republic had instituted.

The people did not accept such retrogression with good grace. The people were stubborn. In 1934 there was a revolt in the Asturias, that was suppressed with a fury and vindictiveness that has no counterpart in our civilized era. And still the people remained stubborn. Every liberal element in Spain combined to form a united front against reaction, and the people went to the polls. Despite corruption of the ballot, despite the constant terrorism of the Army, the landlords and industrialists, despite the fulminations of the Catholic Church, the Popular Front won the elections of February, 1936, by an overwhelming majority. And now it was the turn of those who had always owned Spain, to be stubborn.

The Republic had divorced Church and State (as we have); it had settled tenant farmers on the great estates whose owners lived in luxury on the French Riviera while their peasants worked and starved to death. It had placed public education in the hands of the State (as we have); despite Catholic education, between 60 and 70 per cent of the population was illiterate. It had attempted to ameliorate the lot of its people (as we have). But the owning class was not going to permit such a state of things to come into permanent existence; why, this was Bolshevism! And by the spring of 1936 a rebellion, to be led by the very military men who had sworn allegiance to the new Republic, had been planned. It received the unqualified support of the Army, which was a privileged caste; of the landlords who saw their hitherto unquestioned power slipping from them; of the industrialists, and of the higher clergy. Every priest in Spain had been on the public payroll. The Church was a swollen corporation that owned enormous tracts of land, that possessed factories, power-plants, hotels, department-stores and newspapers. The Republic had stripped it of some of its secular power; it had reduced its subsidies; it had taken the 'education' of Spain's children away from it. Its economic interests therefore determined its political allegiance. And the rebellion, more importantly, received the support of German and Italian Fascism, who saw in Spain possibilities of bolstering their tottering economic structure; who saw raw materials; who saw strategic uses for Spain's geographic position.

The people knew their enemies: the landlords, the Army and police, the manufacturers and the Church. Their enemies were determined to thrust them back into 'their place.' And so, with nothing but their determination as a weapon, they went out to fight their enemies. Little enough support was received from outside. The few arms sent by Mexico and the Soviet Union did not go very far. Germany and Italy began to send in men and materials for Franco—machine-guns and artillery, tanks and aviation. (The first Fascist planes arrived three days after the rebellion broke out.) They thought it would not take very long; they thought it should be relatively easy. But for two and a half years the people fought them with what arms they could get; with the munitions industry they created themselves; with their flesh and blood. It was not easy. The 'rabble' was in arms; like the rabble of the American Revolution, like the rabble of the French Revolution, these people were determined (one hundred and fifty years later) to take the first steps toward civilization and progressive living.

We never felt that they would lose. We did not believe, even near the end, that they could lose. We said, they *must* not lose. We said, *No pasaran!* and we said, *Madrid Will Be the Tomb of Fascism!* Support began to arrive; the best sons of the international working people of the world, came to Spain to fight beside the Spanish people. They knew, in their own lives, in their own bodies, the importance of this fight. The pennies, the nickels and dimes of millions of people who could least afford to part with them, were pooled to buy ambulances and medical supplies, to send food and milk and clothing to the women and children of Spain, blockaded within their borders by four great powers who had solemnly sworn to see that no intervention in the Spanish conflict would take place. And two of these great powers, Italy and Germany, *were* the interveners. There has never been any pretence about it; everybody knew it, and the fact that this piece of cynicism was tolerated by the world will always remain one of the blackest pages in human history. For the Spanish people could not have lost, even temporarily, if they had not been strangled and starved out and sold down the river—by the British ruling class, who worked hand in glove with German and Italian Fascism; by the French ruling class, who worked hand in glove with German and Italian Fascism; by the United States Neutrality Act, which embargoed 'both sides,' but did not forbid the sale of arms to the non-interveners.

The entire democratic world protested as it could; protest meetings were held for two and a half years in every civilized country of the world; the working people knew what was happening, and they exclaimed aloud in horror. They attempted to force their governments to come to the assistance of Spain; they clamored for the opening of the French frontier; they clamored for the lifting of the American embargo;

they demanded Chamberlain's resignation; they cried, *Arms for Spain! Airplanes for Spain! Food for Spain!* But they did not control the avenues of communication; they did not control the press, the radio, the news-reels of their respective countries. They do not yet control them. Opposition therefore came from the most enlightened section of the world's population; and it was stifled, it was diverted, it was aborted, it was suppressed. And intervention proceeded; intervention was intensified. For the people of Spain worked and slaved day and night; they built a munitions industry, they built airplanes and guns, and even more, they built schools; they built child health-clinics and rest-homes; they built hospitals and institutes of cultural advancement; they taught their soldiers to read and write in the trenches; they taught their farmers new agricultural technics; they gave the land to those who worked the land; they were on their way. And so it was not easy. But Great Britain stood aside and France stood aside and the United States stood aside, and more guns arrived for Franco, and more men—regular army corps from Germany and Italy—more airplanes came, more pilots, more technicians, more tanks, until the Spanish Republic had been crushed.

The decent people of this world knew what would happen if Spain died. They said that democratic France would find itself surrounded by Fascism on three sides; it is. They said the death of democracy in Spain would see the end of democracy in Europe; it is dying. They said a Fascist Spain would mean increased Fascist penetration in South America, through economic tie-ups and propaganda; we see it. They said a Fascist Spain would put democracy throughout the world at bay; it is. Austria is gone and Czechoslovakia is gone, and Spain is gone.

But Franco has saved Spain from Bolshevism, as Mussolini saved Italy from Bolshevism (and Ethiopia and Albania), and Hitler saved Germany and Austria and Czechoslavakia, and will try to save others. For it is true that there were Communists in Spain; it is true that there were Communists in the Loyalist Army, some of them in positions of command, many of them in the ranks of the International Brigades. And they were among our most trusted men, they were among our most reliable men; their loyalty to the Spanish Government was unquestioned; they assumed responsibility and fulfilled it; they took on the toughest jobs and did them; their energy and their organizational genius gave cohesive strength to the Army and to the people. And Spain has been saved from them, just as France will be saved from them, and Great Britain, and the United States will be saved from them if the people who pretend to see Communism under every bed and in every teapot (not to mention every piece of liberal legislation and every attempt to ameliorate the suffering of the world's millions) have their way about it.

General Franco has saved Spain, and the late Pope and the present Pope have blessed his arms and his purpose, and committed their children to his tender mercies. Yet wherever he came in Spain to liberate the people they fled from him; and when he marched on Barcelona, blasting his way through human flesh with Italian and German machines, a half a million men, women and children fled over the border into France—and these were only the people who were strong enough to do so, the people who were confined in Catalonia;

for those in the rest of Spain could not escape. And he is beginning the work of reconstruction he has promised for so long, and it would take twenty William P. Carneys, writing in *The New York Times,* to deny what General Franco has himself proclaimed.

In Spain today (tied and bound to German and Italian Fascism) there is no popular representation; there is no freedom of the press; there is no freedom of speech or of assembly; there is no liberty to protest your grievances; there are no labor unions, no workers' organizations; there is one political party, the party of the vast minority; and the land has been given back to the landlords; the factories have been given back to the industrialists; 'education' and its lands, its power and its wealth have been given back to the Church; and the peculiar rights of plunder, of power and of privilege have been given back to the Army and the notorious *Guardia Civil* (the owners' watchdogs) who will take greater care than ever to see that the rabble does not step out of line again. And the 'criminals' and those responsible for 'prolonging the war' by resistance are being punished by the Franco justice—the hundreds of thousands of prisoners that made up the surrendered Loyalist armies are at forced labor, rebuilding what has been destroyed—by Franco (the ultimate irony); hundreds are being court-martialed daily, thousands have had 'information' filed against them by Fascist sympathizers; over a million of undesirable elements had been listed by the General long before he saved his country for Christianity—and these will go to concentration camps or to their death.

You must see these things in terms of human beings, not in words. You would not have needed to go to Spain; you do not need to go to China, to Italy or Japan or Germany, to see how Fascism respects the people it governs. You would not need to see the million dead in Spain, the hundreds of thousands of starved or mangled women, children and babies in Spain and China, to know the name and face of Fascism. You do not even need to go into our own deep South, or into the slums of our great cities, to understand the nature and the aims of Fascism. You only need to look at your next-door neighbor; you only need to look into your heart and ask yourself, what do I want of life? Do I want permanent security for my children and myself? Do I want cultural advancement? Do I want leisure and the time to grow into the sort of human being that I would like to be? Do I want love? And you will know what Fascism is, and what it wants, and what it will do.

The martyrdom of these men, women and children of Spain, of these men from other lands, has not been wasted on the world. Spain is not lost; Spain was a sacrifice. Spain was and is a turning-point in the history of human institutions, and not only for the fact that it demonstrated the invincible and indomitable courage of the working people of the world. If Spain had not resisted, France would have been a Fascist state long since. If Spain had not sacrificed its best sons and daughters and their blood and their future, Fascism would be spread still farther throughout the world. Spain awoke the world to its danger, and the tide is turning. The democratic people of the world saw with their own eyes what could be done to stem the tide of Fascist barbarism, by a people who had nothing to fight with but their hands. Spain awoke millions throughout the many nations of the earth to a realization of the danger that faces them. It held off the monster for two and a half years with its bare hands, starving, block-aded, betrayed by the ruling forces of the great democracies, not by their people. It is one of the great facts of human history, and the world has learned a bitter lesson from this temporary defeat of the working class.

For it *is* temporary, even though the technique of Fascism will be tried again, will be extended and is being extended. And the awareness of the evil that Spain gave to the world may yet result in the fulfillment of the slogan: *Madrid Will Be the Tomb of Fascism!* For the example of Madrid has not been lost upon the world, and every advance of Fascism, every attempt to extend the 'logic' of Fascism, must and will be met by the increasing and the ultimately overpowering determination to resist of all men of good will. For the 'logic' will work again—and the growing discontent of the decent people of this world will be diverted, suppressed, killed—until these people, who have nothing to gain (and everything to lose) by the retention by violence of our present way of life, rise in their majesty and power, destroy their parasites, and reaffirm the beauty and the dignity of human life.

New York City
June 8, 1939

IV

A NOTE FOR 1975

11

I am still thinking about him. For at least four years after we returned from Spain Aaron appeared to me in a dream —always the same dream: We were huddled together for warmth, asleep under that tree the second night after we crossed the Ebro. I awoke in the dream with a start and saw he was not there. I sat up and stared into the darkness, listening. After a moment a figure emerged from among the olive trees. It was Aaron. He came quietly out of the night, stopped a few feet from me. His right arm was extended, his forefinger beckoning. He spoke quietly, saying, "Alvah . . . Alvah . . . come . . . come . . ." I always awoke with a gasp—sometimes with a scream.

This recurrent dream was quite as painful as the visit I made to his family, to tell them how he died. They lived in the Bronx: the father who really looked nothing like Aaron but whose eyes were identical with his; the mother who had not known what he was doing in Spain, but knew now. Throughout the dinner and the long evening—an unmarried brother and one of his sisters and her husband were also present—the mother stared at me with what I felt must be resentment. But like the dream it was probably my own guilt for being alive when he was dead that was staring me in the face.

When I left she said something I will never forget so long as I live and I am 70 today, not the 34 I was that winter night in 1939: She said, "I can't say, Pleased to meet you." Then she and Aaron's father asked me to live with them. "You can have his room," they said. "These are his books. He made this model aeroplane. These are his things. . . . You are the same size."

In 1967 my wife and I tried to find his grave. We found the small town in Gerona province in whose hospital he had died, but there was no grave. For that matter, almost all of the 1,500 comrades we left in Spain had no marked graves and the reason soon became apparent. Ironically enough, it was because they have *not* been forgotten that they have no graves that can be found today. (See *Spain Again*, page 126.)

We used to say that if we survived the war we would get home just in time to fight in a bigger one. World War II started five months after Madrid was betrayed—and occupied. A new organization called The Veterans of the Abraham Lincoln Brigade (VALB) attempted to enlist *en masse* the Monday after Pearl Harbor. Our offer was refused but of the 1,500 who returned (200 did not because they were aliens), at least 1,200 served in World War II, either in the armed forces or the merchant marine.

A cynical charade began the moment these men were inducted. It did not take G-2 long to learn they were in the ranks, and since they were the only Americans with combat experience since World War I they were almost invariably used by their officers to train the men under their command. (For the same reason they had been the raw material of a study of fear and courage under battle conditions, published in 1943 by Yale University's Institute of Human Relations: *Fear in Battle*, by John Dollard, Ph.D., which the War Department found extremely useful.)

The Lincoln men were interviewed by service and local newspapers, put on radio programs, asked to address their comrades-in-arms in orientation classes and were even invited to speak before neighboring "service" organizations like the Chamber of Commerce, Elks, Lions and Odd Fellows. Many were sent to Officers' Candidate Schools, were graduated with high grades and sent back to their original outfits—without commissions.

For the attack on the veterans had begun even before we were withdrawn from the lines by the Spanish government. There had been articles in the Hearst press and in other reactionary publications, denouncing us as international Communist gangsters, soldiers of the Comintern, minions of Moscow who had been sent abroad, first, to "communize" Spain and second, to be trained to take over the U.S.A. for Uncle Joe.

Many of these articles were written by and/or ghosted for men we personally knew to be cowards, deserters and renegades. Some freely admitted they were FBI informers, stool pigeons and police spies. They not only achieved wide publicity in the press, but the House Committee on Un-American Activities gave them an even broader audience. They had a brief spin in the limelight and sank into obscurity, but they surfaced again in 1953 and their "testimony" had an effect on us for years to come.

In the Army of the United States it almost always happened that when the outfit our veterans had helped to train was shipped out, our men were not. Promotions were deliberately withheld, even when earned by hard work and recommended by superior officers. In 1943 and 1944 VALB therefore launched a nationwide campaign that enlisted the support of many VIP's. It brought results: our men were suddenly permitted to move out with their comrades, they won promotions, were sent to OCS again and got commissions—both stateside and on the battlefield.

This did not sit well with such sheets as the *Chicago Tribune*, which attacked the Army for granting us commissions. Testifying before the House Military Affairs Committee in March 1945, Major General Bissell, then head of Army Intelligence (G 2) answered the charge this way:

"The Army's files show the loyalty of each of these officers. . . . These officers have shown by their deeds that they are upholding the United States by force and violence."

Testifying before the same committee, Assistant Secretary of War John J. McCloy was asked by a Republican congressman and member of the American Legion: "Is it possible that an exceptional soldier may turn out to be a Communist?"

The Congressman was referring to Herman Bottcher, a naturalized American anti-Nazi who had fought in Spain, was shipped to the South Pacific as a private and became known as "the one-man army of Buna."

Said McCloy, in reply, ". . . [he was] suspected of being a member of the Communist Party. He went to the South Pacific, there he was promoted to sergeant, then made captain in the field. He was wounded, decorated, and killed in action at Leyte."

But before records like this became known, we had experiences like these: Joe Hecht, interviewed in press and on the radio, sent to OCS, returned without a commission. At OCS itself, when an instructor was explaining the importance of the battle of Stalingrad—"A matter of saving face for the Russians because the city is named after Stalin; that is all . . ." —Joe stood up and begged leave to disagree. The instructor handed him his pointer and Joe said that the city was both tactically and strategically important. He explained that if the Nazis could take this crucial communications hub, they could join forces with their Japanese allies and outflank the entire Soviet front. The instructor asked sarcastically if Joe had been there and Joe said, "No, sir, but it's obvious from the map." "I can read a map, too," snapped the instructor. "Sit down!" Joe sat. On his return to camp he told his Commanding Officer that probably his grades hadn't been good enough. His CO said it wasn't his grades and showed him his personnel card, in the corner of which there were the initials, S.D. Joe asked what that meant and was told, "Suspected of disloyalty."

Now rated sergeant, Joe was transferred to a hospital in New Jersey where he kept medical records and started to do some independent research on the incidence of "combat fatigue" in American troops in training and in action. He even wrote a paper for his new CO, a doctor, demonstrating that such a condition had been practically unknown in the Spanish Republican Army and less so in the International Brigades. He cited Dollard's study and explained that an understanding of one's cause and dedication to it made it practically impossible for such things to happen. He suggested and even outlined an orientation and education course that would go more deeply into the origin and causes of the war and the nature of Nazism and Japanese and Italian fascism.

Perhaps to be rid of so uncomfortable a fellow, after two and a half years in the Army Joe was finally assigned to a combat unit and went to Europe in early spring of 1945.

At Saarlautern in Germany, in command of a company rifle squad, Joe and his men were "caught in the open by grazing fire from a German machine-gun emplacement which was also inflicting casualties on the entire platoon," the citation reads.

"Showing no hesitancy, and at the cost of his life, Sgt. Hecht charged the gun emplacement single-handedly in an effort to destroy it. As a result of his heroic action, his men were afforded the needed time to secure cover. His undaunted courage in sacrificing his life for the men of his squad reflects the highest credit upon Sgt. Hecht and the military service." His family received his posthumous Silver Star. Joe was a Communist.

Milton Wolff was the last commander of the Abraham Lincoln Battalion, a major at the age of 23. He had impressed a number of U.S. military men, stateside politicians and foreign correspondents by his natural-born qualities of military leadership, his achievements and his obvious potential. They tried to get him an appointment to West Point and/or a commission and failed, but with the aid of General William (Wild Bill) Donovan, head of the Office of Strategic Services, they managed to place Wolff with *British* Special Services after the fall of Paris and the Nazi invasion of Yugoslavia.

He served as a civilian with Major equivalency recruiting "proved" antifascists (International Brigade veterans) for behind-the-lines work in occupied Europe. After Pearl Harbor he was transferred (in rank) to OSS and recruited Lincoln men for the same type of work: men like Irving Goff, Vincent Losowski, Bill Aalto and Mike Jiminez, three of whom had been among the handful of American *guerrilleros* in Spain.

When he discovered that OSS was also recruiting the ragtags of European royalty, nationalists, actual neo-fascists and other off-scourings of alleged "resistance" groups, he quit the outfit in disgust and enlisted in the Army of the United States as a private.

He was then held at Camps Dix and Wheeler with men suspected of disloyalty: German and Italian nationals, pimps and criminals. He protested and was ultimately co-opted for OCS—and thrown out eight weeks later, like others of similar background. He then launched a long fight to get into action and was assigned in swift succession to Chemical Warfare, Alaskan Replacement, Puget Sound Patrol (watching for invading Japanese submarines) and to a longshore battalion in North Africa.

In desperation he appealed to Donovan but was shifted to longshore work in India, missing a plane the General had sent for him. He had risen in rank, by this time, to corporal, sergeant and second lieutenant. In India he managed to hook up with General (Vinegar Joe) Stilwell as liaison officer with the Chinese engaged in long-range penetration into Burma, and came down with malaria. It was there that Donovan finally caught up with him and had him flown to Italy where Goff, Losowski and his other comrades had met the General and said they needed him.

Frozen in rank for the rest of the war, Wolff and his comrades successfully dropped men, money, munitions and propaganda behind the lines in Austria, Yugoslavia and Greece, as well as in Italy. He went on one mission behind the Nazi lines in northern Italy and all the men—except for Wolff and the guide—were captured. When the defeat of Germany was imminent, he attempted to get help for the Spanish Maquis who were all set to march from the Haute-Savoie to the Pyrenees in an attempt to liberate Spain. This operation was said to have been approved not only by Donovan but by Franklin Roosevelt, but it was overruled by Eisenhower at the insistence of Churchill. Wolff was rushed out of Europe and shipped home.

While they were still in Italy working for OSS to help the Italian guerrillas under the command of Luigi Longo (known as Gallo in Spain where he was Inspector General of the International Brigades), the VALB men discovered that while the Army of the United States wanted a general strike throughout northern Italy—under the guidance of social-democratic labor leaders on the scene—said strike to coincide with the start of our offensive up the Italian boot, it was also our intention to arrest as many as possible of the guerrillas fighting the Nazis to hold the towns and cities for us. What the hell, they were Reds, weren't they? (Most of them were not.) Longo himself had learned of this and the guerrillas had been warned to do their job and vanish the moment they heard American troops in the vicinity.

The morality of our Establishment does not seem to have changed very much in the last four administrations. And when the VALB-OSS men were home Donovan decorated them with the Legion of Merit and issued them fine-sounding personal letters praising their contribution to the war effort. He told them they could call on him any time they needed work—he had contacts—and one of them said, Thanks, but he could always get a job with his union, the United Electrical, Radio and Machine Workers-CIO and another said, Thanks, he could always go back to being an organizer for the Communist Party.

Wolff himself served as National Commander of the Veterans for many years after the war, working also with the Civil Rights Congress and every committee set up to aid Spanish refugees or political prisoners. He was the sparkplug of VALB's campaign to keep fascist Spain out of the United

Nations during 1946-48, and he was involved in the Willie McGee case in Jackson, Mississippi, touring the south before the Freedom Marchers were organized, helping save the lives of the Martinsville Seven and raising $2,000,000 in bail money for Smith Act victims and helping to save the XVth Brigade's commissar Steve Nelson from literal death in a Pittsburgh dungeon. Nelson was held under a Pennsylvania "sedition" act frame-up and had been sentenced to 20 years by a judge who was an outspoken admirer of Benito Mussolini.

But the attack on the veterans surfaced again in 1953 when a governmental agency, created to forward the Cold War at home and which was the brainchild of the late Senator Pat McCarran (decorated by Franco for his sterling aid to the dictator) started to hear charges against VALB that had been voiced before.

This was the Subversive Activities Control Board, a creature of the McCarran Act that was passed over President Harry Truman's veto in 1950. The allegation—advanced by six deserters from the Brigade and other professional witnesses—was that the Lincoln Battalion and its successor, The Veterans of the Abraham Lincoln Brigade, were subversive organizations probably under the domination of and certainly doing the work of the U.S. Communist Party. This particular fight went on throughout most of 1954 and in 1955 SACB ordered the organization to register as a Communist front, which it promptly refused to do.

Individual veterans were also persecuted under the Smith Act which was allegedly designed to punish—*not* overt attempts to overthrow the government by force and violence, *not* teaching and/or advocating the overthrow . . ., but *conspiring* to teach and advocate . . . . Any lawyer will tell you it is far easier to "prove" conspiracy than it is to prove a man or an organization committed an overt act—when he or it didn't.

12

Lincoln victims spent many years in jail for committing so nebulous a crime. They included:

• Robert Thompson, captain in Spain where he was wounded twice, soldier in the South Pacific in World War II where he was decorated (like Herman Bottcher) with the Distinguished Service Cross by General Clark Eichelberger for service "above and beyond the call of duty." To make the cheese more binding, jail officials in New York were suspected of inspiring a physical attack on Thompson by a Yugoslav fascist inmate who had reason to believe he would be dealt with more lightly under the immigration laws. He fractured Thompson's skull with an iron pipe. After he recovered from that—and he very nearly didn't—and was sent to Federal prison for seven years, the Veterans Administration attempted to take away his 100 percent disability pension (malaria and a new attack of an apparently arrested case of tuberculosis). Once he was safely dead, much too young, our august government attempted to deny his widow his pension and prevent his burial in Arlington National Cemetery. In each instance, it took a nationwide campaign to redress these grievances.

• Irving Weissman, twice wounded in Spain, three years in the Army of the United States, holder of six battle stars and veteran of the invasions of Anzio, Salerno and southern

France. (Five years under Pennsylvania's "sedition" act, reversed by a higher court.)

• John Gates, Lieutenant-Colonel in Spain (political commissar of the XVth International Brigade), paratrooper in World War II. (Five years.) Gates later had a change of heart about his political affiliations but has never denounced and/or renounced his pride in his record in Spain.

• Saul Wellman, officer in Spain, wounded at Bastogne, eight months in hospital and rated 100 percent disabled. This was later reduced to 50-percent disability and once he was convicted (1954) the Veterans Administration not only stopped his pension but billed him in the sum of $9,581.85 for the benefits it had already paid him! (Conviction reversed by a higher court.)

(James Kutcher and Robert Klonsky, both World War II veterans as well, met similar treatment at the hands of the Veterans Administration. At the same time, veterans of Hitler's Condor Legion which had devastated much of Spain, were voted pensions by the new government of West Germany.)

These four men—and Steve Nelson (also convicted under the Smith Act)—were among the handful of VALB men who became Communist Party functionaries, but there were many others who were similarly charged and similarly imprisoned. For it is really very easy to convict people who have committed no crime if you make use of that classic diagnosis-by-parallel beloved of the John Birch Society and American Legion brass hats, and both the government and the many witch-hunting committees throughout the land have used it regularly: "If it looks like a duck, walks like a duck, swims like a duck and quacks like a duck, it must be a duck."

In other words, if the Communist Party opposed our adventures in Korea, Guatemala, Vietnam and Cambodia, our invasion of Cuba, our support of Chiang Kai-shek and Franco, the Smith and McCarran Acts and Spain's admission to the United Nations, and if it favored the graduated income tax, the organization of labor unions, Social Security and unemployment insurance and unemployed councils during the Depression, the support of Republican Spain and such remedial patchwork measures as WPA and the like, then anyone who opposed or supported any of these items must, *ipso facto*, be a Communist, a fellow traveler or a dupe. To make the label stick, you merely forget the millions of individuals who arrived at the same positions on these issues through contemplation, bitter experience or arguments with their fellowmen.

Other Spanish veterans who were naturalized citizens or legally resident aliens were put to enormous expense and emotional suffering when the Immigration Service tried to get them deported. (Allan McNeil—the Major Johnson of this book—Felix Kusman, Willy Busch, Frank Bonetti, Pierre du Valle, among others.) One veteran (Alvah Bessie) was caught up in HUAC's investigation of "Communist influences" in the Hollywood motion-picture industry in 1947 and served a year's sentence for "contempt" of Congress, and others were victimized by HUAC in other investigations in other cities.

The distinguished surgeon, Dr. Edward K. Barsky, who had headed all American medical services in Spain and later served as chairman of the Joint Antifascist Refugee Committee, was jailed for six months and his medical license was temporarily revoked for refusing to turn over to that same committee the list of thousands of contributors to JARC's campaigns.

There can be little doubt that the SACB attack on the

Spanish veterans was part of an attempt to justify our alliance with Franco Spain which began in 1950 with an "import-export" loan of $62,500,000 promoted by Senator McCarran himself.

The United Nations had voted (with American support) in 1946 to *exclude* Spain from all UN organizations because it had come to power thanks to Nazi-Fascist military aggression. By 1952 the USA was leading the fight to have Spain admitted to the Educational, Scientific & Cultural Organization of the UN. And that same year McCarran forced an additional $100,000,000 appropriation for Franco as a condition for passage of a foreign-aid bill. In 1953 and 1954 an additional $226,000,000 was proposed for the use of air, naval and military bases in what could be called a Spanish *place d'armes*, a safe base dominating the Middle East, Africa and even the U.S.S.R.

In his eloquent defense of the American veterans' organization before SACB (13 September 1954), Commander Milton Wolff said:

> We have listened to the petitioner (then U.S. Attorney General Herbert J. Brownell) and to the petitioner's witnesses, and from their lips we have heard all the old tales and lies of the defeated Axis, once more resurrected, as the petitioner attempted to rewrite history to fit the fancy of this hearing. Perhaps what happens to those now present and involved in this hearing in the years to come is of little importance. But what is important is that the petitioner, representing the administration now in power, an administration which has entered into a military alliance with Franco Spain, is determined to rewrite history in such a fashion as to accommodate that alliance and its purposes. And perhaps the panel sitting here as a result of the efforts of Senator McCarran, who is the evil genius of the military alliance . . . and at the same time the author of the Act under which

we are being heard, can do little, under these circumstances, but serve the same ends as does counsel for the petitioner. While what has been happening in this hearing has been obscured by a conspiracy of silence, it has served to set the stage for such events as took place in the historical closing days of the 83rd Congress, and in the forging of closer links with the remnants of resurgent fascism throughout the world.

What is generally forgotten is that the Subversive Activities Control Act, authored by McCarran, was originally proposed by Richard Nixon and Karl Mundt as the Mundt-Nixon Act, and the 24-year life of the Act was finally ended on 30 May 1974 by an order signed by a man whose life became inextricably involved with the same Nixon: Judge John J. Sirica, later of Watergate fame.

Of course, the Lincoln veterans have always had many advocates and we could list them for pages, but singly and together they were unable to stem the attack on us as premature antifascists, international Communist gangsters and agents of the Comintern so long as the Cold War was so effective a tool in American efforts to dominate the world economically and politically—as well as militarily.

Number among them, for the record:

• Justice William O. Douglas (commenting on the Barsky case): "When a doctor cannot save lives in America because he is opposed to Franco in Spain, it is time to call a halt and look critically at the neurosis that has possessed us."

• "They (the veterans) were among the first to see the menace of fascism and certainly among the first to offer their lives to fight this menace. . . . In the last decade they have been in the forefront of all the battles for democracy, and they deserve the best this country has to offer."—Harold L. Ickes,

Secretary of the Interior under Franklin Roosevelt.

• "The Brigade has long since taken its place in the history of our times and become a tireless symbol of man's resistance to exploitation and oppression. The Brigade was right when most of the world proved tragically wrong." —Louis Bromfield, novelist.

• "If the world has a future, they have preserved it." —Vincent Sheean, author and foreign correspondent.

• "The Ebro was a heroic, bloody, costly battle, a truly magnificent example of human courage. The defense by the Americans of Hill 666 above Gandesa against just about the heaviest artillery barrage, bombing and strafing of the war and against Franco's crack Moorish troops, was a proud achievement." —Herbert L. Matthews, *New York Times* correspondent, chief editorial writer and author.

• Pete Hamill, *New York Post* columnist, reporting on the Brigade's annual dinner in New York in 1971: "They went upstairs to a large bright room, and drank a lot of whiskey at the bar, and there was nothing at all to indicate that they were the best Americans of their generation. /"They were the Veterans of the Abraham Lincoln Brigade, and to be able to say that about yourself might be the only badge of honor that is worth having . . . / "It has been a long, lonely time for them in the years since Franco's legions finally marched into Barcelona. Never have so many good men been treated so badly by a supposedly civilized nation. . . . They had gone to Spain because they loved America and wanted its honor preserved; when they came home, America kicked them in the teeth . . . / "When the evening was over, they exchanged addresses and phone numbers, and collected the coats and went back into the strange country that America has become in the years since they were young. That country had done badly by them, but honor is not something that is pinned on you by the likes of Richard Nixon. . . ."

We won and lost many battles in Spain and we lost and won many legal battles once we had come home. Each and every one of them commanded every dollar we could beg, borrow and raise from among our surviving members and our friends; and most of these battles had to go all the way to the United States Supreme Court.

Steve Nelson's conviction in the framed-up "sedition" case in Pennsylvania was overturned and he was vindicated by the Supreme Court in 1956—but that was also the year Franco Spain was admitted to the United Nations.

On 20 April 1966, after 13 years of litigation, the Supreme Court vacated the SACB order requiring VALB to register as a Communist-front organization. Having accomplished absolutely nothing in its more than 20 years except to pay its members salaries of $36,000 a year each, and having been able neither to control subversion nor even to define it, it was abandoned in 1973 and expired for lack of further appropriations. Homer C. Clay was VALB's successful and devoted attorney. An identical fate was met by HUAC in January 1975 when a new Congress "retired" it to deserved oblivion.

The Emergency Civil Liberties Committee of New York undertook the fight to get our name removed from the Attorney General's idiotic list of subversive organizations, first promulgated by Tom Clark in 1948 and since used as a basis for loyalty oaths by federal, state and municipal governments, and as material for blacklisting in defense and private industry. It took another six years before the U.S. Court of Appeals in a unanimous decision ordered the Attorney General to remove the name of our organization from his list.

But Nixon's administration, like those that preceded him since World War II ended, had coddled, nursed and nourished the last reigning fascist dictator in Europe. Even the Greek colonels, taking a leaf from their Portugese counterparts and behaving totally unlike military men anywhere in the world, have returned democracy to their countrymen. It will take Franco's death to accomplish as much in Spain. What happens then will be determined by the Spanish people, who have made their intentions plain and who are in action. (Cf. *Spain Again.*) And those of us who survive are more confident than ever that we will live to return to Barcelona to claim the honorary citizenship in the third Spanish Republic which Dolores Ibárruri, *La Pasionaría*, speaking in the name of her government, promised us in her farewell speech 37 years ago. And we are almost equally sure that we will see her again on *El Diagonal*, where we marched in that final parade on 29 October 1938, and that great avenue will also have reclaimed its original name and will no longer be known as Avenue of The Most General, Francisco Franco.

Of the 1,300 American volunteers who returned from Spain, we lost another 400 in World War II, and it is said we won more combat decorations than any other comparable group of men has ever earned. This may be true but there never has been a group to compare to us, in the sense that we and our comrades of the other brigades were the first and only spontaneously gathered international volunteer army in the history of the world.

Of the men mentioned in this narrative, many have died since 1939, and some of them, like Aaron, cannot be forgotten. One turned up at a party at Vincent Sheean's New York house early in 1939. He was hilariously funny that night and the next morning we read that he had hanged himself: Ernst

Toller, the anti-Nazi dramatist and poet. He had been unable to adjust himself to what he saw as a life in exile and which need not have been one at all—had he only waited.

John Kozar, the seaman-*mecánico* at the 35th Division hospital, went back to sea in World War II but he never got another chance to swim ashore with a pound of coffee in his teeth: he froze to death in a lifeboat in January 1942 when his ship was torpedoed on the Murmansk run. He left a wife and child in Canada.

Edwin Rolfe, poet and author of the first history of the Lincoln Battalion, whose eloquent volume of poems, *First Love*, expressed what all of us have always felt about Spain, was in Hollywood, blacklisted and unemployable when he was taken by a heart attack on 25 May 1954. Two wars (for he was in the AUS also) were too much for so physically frail a man and unemployability added final insult to the injury.

Ernest Hemingway committed suicide on 2 July 1961. He had apparently felt that he was through—both as a writer and a man. His dedication to the cause of the Spanish Republic was never questioned, even though the VALB men attacked his novel, *For Whom the Bell Tolls*, as a piece of romantic nonsense when it was not slanderous of many Spanish leaders we all revered, and scarcely representative of what the war was all about. (But see below.)

A second heart attack killed Allan McNeil (our training officer in Tarazona) after 11 years under threat of deportation, in January 1966.

Harold Smith, our Company 2 commissar, who was wounded twice and always took up too much room in the *chabola* he shared for awhile with Aaron and me, is gone. So are Moishe Taubman and Dave Gordon. So is Juan Negrín, last Prime Minister of the Republic, and so is Manuel Azaña, its last and most defeatist President.

Colonel (and later General) Juan Modesto, former woodcutter who gained some experience in the Moroccan Foreign Legion under Franco himself, was a military genius who rose to command three army corps: the Army of the Ebro with its 70,000 men. He died in exile in Prague in 1969. (See *Spain Again*.)

Another exile died in Mexico on 14 January 1958. I had never seen him in Spain but his name was on our lips whenever we sang the song, *No pasarán*. For a time after we returned I was unable to eat in any New York restaurant that was not authentically Spanish. There were few enough of them and in one such place—and a poor one at that—I saw a man one night whose face was world famous. He was sitting with three younger men and all were obviously Spaniards. I approached the oldest, introduced myself and asked if he were not General José Miaja. He stood and said he was and embraced me in the Spanish fashion. He was on his way to Mexico, he said. He thanked me for fighting for his country!

All our men who fought—or fought and died in Spain or World War II or who survived both wars were, of course, fighting for our own country. We are still fighting for it in one way or another. As an organization and as individuals we have fought our "country" itself when it was misled into Korea and Guatemala and Cuba and Vietnam and Cambodia and Laos. And we are still fighting for the liberation of the Spanish people in the only ways now open to us—and there are many.

There are very few of us left—perhaps 700, perhaps less. But whether they died in Spain or on the high seas, in any of the later battles of the second World War, or of the passage of time, Ernest Hemingway was speaking for them—and about them—in 1939 when he wrote:

"For our dead are a part of the earth of Spain now and the earth of Spain can never die. . . . Our dead will live in it forever.

"Just as the earth can never die, neither will those who have ever been free return to slavery. The peasants who work the earth where our dead lie know what these dead died for. There was time during the war for them to learn these things, and there is forever for them to remember them in.

"Our dead live in the hearts and the minds of the Spanish peasants, of the Spanish workers, of all the good simple honest people who believed in and fought for the Spanish republic. And as long as all our dead live in the Spanish earth, and they will live as long as the earth lives, no system of tyranny ever will prevail in Spain. . . .

"The Spanish people will rise again as they have always risen before tyranny.

"The dead do not need to rise. They are a part of the earth now and the earth can never be conquered. . . .

"Those who have entered it honorably, and no men ever entered earth more honorably than those who died in Spain, already have achieved immortality."*

It is too bad Hemingway could not have waited, too. He would have enjoyed this time. This is the time when many of the world's most dishonorable men—from Seoul, Saigon and Taipei through Washington to Lisbon, Madrid, Athens and the Middle East—are being cashiered, driven from positions of power they bought or stole from the people by force and

---

* From *New Masses*, Vol. XXX, No. 8 (February 14, 1939), page 3.

violence, and they are approaching their own graves, which will also be unmarked—but for entirely different reasons.

San Rafael, California
30 January 1975

V

CHRONOLOGY

A Brief Chronology of the
Spanish Civil War*

1931: *12 April*—Republican parties triumph in city elections throughout Spain.

14 April—The second Republic is proclaimed; King Alfonso XIII abdicates, leaves for exile.

May-June—Education made free and secular; rural reforms give land to the landless.

28 June—Elections held for the Cortes (Parliament).

Summer—Considerable unrest, strikes in telephone and a general strike in Sevilla as workers express discontent with slowness of Republican reforms.

9 December—New constitution promulgated, based in large part on U.S. Constitution.

1932-33: General unrest continues as new Republic moves slowly to implement reforms and *provocateurs* are also active; more strikes and demonstrations. Reactionaries start to organize. The *Falange* (fascist party) is founded by José Antonio Primo de Rivera.

19 November—Electoral victory for the right makes Alejandro Lerroux prime minister.

December—Anarchist risings in Aragón and Catalonia.

---

* From *The Spanish Republic and the Civil War, 1931–1939*, by Gabriel Jackson (copyright ©1965 by Princeton University Press; Princeton Paperback, 1967): A chronology, pp. 101-109, in condensed and somewhat rewritten version. Reprinted by permission of Princeton University Press and Gabriel Jackson.

1934: *31 March*—Mussolini meets with Spanish monarchists, agrees to help with military means if necessary, in their plans to overthrow Republic, reinstitute monarchy.

25 April—Lerroux cabinet resigns.

June—Peasant strikes in Extramadura and Andalucía.

6 October—Rising of Asturian miners, workers in Catalonia also; African troops and Foreign Legionaires under command of Francisco Franco are sent to Asturias, suppress the rebellion with unparalleled brutality.

1935: *February*—Executions in Oviedo (Asturias) of strike leaders; a year of internal crises and political maneuvering—the left attempting to unite, the right moving to take power, "legally," if possible, otherwise, if not.

29 October—Lerroux resignation forced by his involvement in financial scandals, bribery, and the like.

1936: *16 February*—New elections bring sweeping victory for Popular Front (coalition of parties from extreme left to middle).

15 March—*Falange* outlawed; its creator, José Antonio, arrested.

June—Many assassinations of left and right leaders, strikes in building trades and by elevator workers (Madrid), others in Málaga, Cádiz and Spanish Morocco.

16 June—Calvo Sotelo (monarchist) and Gil Robles (Catholic) denounce public disorder in Cortes.

13 July—Sotelo assassinated.

17 July—War (long prepared) proclaimed from Morocco; Republic arms its citizens in the streets and people take control in Madrid, Valencia, Barcelona, other cities.

20 July—New cabinet formed by José Giral; asks France for help and Franco sends envoys to Hitler and Mussolini.

27 July—Sevilla taken by fascists who are reinforced by air from Morocco. German and Italian war planes arrive in

Morocco and Sevilla; France sends a few ancient aircraft to Madrid.

8 August—France seals border to Spain.

14 August—Badajoz taken by fascists; massacre of civilians.

4 September—Largo Caballero forms cabinet including socialists, Communists and Republican representatives.

9 September—The "Non-Intervention" Committee is formed in London.

6 October—USSR says it won't be bound by Non-Intervention agreement since Germany and Italy are plainly intervening.

2 November—Fascists reach Manzanares River outside Madrid; first Soviet planes appear over the city.

6 November—Capital moved to Valencia; General José Miaja appointed to defend Madrid.

8 November—Fascists make all-out assault on Madrid, are stopped cold by Republican militia and first units of the International Brigade (mostly French and German).

18 November—Hitler and Mussolini recognize Franco's *junta*.

20 November—José Antonio, founder of *Falange*, tried and executed.

December—Condor Legion (Nazi aircraft, artillery, tanks, staff officers) formed in Sevilla.

18 December—Mussolini's Blackshirts leave Naples to fight in Spain as "volunteers," thinking they are on their way to Ethiopia.

1937: *6-15 February*—Battle of Jarama (outside Madrid); baptism of fire for first American volunteers of Lincoln Battalion.

8-18 February—Italian troops routed at Guadalajara by Republican army including *Garibaldini* (antifascist Italians).

19 April—Non-Intervention Committee sets up land and sea patrol—which stops nothing going to Franco.

26 April—Guernica, holy city of the Basques, destroyed

from the air by Condor Legion; an early test of equipment and terror tactics.

8 May—Riots in Barcelona, sparked by "superrevolutionary" P.O.U.M. (Trotskyists), are put down by the Republic.

19 May—Bilbao (Basque country) falls to fascists.

23-30 June—Germany and Italy withdraw from sea patrol and Portugal ends land patrol on border. France follows suit in two weeks.

7-26 July—Battle of Brunete; Lincoln and Washington Battalions distinguish themselves.

24 August—Quinto-Belchite campaign; more American action.

1 October—Caballero out, new government formed with Juan Negrín as prime minister, moves to Barcelona 31 October.

14 December—Republic launches offensive, takes Teruel.

1938: *22 February*—Fascists recapture Teruel, launch Aragón offensive (9 March).

11 March—Hitler occupies Austria; French prime minister Léon Blum briefly opens border to Spain. During balance of month fascist offensive in Aragón pushes Spanish and Internationals before it. Big retreats.

15 April—Franco reaches the Mediterranean, cutting Republican Spain in half. Shortly thereafter, French close their border again.

24 July—After months of regrouping and retraining, Republic launches its biggest offensive of the war—crossing the Ebro River to relieve pressure on Valencia and trying to reopen communication between north and south. Hitler pours more *matériel* into Spain.

30 September—Munich pact dooms Czechoslovakia.

15 November—Under inexorable pressure, Ebro sector collapses; the International Brigades are withdrawn from war.

23 December—Fascists launch offensive to take Catalonia.

1939: *26 January*—Barcelona occupied by fascists.

9 February—Mass flight in midwinter over French border of more than 450,000 refugees and Republican troops in Catalonia. France internes them in barbed-wire enclosures on the beaches, where no shelter exists for months.

27 February—France and Britain recognize Franco; Azaña resigns as President.

2 March—Negrín vows to continue war, forms new cabinet, flies to Madrid.

15 March—Hitler occupies Czechoslovakia.

28 March—Franco's troops enter Madrid after its betrayal by a *junta* led by General Casado.

1 April—Surrender of Republican armies continues and the eventual liquidation by Franco of over 200,000 "criminals" who had fought to defend their Republic begins.

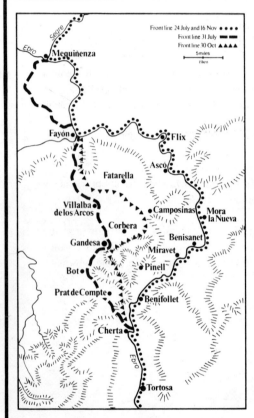

Map of the battle of the river Ebro, showing
the fluctuations of the battle-fronts. The
sketch on the right illustrates the rapid
progress of Franco's final thrust forward in
Catalonia from positions established during
the fighting in the summer and fall of 1938.

**Reprinted by permission of the author and the publisher from *A Concise
History of the Spanish Civil War* by Gabriel Jackson, copyright ©1974
and published by The John Day Company, Inc. The maps were drawn
by Claus Henning.**

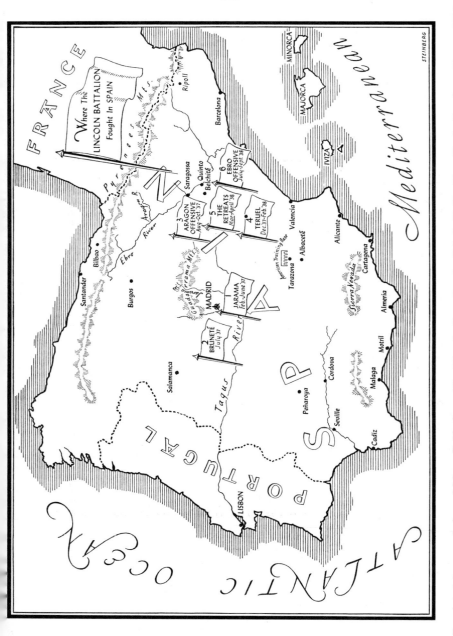

Reprinted by permission of Mary Rolfe from *The Lincoln Battalion* by Edwin Rolfe (New York: Random House, 1939).